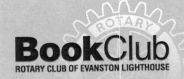

BookClub
ROTARY CLUB OF EVANSTON LIGHTHOUSE

Presented in Honor of

Paul Harvey, Beth McCostlin
UNICEF, USA
October 31, 2017

Rotary Club
of Evanston Lighthouse

The Origins of UNICEF, 1946–1953

The Origins of UNICEF, 1946–1953

Jennifer M. Morris

LEXINGTON BOOKS
Lanham • Boulder • New York • London

Cover photo, UNICEF informational pamphlet. Photospread images 1–11. Series 1: Personal Papers; 1904–1985; Maurice Pate Papers, Public Policy Papers, Department of Rare Books and Special Collections, Princeton University Library.

Photospread images 12–14. Library of Congress, Prints & Photographs Division, photograph by Harris & Ewing, [reproduction number, e.g., LC-USZ62-123456].

Published by Lexington Books
An imprint of The Rowman & Littlefield Publishing Group, Inc.
4501 Forbes Boulevard, Suite 200, Lanham, Maryland 20706
www.rowman.com

Unit A, Whitacre Mews, 26-34 Stannary Street, London SE11 4AB

British Library Cataloguing in Publication Information Available

Library of Congress Cataloging-in-Publication Data

Library of Congress Cataloging-in-Publication Data Available

ISBN 978-0-7391-7624-5 (cloth : alk. paper)
ISBN 978-0-7391-7625-2 (electronic)

∞ ™ The paper used in this publication meets the minimum requirements of American National Standard for Information Sciences Permanence of Paper for Printed Library Materials, ANSI/NISO Z39.48-1992.

Printed in the United States of America

For Emily and Elyse

Contents

Acknowledgments

This book began during a graduate seminar on women and the United Nations at Miami University. I had returned to graduate school after twelve years as a mortgage banker, and found myself once again drawn to the international politics and histories I had studied as an undergraduate. While reading about UN organizations and their policies regarding women, I simultaneously read another text about the Cold War in the United States in another seminar. Elaine Tyler May's book on the post-war American family echoed much of the language in UN documents, which I believed could not be a coincidence. Thus, the way for this work was paved.

Many thanks are owed to all who helped with this project. Thanks go first and foremost to Adiratha Kevin Keefe, who helped me navigate the UNICEF archives in New York. The phenomenal staff at the Mudd Manuscript Library at Princeton University are some of the best archivists I've ever worked with, and for all your efforts I am eternally grateful. Thanks go also to the ladies at the Library of Congress who not only helped me with my cart each morning, but also told me where in the basement labyrinth I could find coffee. Mount St. Joseph University, the University of Cincinnati, and Miami University all provided funds for conducting research, and my editors at Lexington Books have been patient and kind as I slogged through the final versions. To the anonymous reviewer who helped me make important revisions and find new sources, your efforts are greatly appreciated.

Heartfelt thanks go to my mentor and friend, Judith Zinsser, for supporting me through this long, long, process. Finally, to Bryan, Emilie, and Elyse, thanks for your understanding and for doing without me while I worked. I could never have made it to this point without you.

Introduction

The United Nations Children's Fund, more commonly known as UNICEF, embodies the apolitical, international effort to provide relief aid for children and mothers throughout the world. Begun as a temporary relief agency to provide food and clothing to Europe and China in 1946, UNICEF became a permanent UN organization in 1953 and currently operates in more than 190 countries, advocating for maternal and child health and welfare while still upholding its original commitment to provide emergency relief aid to children and mothers in conflict regions.

UNICEF, like its UN counterparts the Food and Agriculture Organization (FAO) and the World Health Organization (WHO), came to be in 1946 due to its synchronicity with the UN's stated purpose—to maintain peace in the world—as well as its own commitment to focus on and resolve issues identified as critical to the survival of children and mothers at the end of World War II. Historian Paul Kennedy posits that organizations like these three comprised a "softer face" of the UN's overall mission, noting that they focused primarily on social, cultural, and environmental issues.[1] And indeed, UNICEF launched its operations to provide temporary emergency relief aid for children and mothers displaced and disadvantaged by war, addressing one of the most pressing social issues of the day. It then continued its existence beyond its original end date of 1950 by continuing to address social, cultural, and environmental issues that impeded the well-being of children, including famine relief, disease prevention, and relief aid for children and mothers in regions engulfed in localized armed conflicts.

By examining UNICEF's founding, early operations, and eventual sanction to become a permanent UN organization, it becomes clear that despite UNICEF's "softer face" it was both influenced by and an influence on the concurrent political and social issues in the years between 1946 and 1953.

1

That Kennedy devotes only thirty-three pages of his book to these agencies that, according to him, dissolve into "alphabet soup" is appropriate, given that his work and the work of others focuses primarily on the creation of a "new world order."[2] By concentrating primarily on politics and economics, histories of the period remain rooted in their analyses of the Marshall Plan and the politics of the Cold War, focusing on how these impacted European and subsequent global economic recovery and political stability. Most notable among these are the work of U.S. historian Michael Hogan and modern European historians Mark Mazower, Keith Middlemas, Arnold Offner, Theodore Wilson, and John Young.[3] It is nevertheless important to acknowledge that UNICEF, and other organizations like it, ran programs that were complicit not only in supporting U.S. foreign policy efforts, but also for influencing social norms by perpetuating the U.S. post-war family ideal as well.

Diverging from these traditional histories yet acknowledging some of their political sentiments, this examination of UNICEF's early years elucidates how, by accepting U.S. funding and remaining in line with U.S. policies, the organization faced difficulties as it negotiated the increasingly polarized terrain of the first decade of the Cold War. Deeply invested in its efforts to thwart the spread of Communism around the world by 1946, the United States often forced UNICEF to maneuver through a political quagmire in order to receive U.S. funding critical to achieving its goals. Political tensions, too, affected UNICEF both internally and externally, subjecting its staff to extreme scrutiny and requiring it to defend providing aid to Communist countries. Its early operations, then, expand our understanding of how an apolitical relief aid organization could be subject to and augment the tensions created by the Cold War both internally and externally; how this created the dilemmas it faced in attempting to procure funding and remain adequately staffed; how it provided relief aid that was often viewed as highly political and therefore suspect; and how these accusations eventually caused amendments to UNICEF's programs so that it could remain a viable entity beyond 1950.

In addition to its sometimes uncomfortable concomitance with U.S. foreign policy, UNICEF's programs also reinforced what historian Elaine Tyler May identifies as the ideal American post-war family. May notes that after the war, the American family came to be viewed as a "fragile institution" that had to be upheld due to its ability to "shape the future" and its corresponding role in containing Communism.[4] Political scientist Cynthia Enloe echoes this sentiment, noting that the Cold War created a "deeply militarized understanding of identity and security . . . [relying] on distinct notions of masculinity [and femininity]" that directed U.S. policy both at home and abroad.[5] Perpetuating the America post-war family ideal also reinforced the notion of the dependence of women and children, supported the assumption that children should be the focus of a family, and relied on the assumption that mothers were the best hope for children to survive and thrive, thereby relegating them to a role inextricably tied to their biological reproductive function and little else. UNICEF, easily assuming the role of the provider for displaced mothers and children after the war, relied on this U.S. prescription regarding the family to justify distributing aid to children and mothers only, even when challenged by nations whose notion of the family differed. Finally, perpetuating this ideal, despite its drawbacks, helped UNICEF retain its U.S. funding during the period between 1946 and 1950.

There is ample proof that children and mothers had been the focus of many of UNICEF's predecessor relief aid organizations, including the Commission for Relief in Belgium and Save the Children, revealing that the reinforcement of roles for family members was not a phenomenon unique to the United States. Indeed, it can be argued that, after World War II, UNICEF's policies and programs received wide acceptance in Western Europe because of their alignment with post-war social programs in Europe that relied on similar prescriptions for the family.[6] These programs, too, relied on specific gender norms as noted in the work of social historians Robert Moeller, Seth Koven, and Sonya Michel, sociologist Terry Kandal, gender historian Anne Digby, and labor historians Frances Fox Piven and Richard Cloward. All have analyzed how social programs in the West developed with clear gender biases based on notions of masculinity and femininity, which in turn determined both their relief aid recipient clientele and what type of relief aid would be provided.[7]

In addition to social programs that reinforced family roles, May claims that the post-war U.S. family structure kept women out of the public realm of men. This trend, analyzed, too, by social historians Berte Siim and Jet Bussemaker, had an effect on post-war definitions of *citizenship* as well. These examinations have concluded that, in spite of declarations of equal rights for men and women in most Western nations as well as by the United Nations, one's sex remained a critical factor in determining one's civil rights.[8] UNICEF's programs can help us better understand how ideas regarding equality and citizenship were upheld due to the reliance on the U.S. family model that relegated women to the private sphere and to the job of caring for children. Its programs can also illustrate how these citizenship parameters could be challenged by UNICEF's unwillingness to extend its relief aid to men.

A study of UNICEF, then, adds another dimension to the political and social history of the immediate post–World War II period, providing an analytical approach not present in the two previously published histories of UNICEF. Written by former UNICEF employee Maggie Black, these two texts—*The Children and the Nations: The Story of UNICEF* and *Children First: The Story of UNICEF*—chronicle UNICEF's operations after 1953 and focus primarily on the successes of UNICEF's yaws and tuberculosis treatment programs. Filled with laudatory biographical information on the Executive Directors of UNICEF since 1965, they focus not on UNICEF's founding or early struggles, but on medical aid triumphs. It is no coincidence that Black begins her histories here, since 1965 was the year UNICEF won the Nobel Peace Prize. It was also the year that UNICEF's first executive director, Maurice Pate, died, and Black barely mentions Pate's contributions to establishing the organization. This book, therefore, returns to UNICEF's origins, examining the specific events that took place between 1946 and 1953 that made the temporary organization a permanent one. Each of the six chapters chronicles a specific aspect of UNICEF's early development and examines the organization's intersections with U.S. policies, gender prescriptions, and Cold War challenges.

The first of these chapters examines UNICEF's predecessor organizations and how these influenced the process for establishing the new UN organization. The operations carried out via these organizations set a precedent for funding, acquiring, and distributing emergency relief aid on an international scale that UNICEF adopted during the first few years of its operation. They also created many of the key concepts on which UNICEF was based, most notably that UNICEF limited its target population to children and their mothers. These in turn influenced UNICEF's early goals and methods of operation, as well as its institutional identity. One of these previous organizations in particular played a larger role than the others in its influence. UNICEF not only borrowed its policies and procedures, but also benefitted by employing several of the individuals who had helped carry out those policies as volunteer employees of the organization. The Commission for Relief in Belgium (CRB) provided UNICEF with its first executive director, Maurice Pate. He gained his initial experiences in providing international relief aid to individuals living in war and under occupation as a CRB volunteer, and applied much of what he learned in Belgium to every aspect of UNICEF's founding and initial operations. The American Relief Administration (ARA), which provided relief aid to the Soviet Union during the famine that occurred there during the 1920s, also informed Pate's experiences.

UNICEF also utilized much of the processes put forth by another organization founded immediately following World War I. Called Save the Children, it established the concept that an apolitical, international relief aid organization for children had become indispensable, touting children as the best hope for the future. UNICEF took up this cause after World War II, and relied on Save the Children's list of children's rights to inform rhetoric and practice during UNICEF's early operations as well as in its declarations and publications in the later years of the twentieth century.

The work of the United Nations Relief and Rehabilitation Administration (UNRRA) at the end of World War II and into the post-war period provided

UNICEF with the basis for a proposal to continue its work by founding an organization that focused specifically on children and their mothers to the newly created UN General Assembly. UNRRA promised funding, supplies, and staff once its operations ceased, exerting further influence over UNICEF. At about the same time, President Harry Truman commissioned a World Food Survey to assess the global need to provide relief aid. Maurice Pate's participation in this survey immediately following the end of World War II further expanded his experience in calculating the need for and distribution of relief aid, and solidified many of the principles UNICEF would adopt to fund its operations and distribution efforts.

UNICEF borrowed liberally from these predecessor organizations in creating a proposal to become one of their numbers. According to historians of state-sponsored assistance programs Pat Thane, Susan Pedersen, and Gisela Bock, this trend was not unusual. Relief aid programs frequently borrowed from one another, forming an informal community of institutions and individuals, public and private, that exchanged ideas as they worked to alleviate the suffering of the poor and disadvantaged at local, state, and international levels—a tradition copied by UNICEF in establishing its aid programs.[9] Their work, combined with the rich history of these predecessor organizations found in numerous sources including Maurice Pate's correspondence and diaries, records of UNRRA's operations, biographies of Eglantyne Jebb, founder of Save the Children, and the copious records of the ARA, establish how a proposal to create UNICEF could be established and approved.

Chapter 2 recounts UNICEF's approval as a temporary relief aid organization sanctioned by the United Nations General Assembly. During the first few months after its approval, UNICEF struggled to create its institutional identity as individual experience brought to the table by a host of disparate contributors collided to try and determine the course of UNICEF's programs. UNICEF's original charter, along with correspondence, oral histories, and UNICEF's meeting minutes, reveals a great deal about the type of organization each contributor had in mind, evincing that no two individuals held the same image or had the same goals for the organization. The charter that became the resolution passed by the General Assembly that created UNICEF had many authors, and relied on rather vague and sweeping language to establish its intended clientele, the type of relief aid it would distribute, and the conditions under which aid could be provided. UNICEF documents, oral histories, and records from the U.S. Children's Bureau illustrate the process by which UNICEF came to be.

Creating a work plan, the subject of chapter 3, became the focus UNICEF's Executive Board meetings during its first months of existence. Official meeting minutes attest to the myriad suggestions, from facilitating adoptions to providing dried milk to school feeding programs, that received consideration. Along with these meeting minutes, unpublished histories of

UNICEF and oral histories from its original staffers provide a vivid picture of the debates that took place. These debates not only demonstrate that no two individuals on the board had a like plan of action in mind, but that the vague language contained in the charter allowed for such contrasting proposals. This chapter also illustrates that, from the start, the United States exerted a great deal of influence on UNICEF's programs and policies. First, Maurice Pate's appointment as executive director meant that his CRB and ARA experiences would guide UNICEF's creation of relief aid programs. Second, Katharine Lenroot, chief of the U.S. Children's Bureau, became the first permanent U.S. representative to the UNICEF Executive Board, introducing the influence of the Children's Bureau to the process of establishing policy and programs. Finally, hiring Dr. Martha Eliot, a maternal and child health care expert and assistant chief of the U.S. Children's Bureau, to conduct a medical survey of Europe, meant that UNICEF's health care programs would most closely align with those carried out by the bureau. And, though Eliot obtained the first financial contribution to UNICEF from the United States as a grant-in-aid, continued funding became the subject of much debate when members of the U.S. Congress questioned UNICEF's distribution of relief aid to Communist nations. In the end, the board rather narrowly defined two primary goals that, at least tentatively, seemed less controversial and most likely to garner the support of those who could provide financial backing. UNICEF, with its U.S. funding, would move forward with its two programs: providing food and medical care.

Chapter 4 examines UNICEF's initial food aid programs, put into action once it received a grant-in-aid from the U.S. government. Modeled after the Commission for Relief in Belgium, the American Relief Administration, and the United Nations Relief and Rehabilitation Administration's programs, these offered aid directly to children via already existing infrastructures such as schools. In order to ensure its clientele received what it needed, UNICEF's Executive Board spent a great deal of time reviewing decades of research on proper nutrition conducted by the U.S. Children's Bureau, as well as the results of the World Food Survey, to determine exactly what UNICEF should provide given its limited resources. Food distributions programs for children and their mothers in Europe began to reveal UNICEF's association with U.S. policy as well as the ways in which UNICEF reinforced the image of the ideal U.S. post-war family. For example, repeated challenges by Communist nations to UNICEF's exclusion of any person from its programs reveals the ways in which Cold War tensions as well as gender prescriptions for the family impacted UNICEF relief aid distribution. Faced with multiples challenges, UNICEF found the cooperation of the Food and Agriculture Administration (FAA) extremely helpful in obtaining nutrition information and in borrowing staff to assist with distribution. Evidence of these events unfolds in UNICEF board meeting minutes, individual country applications for

UNICEF relief aid, correspondence, and testimonies from UNICEF and FAO staff.

UNICEF had, in addition to food aid, also agreed to provide medical aid. Initially, this proved to be a complicated task because of the presence of an interim UN health organization that vehemently disagreed with the inclusion of medical programs as a part of UNICEF's functions. Chapter 5 examines the two primary programs UNICEF established in 1947—anti-tuberculosis and anti-syphilis campaigns—as well as the sometimes rocky relationship it shared with the new World Health Organization (WHO). This relationship unfolds haltingly in Executive Board meeting minutes, correspondence, testimony, oral histories, and UNICEF histories. UNICEF and WHO worked together grudgingly, due in large part to the fact that WHO, anxious to take over UNICEF's health programs, did little to support UNICEF in its quest to become a permanent UN agency in 1950. UNICEF's medical programs, too, reveal the Cold War tensions that existed between the United States and territories that became part of the Soviet bloc after the war. Proposals from Eastern bloc nations to receive UNICEF relief aid almost always included requests for treatment of both men and women, illustrating how these countries pushed UNICEF's boundaries, and how, by refusing this treatment and providing it to mothers only, UNICEF remained committed to U.S. policy and the ideal U.S. post-war family model.

Having logged several successes in distributing its relief aid by 1950 despite some sizeable roadblocks, UNICEF launched a concerted effort to obtain approval from the General Assembly to be made a permanent UN organization. During 1950, the Executive Board focused its energies almost entirely on ensuring that UNICEF's programs became both global and indispensable. UNICEF also began to receive funding from a variety of sources ranging from national governments to private fund-raising efforts. In addition to its struggle to obtain permanent status, UNICEF had also begun establishing operations throughout Asia and Latin America in 1950 and found that relying on its initial operational structure and the image of the ideal post-war U.S. family did not always yield desired results as it confronted cultural differences in these regions. Chapter 6 reviews this process, examining the multiple efforts made to keep UNICEF alive and to prove that it deserved permanent status.

The years between 1951 and 1953, during which UNICEF's leadership, programs, and operations underwent change, further reveals how issues such as Cold War politics and the need to keep in step with changes in the larger United Nations caused shifts to take place concurrently with UNICEF's innovative, global attempts to publicize its programs. High-profile projects such as the sale of holiday greeting cards, fundraising efforts by newly formed country committees for UNICEF, and the appointment of UNICEF's first goodwill ambassador, Danny Kaye, all helped UNICEF accomplish its goal of worldwide name recognition. This in turn helped UNICEF form ties with developing nations, and these relationships became important given that UNICEF's support from Western nations had begun to decline due to Cold War–fueled objections to UNICEF's staff and programs.[10] These new ties assured that when the discussion about its fate came before the General Assembly again in 1953, there would be overwhelming support from these developing nations to approve its status as a permanent UN organization. UNICEF's own pamphlets and pictorial histories, UNICEF official documents and publications, Maurice Pate's personal papers, and testimonies from UNICEF employees and volunteers recount the story of the final push for permanence, which UNICEF received from the General Assembly in 1953.

For more than a decade after 1953, UNICEF's programs still relied on their association with U.S. policies in both foreign relations and gender definitions while they moved into parts of the world very different culturally, socially, and politically from the United States and the West. Slow to change, UNICEF found itself facing embarrassing program failures due to its belligerent adherence to a one-size-fits-all mindset. It eventually began to modify its programs in the 1970s when confronted with the demands from a powerful Western women's movement that it change its views on women and their role in the care of children. This led UNICEF to acknowledge that children and their parents needed different rights and protections, that mothers functioned as farmers, entrepreneurs, and primary providers for their children and families, and that children and their mothers had a right to things like education and clean water in addition to basic relief aid. The UN declared 1979 the International Year of the Child, showcasing UNICEF's work in post-colonial and developing regions. A little more than a decade later, UNICEF sponsored the Word Summit for Children in 1990, the largest meeting of its kind in both attendance and scope. This summit illustrated how far UNICEF's programs had come, but also how much farther they needed to reach to assist children and mothers facing poverty, violence, disease, and discrimination. UNICEF still faces opposition to its programs today as it did in the 1940s and 1950s, but relies on the original resolution that made it an organization to declare that it is "the driving force that helps build a world where the rights of every child are realized."[11]

NOTES

1. Paul Kennedy, *The Parliament of Man: The Past, Present and Future of the United Nations* (New York: Random House, 2006), 143–76.

2. Kennedy, 3.

3. Keith Middlemas, *Power, Competition and the State: Britain in Search of Balance, 1940-61* (Stanford: Hoover Institution Press, 1986); Mark Mazower, *No Enchanted Palace: The End of Empire and the Ideological Origins of the United Nations* (Princeton and Oxford:

Princeton University Press, 2009), and *Governing the World: The History of an Idea, 1815 to the Present* (New York: Penguin Books, 2012); Arnold A. Offner and Theodore A. Wilson, *Victory in Europe, 1945: From World War to Cold War* (Lawrence: University Press of Kansas, 2000); John W. Young, *France, the Cold War and the Western Alliance, 1944-1949: French Foreign Policy and Post-War Europe* (New York: St. Martin's Press, 1990).

4. Elaine Tyler May, *Homeward Bound: American Families in the Cold War Era* (New York: Basic Books, Inc., 1988), 22–24.

5. Cynthia Enloe, *The Morning After: Sexual Politics at the End of the Cold War* (Berkeley: University of California Press, 1993), 3.

6. Robert G. Moeller, *Protecting Motherhood: Women and the Family in the Politics of Postwar West Germany* (Berkeley: University of California Press, 1993); Seth Koven and Sonya Michel, eds., *Mothers of a New World: Maternalist Politics and the Origins of Welfare States* (New York: Routledge, 1993).

7. Terry R. Kandal, *The Woman Question in Classical Sociological Theory* (Miami: Florida International University Press, 1998); Anne Digby and John Stewart, eds., *Gender, Health and Welfare* (New York: Routledge, 1996); Frances Fox Piven and Richard A. Cloward, *Regulating the Poor: The Functions of Public Welfare* (New York: Pantheon Books, 1971).

8. See Birte Siim, *Gender and Citizenship: Politics and Agency in France, Britain and Denmark* (Cambridge: Cambridge University Press, 2000); Jet Bussemaker, "Citizenship, Welfare State Regimes and Breadwinner Arrangements: Various Backgrounds of Equality Policy." In *Sex Equality Policy in Western Europe*, Frances Gardiner, ed. (New York: Routledge, 1997); Alice Kessler-Harris, *In Pursuit of Equity: Women, Men, and the Quest for Economic Citizenship in Twentieth-Century America* (Oxford: Oxford University Press, 2001); and Frances Fox Piven and Richard A. Cloward, *Poor People's Movements: Why They Succeed, How They Fail* (New York: Pantheon Books, 1977).

9. Social welfare programs and the ways they exhibit gender biases have been the object of study in many fields during the last fifteen to twenty years. Economists, sociologists, historians, and psychologists have examined the bases for establishing social welfare relief, how programs changed over time due to economic and social factors, why basic assumptions about providing relief on the basis of sex have remained largely unchanged for over one hundred years, and how this disadvantages women in particular in their role as wage earner and primary provider. Pat Thane, *Foundations of the Welfare State* (New York: Longman, 1982); Susan Pedersen, *Family, Dependence and the Origins of the Welfare State, Britain and France, 1914-1945* (New York: Cambridge University Press, 1993); Gisela Bock and Pat Thane, eds., *Maternity and Gender Policies: Women and the Rise of the European Welfare States, 1880s-1950s* (London: Routledge, 1991).

10. Akira Iriye argues that, in 1946, UNICEF recognized its mandate to provide relief aid to children could reach far beyond Europe, which would require funding from a more diverse base than its original U.S. backers. In Akira Iriye, *Global Community: The Role of International Organizations in the Making of the Contemporary World* (Berkeley and Los Angeles: University of California Press, 2002), 50.

11. http://www.unicef.org/about/who/index_introduction.html.

Chapter One

Charity for Children

When the UN sanctioned the creation of a relief aid organization for children and their mothers in 1946, it generated a new chapter in the long history of maternal and child health and welfare. The new organization, originally called the International Children's Emergency Fund, relied on the traditions built by its predecessor organizations to establish its administrative structure, define its clientele, and determine how it would fund, procure, and distribute relief aid. Only the second international, institutionalized relief aid organization founded to specifically serve the needs of children, UNICEF, as it would eventually be known, adopted an organizational structure developed by similar twentieth-century relief aid organizations, such as the Commission for Relief in Belgium and the American Relief Administration. Its clientele had also been the focus of Save the Children International Union and of the United Nations Relief and Rehabilitation Administration, which eventually included mothers in its child aid programs due to their importance to the survival of children. Funding, procurement, and distribution efforts relied on the knowledge gained from these organizations and built on a history of mother and child health and welfare care that had first emerged in the West from the Christian tradition in Europe that called for ministering to the poor.

The tradition of providing charity for children and mothers in the West began with the work of churches, which, until the start of the nineteenth century, provided the bulk of this kind of assistance. Often motivated by a call from scripture to care for the poor, churches distributed food and clothing to care for children whose families could not provide for them and established orphanages for children without families. By the nineteenth century, child relief aid expanded beyond the church when, supported by studies conducted by medical practitioners and social scientists, poverty began to be viewed as a social problem rather than an ongoing, unchangeable situation to

be ameliorated by providing for basic human needs. As a result, both private
charity and government sponsored assistance appeared in the nineteenth century, most often in response to studies concerning social problems identified
and assessed by practitioners in the fields of medicine and the social sciences. These studies enumerated the underlying causes for social problems as
well as the prescriptions for correcting them.

Charity for children and mothers therefore became less about providing
basic necessities to the poor and more about eliminating poverty by carefully
analyzing its component causes and prescribing a cure. This often meant that
individual members of a family began to be defined by their specific roles in
and responsibilities to the family, regardless of the family's financial status.
If each member of the family adhered to his or her prescribed role, it was
believed that the family would survive. More promising was the idea that
poor families could even eliminate their need for assistance. Curing poverty
evolved to include reform movements and legislation on both local and national levels meant to carry out prescriptions for its elimination.[1] Conducted
in a scientific manner and focused on the inevitability of their progress, the
primary goal of each movement, organization, and piece of legislation was to
provide individualized relief aid that would supply individual members of a
family with what was required for them to fulfill their individual roles. This
assistance would, it was believed, preserve the family as a whole and, from
1800 to 1913, an abundance of examples of efforts to eliminate poverty and
preserve the family appeared throughout the West.

Reform movements sprang into action to ensure individuals followed
prescriptions, and helped not only with the distribution of temporary relief
aid in the form of food, clothing, and medical care, but with sponsoring
legislation on both local and national levels as well. Of primary importance
was the protection of the family as defined by the experts, and, when necessary, the provision of temporary relief aid for its individual members.[2] Prior
to the outbreak of World War I, specific examples of this push to protect the
family, whether via charitable efforts or government actions, proliferate. In
the United States, political Progressives had taken it upon themselves to care
for the poor through private charities, residence and settlement houses, and
community education programs. Historian Kriste Lindenmeyer argues that it
was due to their dogged lobbying that the U.S. government began to take
notice of the plight of the poor.[3] Actions taken to alleviate their suffering
included passing legislation regarding work hours and education, and creating government departments such as the U.S. Children's Bureau, established
to study, make recommendations regarding programs, and provide assistance
to families living in poverty. At the same time, European nations had created
more substantial social welfare organizations funded and administered by the
state. Most of these provided for family relief and had already established

food distribution programs and rudimentary medical care for families in need.

In addition to the pressure brought to bear by political activists on both continents to help the poor, governments in both the United States and Europe had begun to feel the pressure of the growing presence of a women's movement that asserted that children and mothers be regarded as separate groups when conceiving and implementing social welfare programs.[4] In particular, activists called for better aid for women in poverty, as well as for changing the definition of those considered to be impoverished to make the rather malleable and amorphous group more inclusive and easier to identify.[5] In the United States, government departments designed specifically to assist children began to form, filling their ranks with Progressive men and women who had spent their careers in service to the poor.[6] France, Britain, Norway, Sweden, Italy, Spain, and Germany also found themselves urged to consider children and mothers as groups possessing specific needs within their social welfare policies by individuals who believed it was possible to change the existing order for the better. Compelled by a group of well-educated activist individuals, governments debated how to provide adequate care for children and mothers living within their borders, most often identified by the state as dependent.[7]

Government agencies began to consider multiple options in their quest to provide relief aid to mothers and children. From providing an additional wage increase for families with children to giving an allowance for the maintenance of children, government aid programs most often reflected the form it expected a family to take.[8] For example, the income-supplement type of assistance program assumed the family structure included a father who earned a wage to support his family, a mother whose primary focus was the care of her children, and the children themselves, who were to attend school and defer to the various authorities with which they came in contact, including parents, teachers, and various church officials. Providing a supplement to the household income marked a distinct departure from food and clothing distribution programs already in existence, which had given assistance directly to mothers, which they in turn used to feed and clothe their children. Other programs provided a mother's pension, which paid a small sum to mothers directly. These programs appeared in at least twenty-two countries including the United States at the start of the twentieth century according to a U.S. Children's Bureau study published in 1914.[9] Pamphlets appeared, covering every topic from infant mortality to child health conferences to prenatal care for mothers, and the trans-Atlantic conversation on how to best care for the children and mothers crackled with energy. Numerous agencies and individuals searched for the best ways to guarantee what had by 1914 informally been identified as a right to a healthy, happy childhood, and depended almost exclusively on the presence of a caring, competent mother.[10]

The progression of this discussion over how to care for mothers and children slowed considerably, however, when in 1914 war quickly engulfed Europe. Relief aid organization priorities subsequently shifted from dealing with the poor to providing relief to those living with war and occupation. As the conflict dragged on rather than coming to a swift end as had been predicted, organizations began to focus their efforts more narrowly in order to assist specifically defined groups, including children. The war also allowed a shift to begin in how destitute populations were defined. Instead of viewing poor families as requiring temporary assistance to return to a more normal existence, war defined families as unable to survive if they were not provided basic relief assistance in the form of food, clothing, and medical care. Total war and its accompanying devastation of infrastructure, agriculture, and society compelled aid organizations to focus not on providing temporary assistance meant to alleviate suffering due to a temporary crisis, but to try and save countless lives—innocent lives made miserable through no fault of their own—with the distribution of food, clothing, and medical care.

Another unintended consequence of this outpouring of transnational charity emerged in the form of experience for the individuals who organized, funded, and distributed aid. Hundreds of aid workers emerged from the war with a different understanding of the enormity of the task of establishing and running transnational and international relief organizations. One of the most prominent and successful of these organizations, founded by Herbert Hoover and administered by a hand-picked group of American men, helped bring relief assistance to Belgians after the German army's invasion and occupation began in August, 1914. By October, 1914—a mere two months after German troops entered the country—virtually all of Belgium had fallen under German control. As a result, factories closed, commerce became paralyzed, and postal and telegraphic communication all but ceased. Food supplies had been looted or requisitioned by German troops, creating a desperate situation since, prior to the war, Belgium had only produced one-fourth of the food supply needed to feed its population, the balance coming from exports. These circumstances led to the creation of the Commission for Relief in Belgium (CRB). While not originally conceived as a child-aid organization, the CRB eventually focused much of its efforts on the child population in Belgium.

The CRB came into being once it became clear that German troops intended to provide little, if any, assistance to Belgians during the occupation, and Hoover made his first visit to occupied Belgium to ascertain the extent of need. Vernon Kellogg, a chief CRB administrator, recalled that Hoover was "deeply touched by the distress of children, and [was] impelled by this to use all of his intelligence and energy to relief this distress."[11] Once established, however, the CRB's day-to-day operations relied on that group of young American men who would reside in Belgium and ensure the distribution of the supplies that arrived via ship. The men who participated in the CRB's efforts in Belgium included a twenty-two-year-old Denver native named Maurice Pate. He began his CRB work with impressive Ivy League credentials but little to no experience in providing relief aid anywhere prior to his appointment to the CRB. [12]

Volunteering to work with the CRB appealed to Pate, who, according to Judith Spiegelman, experienced his first philanthropic impulse at the age of four while attending church. Hearing about the plight of poor children in his neighborhood who lacked food, Spiegelman writes that Pate overcame shyness and a "serious stammer" to knock on doors, helping his family to collect money for the needy. [13] After his graduation from East Denver High School, Pate went east to attend Princeton University, where he first experienced volunteering for an international relief aid organization. He participated in the activities of the Princeton chapter of the International Red Cross in addition to studying physics and mathematics, graduating with honors in 1915. Returning to Denver after graduation to work in banking for his uncle, Pate became interested in finding a way to participate in the war in Europe. The CRB would allow him to continue the relief aid work he had begun with the Red Cross at Princeton and, after receiving his appointment as an administrator and his travel orders, he left Denver on May 14, 1916, headed for Belgium. An article titled "Denver Man Helps to Feed 50,000 Belgians" claimed Pate was the youngest person chosen to work with the CRB, "One of thirty-five zealous Americans . . . holding death at bay for the starving subjects of King Albert's hapless land." [14] He boarded the *Ryndam* of the Holland-America Line in June, 1916, and began the journey to a job he knew little about but that would set the course of his life' s work. [15]

Traveling to his new post would prove tedious and involved a significant delay in port to accomplish the processing of entry and residence papers, but taught Pate much about what to expect from international travel. A copious writer and recorder of events, he used his idle time on board the ship to pen informative and reassuring letters to his family. While waiting to disembark, he noted in a letter to his mother dated June 27, 1916, that the only persons on board his vessel headed to Belgium were members of the commission; other travelers included women returning to their husbands in Germany and a doctor's party including doctors and nurses bound for Vienna. He went on to describe a shipboard conversation with a fellow Belgian-bound passenger, Mrs. Charlotte Kellogg, wife of CRB administrator Vernon Kellogg, who revealed details about the interworkings of the acquisition and distribution process in which Pate would soon be participating. "The country is divided into districts, each under one, two or three Americans. The chief function of the Americans is to get the food into Belgium: and after it reaches there in sealed cases to see that it is checked and placed in the commission warehouses." [16]

It becomes clear in Pate's letter that his conversation with Mrs. Kellogg may have revealed details about the basic duties and responsibilities of a CRB administrator that had been previously unknown to him. Describing the CRB's relief aid processes, Pate made known that, once in Belgium, the CRB's main task involved providing aid to the Belgian authorities who either gave or sold that relief aid to individuals, making sure to provide "just enough for necessary sustenance."[17]

This passage in Pate's letter provides important insight into relief aid distribution in two ways. The first concerns the economic and scientific principles used to determine the scope of supplies needed as well as how to distribute relief aid in the twentieth century. Whether to individuals or to countries, relief aid organizations established a precedent of requiring some payment or promise of payment for the relief assistance being provided. The CRB and other international relief aid organizations that followed it, including UNRRA and UNICEF, adopted this payment-for-aid procedure. Instead of procuring relief aid items then simply distributing them to individuals in need, assistance came with expectation of payment. In its "Manual for Information for the Representatives of the Commission for Relief in Belgium," the CRB's instructions to its operatives made it clear that "the people in general lacked not money but rather the opportunity to spend it for much-needed food." The "well-to-do," it claimed, could purchase food, and that "slight profit," combined with the "generous gifts from all over the world enabled the Commission to furnish food . . . to the poorer classes." In spite of the fact that persons living in war or occupied territories had come to their situation through no fault of their own, those with means as well as governments of these combatant nations and occupied territories were expected to contribute to, not take from, relief aid programs.[18] To provide relief assistance without extracting funds countered the idea that aid was a form of temporary relief, meant solely to help a return to self-sufficiency.[19]

In addition to economic principles, Pate's phrase "just enough for necessary sustenance" reflects the countless hours of scientific research performed by both public and private organizations regarding proper nutrition, the types of food that would provide this nutrition, and the exact amounts required to meet basic nutrition needs. Robinson Smith reinforced this in his summary of the work of the CRB. He wrote: "Rationing, if rightly played, is the finest game in the world . . . it ensures that everyone shall have his due amount of food at minimum cost."[20] Studies like these would proliferate as relief aid organizations, both domestic and international, began to expand their scope in the twentieth century. Both the America Relief Administration (ARA) and the Save the Children International Union proposed weekly rations based on nutritional studies, touting items such as tinned milk, cheeses, and dried milk and vegetables as necessary to provide minimum levels of nutrition. Subsequent proposals from other child relief aid organizations, including UNICEF, would include similar lists backed by the most current nutritional information, all of which included milk as a primary item necessary for good child nutrition.[21] These lists not only became important for replicating studies that determined basic nutritional needs, but also became shopping lists of a sort, allowing organizations to establish a budget that assisted them in raising funds and determining the fees countries would need to pay for relief aid.

Insight into the food-distribution operations of the CRB notwithstanding, Pate's letters make great effort to try and reassure his parents that his work would also provide him with cultural and social opportunities and would add to his experience and would, above all, be safe. He notes in his first letter after arriving in Rotterdam that, while the men waited for their passes, "the Commission is quartering us at the Maas, the finest hotel in Rotterdam." Rotterdam, he continued, housed the most important of the CRB offices, as "every pound of food for Belgium goes through here." Emphasizing the importance of his task, he reminds his parents: "It is impossible for us in the United States to comprehend the enormity of the commission's work—outside of the war itself is the biggest undertaking in the world at present."[22] Pate had discovered during his conversation with Charlotte Kellogg that he would be boarding with a Belgian family. This, he wrote, pleased him a great deal as he "wish[ed] to acquire his French this way." And, when asked about the type of homes in which CRB staffers were housed, Charlotte Kellogg "said that the Commission members wherever they go are given the finest Belgian homes or chateaux for individual use." He does his best to soothe his parents' concerns, writing that "Mrs. K told us that there was nothing which the Belgians would not do for the Americans with the Commission in providing every convenience, so you can be sure I will be all right."[23]

Pate's letters, replete with their work details and kind reassurances, tell us much about Pate the individual and how his role as one of the most well-known relief aid providers of his generation evolved as a result of his work with the CRB. In July, 1916, his diary entry includes the idea that part of the goal of the CRB's "function is to serve—not to judge."[24] He seems to have understood that the juxtaposition between his status as a privileged American who played tennis, ordered custom tailored suits, and ate luxuriously as the guest of Belgian notables made providing basic food aid to desperate Belgians possible.[25] And, even though he attended dinners he described as "prosperous" making "Thanksgiving repast small in proportion," he made the decision to eat the rations provided to the Belgians for a six-day period, writing that he "decided to make this test in order to be able to judge at first hand whether the more destitute of the population actually receive enough to sustain them."[26] Pate confided to his father that he took on the CRB work in order to "be able to accomplish something and be a part of this undertaking," and learning to negotiate between these two poles helped him succeed in his future endeavors as a provider of international relief aid who attended black-tie fundraisers one week then visited relief aid stations in Africa the next. In a 1916 letter to his father, he declared that a colleague told him working with the CRB was "the best experience he has ever had . . . and every man who once starts the work wants to continue it"; and, with the exception of a brief period during which he returned to banking work, Pate continued relief aid work for the rest of his life.[27]

Pate's almost daily diary entries attest to his desire to maintain as detailed a record as possible of his experiences, illustrating how much these affected his vocational path. They also reveal how the neutrality of the United States made it possible for him to travel both inside and outside Belgium, recording his observations on the effects of war from the perspective of a neutral non-combatant-a status on which Pate would rely many times in the future in order to gather information and distribute relief aid. Finally, they provide insight into the principles on which Pate would base his leadership of UNICEF, specifically with regard to food aid assistance. When the United States entered the war in August, 1917, Pate enlisted in the U.S. Army; but, for about a year, Pate learned a great deal about the glaring indignities and inequities of war and how these could be ameliorated by a self-declared non-political organization sanctioned to provide relief aid led by an individual who could maneuver through the chasm between wealthy donors and individuals in need.

The end of the war in 1918 did little to change the availability of basic necessities in Europe, and while Pate began working with another Hoover relief aid program, a young English woman acted on her philanthropic impulses to focus on food aid for children. Eglantyne Jebb, born in 1876 to a wealthy English family whose matriarch spent much of her time in volunteer efforts, received an Oxford education in addition to her home-schooling in charitable work. She began a career in teaching and, upon finding it unsatisfying, remained open to exerting her energies elsewhere. It was in 1913 during a trip to the Balkans to visit Macedonian refugees that Jebb's work became focused on providing relief aid. She and her sister, Dorothy Buxton, would eventually found Save the Children, the first international child relief aid organization of its kind.[28]

Historian Linda Mahood writes in her book about Jebb's life and work with Save the Children: "There was nothing new about a children's charity in 1920," noting that "an elaborate network of voluntary child welfare agencies, homes, ragged school programmes and emigration schemes had evolved" leading states to adopt legislation for "higher standards of child health and education."[29] In this way, she echoes the sentiments of social historians Pat Thane, Susan Pedersen, and Gisela Bock, who have examined the ways in which relief aid organizations in Europe and, to some extent, the United States, shared studies and observations on processes and programs, thereby creating an informal network that traded information but did not come together as one organization to raise funds and provide relief aid.[30] Indeed, the U.S. Children's Bureau published a study in 1914 titled "Laws Relating to Mothers' Pensions in the United States, Denmark and New Zealand" that compared the programs being administered in twenty-two U.S. states to those in Denmark and New Zealand. The study is factual rather than analytical in nature; however, it does reinforce that these transnational networks existed and provided a forum for sharing important information on maternal and child health and welfare and relief aid in general.[31]

It was Edward Fuller, a member of the Save the Children board, who observed that, despite the prevalence of the informal network, the formally institutionalized international scope of Save the Children did have a precedent. In *The Right of the Child: A Chapter in Social History*, Fuller wrote that the International Red Cross Committee in Switzerland not only influenced how Jebb established Save the Children, but also provided "patronage . . . a boon which was to eventuate in the Committee's participation in the formation of the [Save the Children] International Union in January 1920."[32]

Francesca Wilson's 1967 biography of Jebb provides a framework for understanding how, in the 1920s, Save the Children emerged as a formal, permanent, apolitical, institutionalized, international child relief aid organization that began to replace large portions of the informal network and, to some extent, the work of the CRB, that had existed prior to and during the war. Linda Mahood critiques Wilson's work as a "hagiographical representation of her [Jebb's] achievements";[33] nevertheless, Wilson' s recounting of events, which drew from Jebb's personal papers as well as from interviews with her surviving relatives, helps elucidate how Save the Children marks the beginning of a permanent shift in the way relief aid organizations operated, changing them from affable collaborators to cantankerous competitors whose agendas were not always as apolitical as they appeared.

Wilson's claim that Save the Children and Fight the Famine before it were "political: [their goal was] to influence public opinion and above all the Government" supports the notion that apolitical organizations could not avoid the political.[34] Jebb and her sister Dorothy Buxton, who had been working with the Fight the Famine Council in Britain, "were particularly concerned with the lack of food supplies." Echoing the work of the CRB, they viewed the task of alleviating the suffering of Europeans as most urgent and made appeals for the British government to distribute funds to needy nations in order to "get Europe's economy going again," as poverty could prove "deadly to women and children." And, in an effort to emphasize just how great the need had become due to poverty, Jebb recruited Dr. Hector Munro, a public health expert, to accompany her when she appealed to the Archbishop of Canterbury and the Pope to provide funding for both food and medical aid programs.[35]

The Save the Children International Union brought together twenty-seven countries, all dedicated to upholding Jebb's "Declaration of the Rights of the Child," which later became known as the "Declaration of Geneva." Drafted in 1922, Fuller described it as the recognition that "Mankind owes to the Child the best that it has to give." The participating nations promised to provide for a child to develop normally, both materially and spiritually; to feed the hungry, nurse the sick, and shelter the orphaned; to provide relief to children first in times of distress; to protect children from exploitation; and to teach children to serve others.[36] According to Wilson, relief aid work began immediately in post–World War I Europe, then expanded to providing relief to Russia during the famine, and to Greek refugees "displaced by the armed conflict that ensued after WWI."[37] With all its efforts to remain apolitical and focused on a sympathetic, non-controversial demographic, Save the Children nevertheless faced criticisms and protests when its programs began providing aid to countries whose political alignment did not mirror those of its most prominent funders. Finding its distribution of milk to Russian children too "left-leaning," Wilson notes that many in England with the most to contribute balked when asked to donate to the cause. It seems that Jebb spent a great deal of time responding to these critics, relying on the charter to reinforce that Save the Children's mission was to help all children, regardless of their place or race. Jebb's persistent contention that "a child is a child" not only helped Save the Children survive, it also resulted in a League of Nations endorsement accompanied by the recommendation that all League members emulate Save the Children's focus on providing relief aid to children.[38]

Save the Children was not the only organization providing relief aid to Russia during its famine. The American Relief Administration (ARA), established by the U.S. Congress in 1919, distributed relief aid in central and eastern Europe until 1923. According to historian Bertrand Patenaude, Woodrow Wilson named Herbert Hoover program director based on his work with the CRB. Staffed by many CRB alums, the ARA, with its U.S. mandate and its reliance on contributions from Russian republics, could not have peddled itself as apolitical nor as strictly charitable. Relying on the pay-for-aid model and influenced by the anti-Bolshevik sentiments that proliferated in the West, the ARA continued several precedents in the distribution of relief aid by the CRB and inaugurated political tensions that, according to Patenaude, lingered long after the ARA departed from Russia.

Prior to his work with the ARA, Hoover had traveled to Russia for business purposes in 1913. His visit coincided with a period of extreme worker unrest there, during which thousands of strikes were held. Hoover's business interests succeeded regardless, and he noted in his memoirs that "from the moment the fires in the new furnaces were started, the company made money." His satisfaction with the money made, however, could not diminish his dislike for the "hideous social and governmental backgrounds" he observed there.[39] The concern over unrest in Russia and what it meant for the future stability of the nation had gathered a vast audience of anxious observers. Those concerns turned into very real fears with the Revolution in 1917, but the ongoing war in Europe made it difficult for any action to be taken by the United States or its allies to ascertain the true nature of the situation.

When the war ended, President Wilson invited Hoover, who had worked as Wilson's food administrator since 1917, to accompany the U.S. delegation to Paris. Applying the lessons learned from the CRB, Hoover helped administer U.S. relief aid to Europe and established a relief effort that Patenaude describes as "a marriage of convenience between philanthropy and business."[40] And, like the CRB, the ARA chose credentialed young men to serve as administrators, many of whom had worked for the CRB—including Maurice Pate.

It is interesting to note that, in his own papers as well as the many notices put forth by various individuals and organizations announcing Pate's death, his work with the ARA is rarely mentioned in lists of his achievements. He spent time with the ARA working in Poland as the director of the Children's Relief Bureau, for which he received accolades from heads of state at a banquet held in his honor.[41] Indeed, he receives only a brief mention in Patenaude's more than seven hundred page work on the ARA titled *The Big Show in Bololand*. The single story recounted describes how Pate, along with one of his ARA colleagues, had been instructed to be captured by the Soviet army as it moved west in 1920. This capture was to have supported a larger effort by the ARA to gain access to high-ranking Soviet officials in the hope that conversations to expand the ARA's operations could begin. Though mentions of Pate in the histories of the ARA are fleeting, and his own papers held at Princeton University provide little information about his experiences, this single event is significant. His work with the ARA added to Pate's vocational development and influenced his eventual leadership of UNICEF in several key ways, including negotiating between banquets and field work as well as dealing with challenges to UNICEF personnel delivering supplies to Soviet bloc countries after World War II. The passage also reveals the underlying motives in the ARA's programs, both economic and political, that coexisted with the purely humanitarian aspects of the operation—motives that would resurface in a modified form during the first years of UNICEF's relief aid programs.

The motivation to make the operation financially efficient constituted one of the ARA's primary goals. By collecting donations from a variety of sources, including recipient countries, the continuation of the ARA's programs could be assured while upholding the idea that governments bore financial responsibility for programs in which they participated. This becomes clear in the detailed financial accounts of historian H. H. Fisher as well as the records published by Hoover associates Frank Surface and Raymond Bland. Their notes on the ARA's financials indicate that it collected "$11,357,325.13" in "Gold Funds of the Russian Republics;" "$4,374,893.28" from "sales in Russia to Affiliated Relief and Other Organizations"; "subsidies"; "donations of commodities"; and, "services and facilities" totaling "$14,652,432.21."[42] Patenaude claims that the "ARA delivered food worth over $150 million . . . to twenty-one countries" during the period between 1921 and 1923, handily adapting the CRB model to a much larger, longer-running undertaking to ensure it remained in the black.[43]

Solvency meant continued operations, which coincidentally supported several of the ARA's political motives as well. According to Patenaude, Hoover and the U.S. government that backed the ARA's operations viewed food as a weapon for achieving political ends. A fed population allowed the United States to divest itself of surplus agricultural products and help make the population more productive, thereby supporting an economic recovery. This economic recovery could increase the demand for U.S. manufactured goods as well. Feeding the hungry could also foster political stability, which could succeed in preventing the spread of Bolshevism, which Patenaude insists was a primary factor: "There was in fact nothing neutral about the proposed commission [ARA]. It was designed for intervention of the most extreme kind and was tantamount to ordering the Bolsheviks to call off the Revolution."[44]

The ARA, guided by these motives, carried out its relief aid programs until 1923. Pate remained in Poland, and for the next seventeen years worked in business, according to his friend and relief aid volunteer colleague Helenka Pantaleoni. She first met Pate when she began volunteering for the Polish Relief Commission in 1939 for which Pate served as executive director.[45] She recalled that Pate never really exited his relief aid work, noting his efforts for prisoners of war for the Red Cross during World War II once the Polish Relief Commission ceased its fundraising efforts.[46] Pantaleoni and Pate would combine their efforts once the war ended when the demise of a transnational relief aid organization, the United Nations Relief and Rehabilitation Administration (UNRRA), created a void in providing relief aid to Europeans, specifically to children. UNRRA emerged from the sponsorship of the United States and Britain, its primary objective to provide relief aid to liberated regions of Europe prior to the end of the war. It left legacies to UNICEF in the form of provisions and policies that both helped and hindered UNICEF as it attempted to provide relief aid to children and mothers after the war.

UNRRA operatives followed Allied troops into liberated regions of Europe bearing food, clothing, and medical care for the civilian populations living there. Its operations, begun in 1943, resolved that

immediately upon the liberation of any area by the armed forces of the United
Nations or as a consequence of retreat of the enemy population thereof shall
receive aid and relief from their sufferings, food, clothing, and shelter, aid in
the prevention of pestilence and in the recovery of the health of the people . . .
and for assistance in the resumption of urgently needed agricultural and indus-
trial production and the restoration of essential services. [47]

UNRRA claimed that as a "pioneer organization, doing a job of scope and
significance new to history . . . it had to learn by doing."[48] Its official history
notes that UNRRA brought together staff from many countries to conduct its
relief operations, and, in the end, provided relief assistance to "seventeen
war-warped countries."[49]

Despite its charge to provide relief assistance to liberated regions of Europe, UNRRA's scope was much wider than its press appeared. In addition to
the basics, UNRRA would attempt to restore both in Europe and parts of
Asia "those segments of a nation's economy which were necessary to carry
out the relief program, and to give each country and its people some of the
tools to begin to help themselves."[50] In his first quarterly report on UNRRA
Expenditures and Operations to the U.S. Congress, President Roosevelt reveals this wider mandate, noting that "UNRRA representatives are already
on their way to liberated areas of Europe and are preparing to go the Far
East." Roosevelt's report includes the monetary contributions authorized by
the U.S. Congress. The contributions would be made in three installments,
the first in the amount of $1,350,000,000 and two more, one for
$450,000,000 and a third for $350,000,000. Roosevelt's letter notes that
these contributions, which made up the bulk of UNRRA's funding, would
provide a mere 2 percent of the relief aid required by recipient nations.[51]

The restoration of industry and agriculture destroyed by years of constant
bombing, as well as assisting with education rehabilitation, were also included in UNRRA's mandate, activities that made its apolitical status questionable.[52] A 1945 pamphlet titled "UNRRA: Organization, Aims, Progress"
makes it clear that, when founded in 1943, UNRRA's original organizational
goals had included the "resumption of urgently needed agriculture and indus-
trial production and the restoration of essential services," which would, according to the National Planning Association, help the United States transition into its new role as a creditor nation if careful attention was paid to U.S.
policy on foreign trade.[53]

In addition to its economic interests, UNRRA also made provisions to
assist with education rehabilitation. The report of the director general, Herbert Lehman, submitted in March, 1946, addresses UNRRA's participation
in this effort, which included assessing children in Nazi-occupied regions
upon their liberation, a program that also had been proposed by Save the
Children as early as 1942.[54] Save the Children insisted that, in occupied

regions such as Luxembourg, re-education for children would be necessary in order for them to leave their occupational indoctrination behind, as well as to ensure their ability to productively participate in democratic processes that would emerge after the war. Lehman noted that, while "UNRRA has not been authorized to furnish supplies for general education rehabilitation," it would supply items in support of this effort and would work in concert with the newly formed UN agency, UNESCO (United Nations Educational, Scientific and Cultural Organization), to "coordinate those activities of international educational agencies which are related to educational rehabilitation."[55]

UNRRA's participation in efforts outside the distribution of relief aid further echo the notion that food, clothing, and medical care frequently included political and economic stowaways intended to influence as well as restore. The National Planning Association's 1944 pamphlet titled "Food for Europe After Victory" provides further evidence of this, declaring that the "guiding principle" of any U.S.-supported relief aid program, including UNRRA's, "is the achievement by democratic means of the highest possible material and cultural standard of living for the whole people." Achieving this objective included using U.S. policy on foreign trade to ensure that foreign trade helped both the nation and its workers.[56]

Even with the promise of political and economic benefit to the United States, concerns over the number of countries being served, as well as the type of aid being provided and how it was obtained, placed UNRRA under scrutiny by the U.S. Congress almost immediately when it planned to provide aid to Communist nations. This is evident in UNRRA's appearance before the Senate Subcommittee on Appropriations in November, 1945. The committee, headed by Senator Kenneth McKellar of Tennessee and including Senator Patrick McCarran from Nevada, posed pointed questions about purchases and distribution of goods to the UNRRA administrators, who wished to collect $550,000,000.00 already set aside for UNRRA, as well as procure an additional $1,350,000,000.[57]

The senators inquired about every aspect of UNRRA's operations, including what materials had been purchased, where they had been purchased and for what purpose, as well as the number of individuals employed by UNRRA and the salary of each. Several senators voiced concerns about providing items such as copper to Poland and steel pipes to Greece. In a section of the record titled "Difficulty in Reconciling Purchase of Some Items with a Relief Program," Senator Richard Russell of Georgia asked, "Why was it necessary to ship 1,230 tons of copper to Poland? What was the particular demand for it?" The U.S. UNRRA representative, Mr. David Weintraub, responded, "I don' t know specifically, but I am sure that the general answer applies. That would be in order to reestablish the communications within Poland, and repair other public utilities." Senator McKellar quickly asked, "Well, are we going to do that? The object of this so-called charity is to put up telephone poles and establish communications and build trunk lines and things of that sort? If it is that, why, I think we ought to call a halt. . . . When is this thing going to stop?" Resolving the question regarding limits on what UNRRA would and would not provide eluded Senator McKellar and his committee, since President Truman remained committed to providing assistance to the war-ravaged regions of Europe. However, he, too, had issues with UNRRA, primarily because much of its food relief had ended up in Soviet-controlled territories.[58]

By the fall of 1946, UNRRA's reports went not only to the U.S. Congress, but to the secretary-general of the newly established UN as well given that the UN would be assuming responsibility for continuing UNRRA's operations. By this time the report addressed the issues raised by Senator McKellar, chronicling the progress achieved by providing copper and other raw materials to Poland, Greece, and six other countries, many with close proximity to the Soviet Union. This report also employed dramatic language to underscore the importance of continuing both relief aid and economic assistance. "Without foreign assistance," the report claimed, "governments will be faced with an inexorable choice." This choice, whether to feed its population or to restore its infrastructure, could be eliminated as long as UNRRA continued to support "the twin tasks of relief and rehabilitation." By 1947, the report touted, and with "a limited amount of foreign assistance," each of the countries detailed in the report would be able to "substantially accomplish" restoration of both people and places and would, no doubt, exhibit the influence of its benefactors. One such example is the attention paid to nationalization of industries in Poland, which, the report hoped, could be curbed with both assistance and calls from the West for them to remain private.[59]

This 1946 report also cautions against reducing funding for UNRRA, as this would diminish the very visible relief aid programs but also the undeniable influence on Soviet-controlled territories. As early as March 1946, Herbert Lehman had sounded the alarm for funding in his report, claiming that the residual funds from the first quarter of 1946 would only be "sufficient to permit continued commitments, at best, through a portion of the second quarter." Member governments, having only provided a little less than 3 billion dollars toward UNRRA's operations, would need to reconsider their financial contributions; otherwise, "The effective scheduling if not the full realization of UNRRA's program will be correspondingly threatened." Buried in the pages of Lehman's report between calls for money and cautions about ceasing UNRRA's activities lies information on a group of relief aid recipients identified as "especially vulnerable to the effects of war" and given "special consideration in relief and rehabilitation"—children and their mothers. Lehman notes that UNRRA provided several important services to this group of "children, nursing and expectant mothers . . . and persons without resources," including "supplemental feeding and other welfare supply programs." Given special mention were China, Czechoslovakia, and Poland, two of which were aligned with the Soviet Union, and all of whom desperately needed UNRRA's assistance.[60]

Fiorello LaGuardia replaced Herbert Lehman as director general April 1946, immediately narrowing the focus of UNRRA in the hope that this would encourage the U.S. Congress to continue its monetary support of the organization. Concentrating only on feeding programs in newly liberated countries that had suffered the most depletion in their domestic resources, LaGuardia's report for the third quarter of 1946 indicates that among UNRRA's most important programs was the one "for assistance in meeting the needs of children." He wrote that, while child assistance programs had proliferated between the two world wars, "the consequences of World War II more than offset these social gains" since "the resources of governments to meet this need were enormously curtailed."[61] Even with these changes, UNRRA could not retain the support of the U.S. Congress, its primary source of funds, due to the still unresolved questions about its programs. "At the Fifth Council Session in Geneva in August, 1946, the United States and the United Kingdom," which followed its lead, announced their plans to cease support for the organization' s operations.[62]

The United States provided many reasons to justify why it could no longer support UNRRA. Those given in Geneva included the fact that "most liberated countries" had established "functioning governments," and that these new governments could now turn to the "International Bank and Monetary Fund" for funding to establish their own programs.[63] Another factor was the United States's adoption of the Marshall Plan, which required diverting funds from other types of foreign relief programs for its financing. Knowing its demise would be inevitable, UNRRA planned to make its last U.S. shipment in the spring of 1947.

LaGuardia had anticipated this action in his 1946 report, claiming that even though governments possessed the desire to "carry on child feeding . . . they have neither the food nor the funds necessary for this work, and will need help from the outside for some time beyond the life of UNRRA."[64] And, by the time Lowell Rooks, who became the director general after LaGuardia, filed his report for the fourth quarter of 1946, it included provisions for transferring UNRRA's funds and supplies to "Other International Agencies." This included the newly formed Children's Fund of the United Nations which had been sanctioned by the General Assembly to being operations on December 11, 1946.[65]

NOTES

1. Digby and Stewart write that, especially in Britain, the state did not become involved in welfare assistance to children and mothers until several causal factors appeared, including war, the increased prominence of the Labour Party, and the women's movement. See Anne Digby and John Stewart, eds., *Gender, Health and Welfare* (New York: Routledge, 1996), 1–6.

2. See Digby and Stewart, *Gender, Health and Welfare*, 1–6.

3. Kriste Lindenmeyer writes that the U.S. Children's Bureau, conceived by individuals she identifies as part of the Progressive Child Welfare Movement, reflected the influences of both men and women progressive activists. These included Homer Folks, Emma Lundberg, and John Spargo, all of whose writings had focused on industrialization and urbanization and how these had negatively affected the family and its children. Kriste Lindenmeyer, *"A Right to Childhood": The U.S. Children's Bureau and Child Welfare, 1912-1946* (Urbana: University of Illinois Press, 1997), 10.

4. Digby and Stewart, *Gender, Health and Welfare*, 5–7.

5. In their examination of the relationship of the women's movement to the state, Bock and Thane note that transnational similarities began to emerge, and that tracking these movements on regional and local levels proved less complicated than tracking them between nations. See Gisela Bock and Pat Thane, eds., *Maternity and Gender Policies: Women and the Rise of the European Welfare States, 1880s-1950s* (London: Routledge, 1991), 3–9.

6. Lindenmeyer, "A Right to Childhood," 10.

7. The change in notions of gender equality brought about by the women's movement seem to have caused a shift in the way states viewed women, moving away from focusing on biology and examining them instead on social and cultural terms. Bock and Thane, *Maternity and Gender Policies*, 14–15.

8. For information regarding government policies, see Anne-Lise Seip and Hilde Ibsen, "Family Welfare, Which Policy? Norway's Road to Child Allowances" and Jane Lewis, "Models of Equality for Women: The Case of Support for Children in Twentieth-Century Britain," in Bock and Thane, *Maternity and Gender Policies*, 40–56, 73–89.

9. U.S. Children's Bureau, "Laws relating to 'Mothers' Pensions' in the United States, Denmark and New Zealand," Dependent Children Series No. 1, Bureau Publication No. 7 (Washington: Government Printing Office, 1914).

10. A 1923 U.S. Children's Bureau publication addressed the issue of education for women on proper mothering, noting that young mothers needed help "to become a better home maker and mother." In U.S. Children's Bureau, "Standards of Public Aid to Children in Their Own Homes" by Flora Nesbitt, Bureau Publication No. 118 (Washington, DC: Government Printing Office, 1923), 34.

11. Vernon Kellogg, *Herbert Hoover: The Man and His Work* (New York: Appleton and Company, 1920), 12.

12. Vernon Kellogg's wife, Charlotte, noted in her account of the Belgian relief effort that she was the only woman on the board, and was allowed to enter Belgium in 1916 for a tour of the various sites the CRB managed. She recorded much about the CRB's operations and provided details of her visits to storage facilities and feeding stations. She offered advice to many of the young men who worked as administrators, and she recounted many of her conversations with individuals receiving assistance ranging in age from the very young to the very old, both male and female, and in a variety of settings both rural and urban. In Charlotte Kellogg, *Women of Belgium: Turning Tragedy into Triumph* (New York: Funk and Wagnalls Company, 1917).

13. Judith M. Spiegelman and UNICEF, *We Are the Children: A Celebration of UNICEF's First Forty Years* (New York: The Atlantic Monthly Press, 1986), 352.

14. Don Fitch, "Denver Man Helps to Feed 50,000 Belgians," Series 1: Personal Papers; 1904–1985; Maurice Pate Papers, Public Policy Papers, Department of Rare Books and Special Collections, Princeton University Library, Princeton University, Princeton, New Jersey. Hereafter Maurice Pate Papers, Princeton University Library.

15. Maurice Pate, Diary, 1916–1917. Maurice Pate Papers, Princeton University Library, 1.

16. Maurice Pate, letter to his mother written from the Ryndam on June 27, 1916. Maurice Pate Papers, Princeton University Library.

17. Maurice Pate, letter to his mother written from the Ryndam on June 27, 1916. Maurice Pate Papers, Princeton University Library.

18. *Manual of The Commission for Relief in Belgium* (Belgium: C.R.B., 1917). Maurice Pate Papers, Princeton University Library, 11.

19. Historian Bertrand Patenaude notes that the idea of self-help constituted one of the cornerstones of the ARA's operating principles, despite the fact that many, including George Kennan, found it to be naïve when applied in Russia as part of the famine relief effort after World War I. See Bertrand Patenaude, *The Big Show in Bololand: The American Relief Expedition to Soviet Russia in the Famine of 1921* (Stanford: Stanford University Press, 2002), 40.

20. Robinson Smith, *Food Values and Rationing of a Country* (New York: Commission for Relief in Belgium, 1917), 1.

21. Sir Frederick Mander and Brigadier-General J. G. Browne, *Children in Bondage; A Survey of Child Life in the Occupied Countries of Europe and Finland Conducted by the Save the Children Fund* (London: Longmans, Green and Co., 1942), 10; See also "The Production, Distribution and Food Value of Milk" published by The Milk Committee (Washington, DC: Government Printing Office, 1918).

22. Maurice Pate, letter to his mother and father dated July 11, 1916, from the Mass-Hotel, Rotterdam. Maurice Pate Papers, Princeton University Library.

23. Maurice Pate, letter to his mother dated June 26, 1916, from the Ryndam, Holland-America Line. Maurice Pate Papers, Princeton University Library.

24. Maurice Pate, Diary entry July 10, 1916. Maurice Pate Papers, Princeton University Library, 6.

25. Maurice Pate, letter to his parents dated July 3, 1916, from the Ryndam, Holland-America Line. Maurice Pate Papers, Princeton University Library.

26. Maurice Pate, Diary entries August 28 and 29, 1916, and December 11, 1916. Maurice Pate Papers, Princeton University Library, 23, 58.

27. Maurice Pate, letter to his father dated July 15, 1916, from the Maas-Hotel, Rotterdam. Maurice Pate Papers, Princeton University Library.

28. Linda Mahood, *Feminism and Voluntary Action: Eglantyne Jebb and Save the Children, 1876-1928* (New York: Palgrave Macmillan, 2009), 5, 34, 43, 144.

29. Mahood, *Feminism and Voluntary Action*, 167–68.

30. See Thane, *Foundations of the Welfare State*; Pedersen, *Family, Dependence and the Origins of the Welfare State, Britain and France, 1914-1945*; and Bock and Thane, Eds., *Maternity and Gender Politics: Women and the Rise of the European Welfare States, 1860s-1950s.*

31. U.S. Children's Bureau, "Laws Relating to Mothers' Pensions in the United States, Denmark and New Zealand."

32. Edward Fuller, *The Right of the Child: A Chapter in Social History* (London: Victor Gollancz, Ltd., 1951), 39–40.

33. Mahood, 5.

34. Francesca M. Wilson, *Rebel Daughter of a Country House: The Life of Eglantyne Jebb, Founder of the Save the Children Fund* (London: George Allen and Unwin Ltd., 1967), 173.

35. Wilson, 173–77.

36. Fuller, 10.

37. Wilson, 181.

38. Wilson, 182–83.

39. Herbert C. Hoover, *The Memoirs of Herbert Hoover, Volume I: Years of Adventure, 1874-1920* (New York: The MacMillan Company, 1957), 1–5, 103–5.

40. Patenaude, *The Big Show in Bololand: The American Relief Expedition to Soviet Russia in the Famine of 1921* (Stanford: Stanford University Press, 2002), 29.

41. "Banquet in Honor of Lieutenant Pate," *Morning Courier*, Warsaw, August 29, 1919. Maurice Pate Papers, Princeton University Library.

42. H. H. Fisher, *The Famine in Soviet Russia, 1919-1923: The Operations of the American Relief Administration* (New York: The MacMillan Company, 1927), appendix B, 553; Frank

M. Surface and Raymond L. Bland. *American Food in the World War and Reconstruction Period: Operations of the Organizations under the Direction of Herbert Hoover, 1914-1924* (Stanford: Stanford University Press, 1931), 144.

43. Patenaude. *The Big Show in Bololand*, 30.

44. Patenaude. *The Big Show in Bololand*, 31–32, 34.

45. I. J. Paderwieski to Maurice Pate, January 21, 1941, expressing appreciation for Pate's work as executive director of the Commission for Polish Relief. Maurice Pate Papers, Princeton University Library.

46. Helenka Pantaleoni interviewed by Richard Polsky (New York: Columbia University Oral History Project, 1977), 1–3.

47. U.S. Congressional Record, "Resolution by the U.S. Congress November 9, 1943 approving U.S. participation in UNRRA" (Washington, DC, 1943).

48. *The Story of UNRRA.* Pamphlet issued by the Office of Public Information, United Nations Relief and Rehabilitation Administration (Washington, DC, 1948), 8. (Hereafter referred to as *TSOU.*)

49. *TSOU*, 3.

50. *TSOU*, 5.

51. *Message from the President of the United States transmitting the First Quarterly Report on UNRRA Expenditures and Operations in Accordance with the Act of March 28, 1944, Authorizing United States Participation in the work of the United Nations Relief and Rehabilitation Administration* (Washington, DC: U.S. Government Printing Office, 1944), 5, 12; and U.S. Congressional Record, 79th Congress, 1st Session. House Document No. 139: *Second Report to Congress on United States Participation in UNRRA* (Washington, DC: U.S. Government Printing Office, 1945).

52. Numerous publications by the United Nations Relief and Rehabilitation Administration provided assessments of industry and agriculture. These were accompanied by prescriptions for returning national economies to pre-war status as well as how to ensure these countries would be fit to participate in global trade as quickly as possible. This is well illustrated in the UNRRA publication titled "Economic Recovery in the Countries Assisted by UNRRA: Report Presented by the Director General of UNRRA to the Secretary General of the United Nations," prepared by the Economic Advisor of UNRRA (Washington, DC: United Nations Relief and Rehabilitation Administration, 1946).

53. "UNRRA: Organization, Aims, Progress" (Washington, DC: Press of Graphic Arts Press, Inc., 1945), cover page, and "UNRRA: Gateway to Recovery" (Washington, DC: National Planning Association, 1944), 30–31.

54. *Children in Bondage: A Survey of Child Life in the Occupied Countries of Europe and Finland Conducted by the Save the Children Fund* (London: Longmans, Green and Co., 1942), 59-67.

55. *Report of the Director General to the Council for the Period 1 January 1946 to 31 March 1946* (Washington, DC: UNRRA, 1946), 11, 20.

56. "Food for Europe After Victory," Planning Pamphlet No. 29 (Washington, DC: National Planning Association, 1944), and "America's New Opportunities in World Trade," Planning Pamphlets Nos. 37–38 (Washington, DC: National Planning Association, 1944).

57. U.S. Senate Subcommittee of the Committee on Appropriations. *H.J. Res. 266, A Joint Resolution Making an Additional Appropriation for the United Nations Relief and Rehabilitation Administration for 1946: Hearings Before the Subcommittee of the Committee on Appropriations*, Seventy-Ninth Congress, First Session, 1945, 1.

58. *H.J. Res. 266*, 42–43, 53, 77.

59. *Economic Recovery in the Countries Assisted by UNRRA: Report Presented by the Director General of UNRRA to the Secretary General of the United Nations* (Washington, DC: United Nations Relief and Rehabilitation Administration, 1946), 10, 30, 87.

60. *Report of the Director General to the Council for the Period 1 January 1946 to 21 March 1946* (Washington, DC: UNRRA, 1946), 11, 74, 75, 78.

61. *Report of the Director General to the Council for the Period 1 July to 30 September 1946* (Washington, DC: UNRRA, 1946), 112–13.

62. *TSOU*, 44.

63. *TSOU*, 44–45.

64. *Report of the Director General to the Council for the Period 1 July to 30 September 1946* (Washington, DC: UNRRA, 1946), 114.

65. Report of the director general to the Council for the Period 1 October 1946 to 31 December 1946 (Washington, DC: UNRRA, 1946), 10–11.

Chapter Two

Continuing the Tradition

The United Nations and Post-War
Relief for Children, 1946

The Children's Fund emerged just as UNRRA's work, begun in 1943, started to wind down in 1946. Having continued its programs after the official end of six years of fierce warfare on the European continent, UNRRA struggled to remain financially viable in the face of increased U.S. Congressional scrutiny and reluctance to allocate funds where it could not exert more control over programs. The United Nations alliance that created UNRRA had proudly announced: "The German Armed forces on land, at sea and in the air have been completely defeated . . . and Germany, which bears responsibility for the war, is no longer capable of resisting the will of the victorious Powers."[1] Now, it was time to rally other nations around their will to relieve and rehabilitate the regions that war had all but destroyed.

Having reconquered Europe from the Nazis in May and ended the war in the Pacific by August, the allied United Nations faced several imposing challenges as they began the process of returning the post-war world to normal. UNRRA's role in helping them deal with these goals, albeit with limitations, indicated the willingness not only to provide relief aid, but also to provide the means to rehabilitate roads, rail networks, farms, factories, and society and culture. Human casualties in Europe alone totaled more than 40 million, including civilian deaths in numbers far greater than in any previous armed conflict.[2] These losses left a gaping hole in families, in towns and cities, and in the work force. Other casualties included destruction of economies, agriculture, and infrastructures. The suffering this pressed on survivors profoundly changed Europe both socially and culturally, spurring many European nations to adopt sweeping social welfare programs and to embrace the idea of economic unification that ignored national boundaries, something historian Paul Kennedy argues had begun after World War I but expanded rapidly after World War II.[3] Life in the eastern hemisphere had been disrupted irreversibly as well. The use of the first atomic weapons, which spawned a battle for atomic supremacy between the United States and the Soviet Union that lasted for almost fifty years, had the immediate effect of inflicting massive loss of life and destruction of property in Japan. China, too, required assistance to help it recover from its own losses; therefore, relief aid, reconstruction, and a return to normal in 1945 became a very different enterprise than it had been after former wars since no country could not participate, either as a provider or a recipient of aid. Kennedy writes that after a "great and bloody war," there are usually calls for the creation of a new world order, and cites the creation of the International Committee of the Red Cross in 1864 and the League of Nations in 1919 as examples.[4] However, the United Nations allies faced daunting new challenges its predecessors had not, while at the same time discovering several new opportunities as they planned their course.[5]

The allies, having negotiated terms to end armed conflicts and begun the task of assessing worldwide war damage, came together to form another international organization that they hoped would continue and expand the work of UNRRA in addressing myriad challenges they faced. The newly created United Nations (UN) emerged from the United Nations Conference on International Organization held in San Francisco in June 1945, but traced its roots back to the conference that had founded UNRRA.[6] This is evident in article 3 of the UN's charter, which proclaims, "The original Members of the United Nations shall be the states which [participated] in the United Nations Conference on International Organization at San Francisco, or . . . previously signed the Declaration of the United Nations on 1 January 1942."[7] These original founders called it the United Nations partly to signal their undisputed leadership, and partly to indicate that any nation wishing to join them must agree to their terms in order to "unite" with them in their quest. Article 4, which established the path of entry for other nations, proclaimed: "Membership in the United Nations is open to all other peace-loving states which accept the obligations contained in the present charter and, in the judgment of the Organization, are able and willing to carry out these obligations."[8] The charter enumerated lofty goals for those who signed on. A nation would have to commit to "saving succeeding generations from the scourge of war," maintaining human rights, "promoting social progress," and using "international machinery for the promotion of the economic and social advancement of all peoples."[9] The UN's primary operating principle, that countries could work together to maintain world peace, was put into action immediately after the war. The UN provided financial assistance to rebuild industry and agriculture, assisted in managing occupied Germany and Japan, and ensured the survival of populations in former war regions by providing for basic human needs in the form of relief aid. The organizational structure of the UN emerged during the months following the end of the war, concurrent with its recovery efforts. Its primary organs included the General Assembly, the Security Council, the Economic and Social Council, the Trusteeship Council, the International Court of Justice and the Secretariat, all of which focused on providing assistance now that peace had been achieved.

Five of these six primary UN organs had a clearly defined set of responsibilities. The General Assembly constituted the discussant body, while the Security Council's charge focused on maintaining international peace and security. Monitoring trust territories and ensuring their safe return to self-rule fell to the Trusteeship Council, with the International Court of Justice functioning as the primary judiciary body for the UN. The Secretariat, including the office of the secretary-general, acted as the chief administrative body. Only the Economic and Social Council had a vague albeit vast charge-to monitor "international economic, social, cultural educational, health and related matters . . . [making] recommendations . . . to the General Assembly" and calling international conferences on any matters falling under its competence.[10] All of these organs had the power to establish sub-groups as necessary to carry out their programs and uphold the primary goal of maintaining world peace, and Kennedy claims that the UN had a "broader remit to address the economic, social, and cultural reasons that it believed drove people toward conflict" than had its predecessors.[11] And, with its ambiguous assignments, the Economic and Social Council would create the most sub-organizations by far.

With its organizational structure in place, the United Nations had to resolve one pressing question in order to truly begin its work: where to locate its headquarters. It had been operating out of temporary spaces in London and Flushing, New York, as well as offices in various other cities including Washington, DC, but these, for one reason or another, proved unsuitable. The General Assembly finally decided on February 14, 1946, that a permanent site would be established in the United States in the small village of Lake Success, New York, on Long Island. By the end of 1946 the move to Lake Success had begun, with most UN members assuming it would become the organization's new, permanent home. John D. Rockefeller's offer of a parcel of land in Manhattan proper, however, led members of the General Assembly to move from Lake Success and establish the permanent headquarters there in 1950.[12] The location of its headquarters in the United States meant that individuals in proximity, especially those in New York and Washington, DC, would fill most of the administrative positions, while others with expertise in fields like relief aid, economic development and diplomacy would be available to attend sessions during which operations, programs, and sub-organization applications would be considered by the General Assembly.

Finally inhabiting its newly established headquarters, the General Assembly faced a crushing workload, including tasks both necessary and mundane. It had to decide on a symbol for the new United Nations and manage administrative staff while it also considered myriad proposals from its primary organs for the creation of sub-organizations. These would, in theory, be able to carry out more specific tasks that fell under the purview of each primary organ. The General Assembly, when at last ready to begin hearing proposals, considered one resolution 57 (I) that would create the International Children's Emergency Fund (ICEF), later known as the United Nations Children's Fund (UNICEF).[13]

According to Helenka Pantaleoni, whose appointment as an accredited U.S. observer for the United Nations Council of Women gave her access to discussions regarding the ICEF resolution, supporters of the international organization for children pushed "Delegations to the wall to get going."[14] The resolution, which made its way swiftly through the usual channels, received unanimous approval on December 11, 1946, under the authority of article 55, which stated that "with a view to the creation of conditions of stability and well-being which are necessary for peaceful and friendly relations among nations . . . [the UN] shall promote solutions of international economic, social, and health related problems."[15] The authorship of the resolution has been attributed to several individuals, all of whom worked with the ICEF in various capacities during its early years; however, there can be little doubt that those responsible for having written the document took care to include sentiments from Save the Children, which had proclaimed: "The Nation's greatest asset is the rising generation—the citizens of tomorrow," elements of the CRB's child-feeding operations that had focused on child victims of war, and UNRRA's own commitment to assist the vulnerable, which included children.[16] And, despite Pantaleoni's recollection that Maurice Pate had "barely heard anything about it" and "would like to [visit the UN] very much," Pate's own letters reveal that his involvement may have begun some time before he accompanied her to Lake Success, and would escalate swiftly after September 1946, regardless of his seeming unfamiliarity with the UN.[17]

Pate, at Pantaleoni's invitation, accompanied her as she carried out her duties as a U.S. observer for the United Nations Council of Women. These duties included identifying needs, then assessing how a UN program would affect U.S. policy.[18] Pantaleoni had long been involved in volunteer work at a national level and, as a result of her role as UN observer, she founded the group Women United for the United Nations, which brought together several powerful entities in support of UN initiatives, including the League of Women Voters, the Junior League, and the American Association of University Women.[19] This trip to Lake Success allowed Pantaleoni to share what she knew about the UN with Pate, who had only recently returned from a worldwide trip to compile information on global post-war food needs for President Truman. The consequence, intentional or not, seems to have been that both trips opened the path for his involvement in the effort to provide UN sponsored relief aid to children.

They went into the Third Committee, which Pantaleoni recalled was the Social, Cultural, Humanitarian, Educational Committee—"where Eleanor Roosevelt was the United States Delegate"—and almost immediately, one of the delegates "fished [Pate] out," claiming he needed to speak to Pate about something "very important." That delegate, Ludwik Rajchman, was known to Pantaleoni as a Polish specialist in public health.[20] Approaching Pate about his expertise with relief aid organizations, Pantaleoni recounted that Rajchman claimed he had been "thinking about Pate and wanting to see him, because" he felt Pate an excellent candidate "to think about organizing an action, a fund for the benefit of children, war victims chiefly."[21]

According to Pantaleoni, Pate and Rajchman "disappeared for a couple of hours." She knew they shared mutual concerns regarding the welfare of children, and had discussed Pate's observations from his involvement in the U.S. government's World Food Survey. Conducted at the request of President Truman and led by Herbert Hoover, this trip once again thrust Pate into a role regarding provision and distribution of food relief aid, after which he would be approached not just by Rajchman, but by others as well to apply his skills to the task of overseeing an international relief aid effort.

Attempts by the former CRB and ARA administrators to provide relief aid to Europe during World War II had achieved limited success. In 1941, Hoover, for example, had proposed to Secretary of State Cordell Hull that the United States provide relief aid to Nazi-occupied regions in ARA fashion. Hoover forwarded Hull's rather acerbic denial, dated June 29, 1941, to one of his former relief aid associates, Perrin Galpin, who subsequently provided a copy to their mutual friend Maurice Pate on July 18, 1941. Hull had denied Hoover's request to provide food, arguing: "It is clear that the responsibility and manifest duty to supply relief rests with the occupying authorities"—in other words, the German government. Hull continued, claiming that "Hitler has already brought all continental Europe to the point of starvation," and asserted that if Hoover had any information on "why, when the Hitler regime claims to have an abundance of stocks of food, the rulers of that country have not made provision at least to restore the occupied countries," it "would be of interest to this Department." Hull ended his letter by stating that he could not "elaborate in writing on the highly difficult and highly complicated military and other closely allied considerations involved in this proposal," which prompted Galpin to observe to Pate: "The Secretary was pretty sore when he wrote this I think."[22] Clearly, the impulse to provide relief aid had not waned, and had not excluded Pate. The former relief aid fraternity would find their efforts more welcome with President Truman, who commissioned

36 *Chapter 2*

Hoover to make a survey of the world food situation soon after the end of the war.

Hoover tapped Pate to serve as part of his entourage. Pate served as scribe for the World Food Survey task force and, as was his habit, Pate kept abundant notes that, when typed, totaled more than 136 pages. His unpublished record begins by noting on page 1 that the group accompanying Hoover had covered "82 days, 50,000 air miles, and 38 countries." Pate's first official act as a member of the World Food Survey occurred even before he departed the United States. Word of the trip seems to have spread among the international community in Washington, DC, and "Dr. Ludwick Rajchman, Polish Representative to UNRRA . . . [who] phoned me in my office at the American Red cross" became the first to request that Pate take Poland's concerns to Hoover. Hoover, Pate writes, met with representatives from several countries during the period from March 7 to March 11, noting that "[Polish] Ambassador Lango and Dr. Rajchman were the first to arrive" for those sessions. After concluding the discussions and amassing the necessary information to conduct their study, the group departed on March 17, 1946, from LaGuardia Airport "bound for the Azores." Pate also wistfully included that "we are all going to miss greatly [Hoover's assistant] Bunny Miller, but the Chief has decided to set the simple procedure of men only for this long voyage."[23]

The initial group that excluded Bunny Miller included Hoover, Pate, and seven of their associates from both the CRB and the ARA; a military aide and a flight surgeon tasked with watching over the former president accompanied them as well. They landed in Paris on March 19, arriving in Warsaw via Berlin on March 25. Pate's notes indicate that there is a great deal of attention paid to official protocol for the former U.S. president, and that their primary activities included formal breakfasts, lunches, and dinners. Part of one day, he observed, had been spent on visits to children's institutions and schools with the press corps.[24] Very little time, however, was actually spent with children. The group continued its journey, visiting Sweden, Norway, England, Belgium, Denmark, Austria, and Greece before continuing on to Egypt, India, Thailand, China, Korea, and Japan. They returned with their results on June 19, 1946, which subsequently became a pamphlet titled "The Children Are Hungry." This pamphlet, published by the U.S. Department of Agriculture, comprised "country by country reports on child feeding, health and welfare." Its authorship was attributed to Pate, whom it was noted was "on leave from his post as Red Cross Director of Prisoner of War Relief."[25] Pate's unpublished notes provide insight into the group's miscellaneous expenditures during the trip, including sheets of paper and gallons of gasoline used. Additionally, he kept record of the number of days on the trip lost due to illness—zero—and the failure to answer muster roll at all hours—also zero. Truman and Hoover, Pate claimed, had conducted a "very satisfactory conference," after which Hoover met with the press. A few days later, Truman requested that the group survey South America as well.[26]

This survey of Europe and Asia, and Pate's primary role in publishing and distributing its results, may have been a factor that prompted Arthur C. Ringland of the President's War Relief Control Board to solicit Pate for a job. Ringland wrote to Pate on May 17, 1946, to offer him a position on the Committee on Voluntary Aid. This committee, he wrote, would emerge as a result of the termination of the War Relief Control Board, and would be "wholly advisory" in its function. It would, Ringland mused, benefit from the inclusion of individuals with experience from the Red Cross, UNRRA, and "someone with a Hoover ARA background such as you." He closed by acknowledging that "it is asking a great deal at this particular time," but hoped Pate would consider the position. Pate had very little time to consider Ringland's offer, but most probably provided a swift reply that he would be unable to join the committee at that time; he had already been asked to accompany Hoover on the recently commissioned survey of South America, and departed on May 25, 1946, for Mexico City.[27]

The Latin America survey spanned May and June 1946. Upon its conclusion, Pate compiled another set of results for presentation to the White House. These, as well as projections from UNRRA also put forth in June, made it clear that a global food deficit of around "3,587 tons or 24 percent" existed. Most notable was that millions of children were "in need of supplemental feeding."[28] With all of this information regarding the dire nature of the food supply and how it would affect children worldwide, it seems that efforts would have been made immediately for providing aid to children. UNRRA did continue its work, but could, in the end, only provide a fraction of what the post-war population required. Save the Children, too, participated, but put its efforts toward alleviating the suffering in Europe only. When finally a large-scale relief aid effort for children gained momentum, it would be via the UN, and Pate's involvement seemed inevitable. When they drove back to New York from that meeting in Lake Success, he confided to an unsurprised Pantaleoni that "I've just been asked to organize a fund for the benefit of children." Pantaleoni's recollection was that Pate hadn't even been considering working in relief aid at that time, and had only "touch[ed] on it" in discussions with Hoover. [29] Pate's own letters, however, reveal his involvement in Hoover's unsuccessful attempts to launch relief aid efforts in 1941, and that he most certainly exited the Lake Success meetings in September with a copy of the resolution for the creation of the ICEF for his perusal and input.

Evidence of his involvement with the ICEF resolution appear in Pate's "Points for Discussion with Mr. Hoover" dated October, 1946. These notes contain exact verbiage from the UN resolution as well as Pate's own ideas on the organization. He offered edits to the language that would help clarify the

ICEF's demographic, as well as how it could be funded and staffed, and how it would fit within the UN's administrative structure, all of which reflect Pate's consideration of the policies of the U.S. State Department and UNR-RA. The first of Pate's suggestions, which he notes used "language as proposed in Geneva resolution UNRRA," included providing relief aid to children and adolescents that were the victims of oppression as the clearly defined ICEF demographic. "Or," he noted, the language could be more specific. The ICEF would operate "for the purpose [which he lined through and replaced with "promoting"] of posterity and providing for the rehabilitation, health and welfare of children and adolescents who have suffered as a result of war," language he confirmed had been supplied by the State Department's unit for Labor, Health, and Social Affairs as well as the Advisory Committee on Foreign Aid. Next, Pate references article 13 of the resolution that gives the fund (ICEF) the power to direct its own operations with "foreign and indigenous agencies as did the ARA." If it did not, asserts Pate, then it "would . . . be a mere procurement agency and not a relief agency."[30]

Taking care to ensure the ICEF would indeed become a relief agency, Pate provided his modifications to text taken from the draft resolution for creating the ICEF on the next three pages of his notes. Since some of the language included did not become part of the final resolution, it can be concluded that Pate intended to insert passages that would make the ICEF's programs mirror those of the CRB and the ARA, thereby addressing what he perceived may be issues raised by the U.S. government from which Pate felt the bulk of the ICEF's funding would be made available. What is perhaps most interesting in Pate's version of the resolution is that it only addresses providing "certain types of food aid and equipment which are required to be imported into countries . . . in order to supplement their national programs of assistance to children and adolescents" and does not mention the provision of medical aid at all.[31] This may indicate that, during their discussion in September, Pate and Rajchman had agreed that the ICEF would provide food aid, while Rajchman, who clearly hoped to head a health organization, would cover the medical programs.

Rajchman, in his capacity as UN delegate, seems to have known that at the same time the ICEF's resolution was making its way through the process, China and Brazil had introduced a declaration to the General Assembly to consider organizing a global health agency as well.[32] This declaration had ample precedent, since the League of Nations had included a global health section that operated in Europe and Asia, and the International Committee of the Red Cross had long provided transnational and international health assistance. Therefore, after the requisite consideration and discussion, the General Assembly gave the declaration unanimous approval. It fell to the Economic and Social Council to take the next step, and it convened the Technical

Preparatory Committee to consider proposals for creating what would become the World Health Organization.

This committee brought together individuals who had previously worked in international public health with both the League of Nations and UNRRA, including Dr. Martha M. Eliot, associate chief of the U.S. Children's Bureau and future advocate of the ICEF. Eliot became the alternate to the Standing Technical Committee on Health from the United States.[33] The committee met in Washington, DC, in April 1946, its primary task to consider proposals. One of these had been submitted by Ludwik Rajchman, who had written: "Health is the greatest commodity in the world. There are on earth somewhat more than two billion consumers."[34] Rajchman had been head of the health section of the League of Nations, worked with UNRRA, and came to the UN prepared to lend his expertise to the formation of another international health organization. However, the Technical Committee chose a different path, which, according to one of its members, had much to do with their individual opinions of Rajchman himself and their prior experiences when working with him.

Dr. Henry Van Zile Hyde, chief of the health division of UNRRA, claimed that Rajchman's proposal to the Technical Committee "somehow was buried, and was never considered. I'm not sure I ever saw it."[35] He stated that, although Rajchman "was a man of substance whose document should have been thrown on the table," he believed some "personal resentment" existed between Rajchman and other members of the committee, thereby nullifying Rajchman's contribution. According to Hyde, Rajchman had a reputation for being extremely "high-handed" and demanding while working with the League of Nations.[36] Worse still, Rajchman, who lived in the United States and "was a member of the Cosmos Club here . . . would go to Poland [and] was an all-out Communist there," leading Hyde to conclude that his reputation for being difficult to work with combined with his political reputation had ultimately thwarted his efforts.[37] Given the anti-Communist sentiment that already existed in the United States, there can be little doubt that Rajchman's ties to Poland constituted a primary reason that the technical committee ignored the former director of the health section of the League of Nations. Pantaleoni, too, claimed that many "questioned his political affiliations," and that his role in "the China lobby in Washington" and his work "in China for a while for World Health" made many wary of Rajchman's motives.[38]

What also becomes clear in Hyde's and Pantaleoni's remembrances of this incident is that Cold War tensions had infiltrated the UN from the start. Their comments regarding Rajchman's association with Poland—his country of origin—as well as his work in China illustrate the scrutiny with which U.S. representatives to UN committees, boards, and organizations perused proposals and reviewed staff from reputed Communists. Indeed, it can be argued that Rajchman's attempts to work with the UN, despite his work with the League of Nations or with UNRRA, must have always fallen under suspicion when any U.S. delegate or representative was involved. Regardless of the political intrigue, which Mazower writes emanated from a "Cold War mindset that saw communism everywhere," the fact remained that more than 30 million children lacked adequate food, clothing, and medical care.[39] The effects of years of armed conflict coupled with the looming worry over who would provide for their needs after UNRRA's last shipments, scheduled for the spring of 1947, created the pressing need for another organization to be ready to take over its operations.[40]

There would still be several hurdles to getting the ICEF ready to begin its operations, part of which included the proposal that it assume UNRRA's duties. It needed staff, a place to call its home, and funds—none of which it had in spite of its unanimous support from the General Assembly. Pate, with all his experience and connections, seemed the perfect choice to administer the ICEF, and Pantaleoni asserted that Pate, "a man who was never really quite happy unless he was saving humanity by the millions," only needed Hoover's blessing to take his place as the ICEF's first executive director. In fact, she offered her sizeable energies to help Pate in this cause, and told him: "If you start something for children, I'll drop everything and work for that."[41] Pantaleoni's enthusiastic support notwithstanding, Pate expressed some reservations regarding taking the ICEF job in correspondence with a friend, indicating that he may not have heartily embraced the idea of becoming the ICEF's executive director at first.

That Pate may have been reluctant to assume the duties of executive director appear in a letter to his friend Hallam Tuck in December 1946. He wrote to inform Tuck, whom Pate had known since his CRB days, that the ICEF had been approved, and that a meeting of the "a Committee with representatives of twenty-five nations" would be held at Lake Success later that week. During the meeting, Pate wrote, he guessed that "Dr. Rajchman will probably be elected Chairman, and it is possible that this meeting will also elect a Director of the Fund." His letter indicates that, when Rajchman approached him on the matter in September, Pate "took the liberty of bringing up your [Tuck's] name." Pate asserted that he would be "glad to give my help to the Fund, if it had the backing of the American Government and if you were asked to direct it."[42]

Pate's considerable experience gave him good reason to put forth his friend for the job; both he and Tuck had been involved in U.S.-backed relief aid operations, and both of them understood the skill required to navigate requests for funding, staff, and supplies from governments and their agencies. Pate's role in many of these had been supporting, and even though he had served in a leadership capacity for UNRRA and for the Red Cross, he still expressed initial hesitation to become the ICEF's lead administrator. Later in the letter, Pate acknowledged that despite his desire for Tuck to assume the lead role, "everything was practically set to bring me in as Director of the Fund, that this move had apparently started several months back and I deduce that you had a hand in guiding things in that direction too." Acknowledging defeat, he then appealed to Tuck to become involved in the ICEF in another capacity. Pate wrote that he would "enter into it alone with a very heavy feeling unless I had your backing on the [Executive] Committee" as the American delegate. Tuck, Pate claims, would have the necessary finesse to deal with the State Department and with "developing Congressional support" for the fund, all of which would ease Pate's burden should he be named director.[43] Unfortunately for Pate, his friend would not be named to the ICEF board or committee; Eleanor Roosevelt initially took on that role instead, and subsequent representatives would not include Hallam Tuck among them.

Pate's letter to Tuck also discloses one of the internal UN administrative hurdles preventing the ICEF from moving forward. He wrote that, while Rajchman desired that the ICEF should begin its operations immediately, the secretary-general, Trygvie Lie, "has had a tendency to delay the starting of the Fund, and insists on going through certain further formalities."[44] Pate would, of course, be tapped to direct the ICEF, and would receive a contract from Trygvie Lie in January 1947, for a two-year appointment as the ICEF director that would be renewed biennially until his death in 1965. It originally included a salary of ten thousand dollars a year, and a two thousand five hundred dollar allowance for "representations (including hospitality), housing, education, and children's allowances," which he accepted.[45] The "further formalities" causing delays included some rather contentious discussions regarding to whom Pate would report—issues that had appeared in Pate's notes for discussion with Mr. Hoover the previous October. Pate had written that the executive director would "be subject to the general supervision of the Board" but would "appoint the staff of the Secretariat." With this, Pate seemed to be suggesting that, although the executive director would be the "chief administrative officer" of the ICEF and be responsible to the board, that office would have a dual reporting relationship to the Executive Board and the office of the secretary-general.[46] This matter did achieve eventual resolution, as chronicled in a letter to the soon-to-be ICEF chairman Ludwik Rajchman from Martin Hill, a member of the Executive Office of the secretary-general. Hill stated that it had originally been declared that "Mr. Pate should report direct to the Secretary-General through the Executive Office," but that this assertion had "provoked immediate reaction from the Social Department which has all along considered the Fund its special baby." The debate had been resolved in a private meeting between Pate and Lie, during which it was agreed that Pate would issue the following statement:

> While I should appreciate the assistance of various Department in the Secretar-
> iat and more particularly the Social Department and will naturally consult
> regularly with that Department since my work is so closely bound up with
> much of its work, I should like it to be understood that I and my staff will be
> administratively responsible to you [Lie].

Settling the matter of the oversight of the executive director had required
rather tense discussion, and the matter of seating a permanent Executive
Board still remained. There would be no work until these details could be
resolved.

According to UN protocol, Pate's leadership role in the ICEF could not
become official until an Executive Board had been selected and their nomi-
nations ratified. They, in turn, would approve the nominee for executive
director. The original board that approved Pate's appointment consisted of
representatives from twenty-one member nations, many of whom were selected because they were countries "who had money and that might be
shamed into giving something if they were on the board when the existing
UNRRA money ran out."[47] Board membership changed in number and com-
position repeatedly during the first weeks of the ICEF's existence, explaining
why some records list the initial group as having twenty-one members, while
others list the number as twenty-five or more. In that early period, it was also
apparent that certain nations—the United States among them—had not yet
decided to put their full financial and administrative support behind the organization. This may have been due to several factors, not the least of which
included whether or not relief aid would be supplied to Communist countries,
or that the ICEF may create inefficiencies by duplicating the efforts of other
UN organizations like the better-supported FAO. That the make-up of the
board remained somewhat amorphous prevented the ICEF from moving forward regardless of the reasons for the constant change. Settling it into a more
fixed pattern required a decision by the Economic and Social Council that
representatives from thirty nations, chosen by the Economic and Social
Council, would sit on the board for three-year terms.[48]

Having determined how many members would make up the board and the
length of their terms of service brought with it another complication, since a
seat on the Executive Board did not guarantee that those appointed would
have the ICEF's best interest in mind. Most of the countries whose designees
populated the first ICEF Executive Board had no specific selection criteria
for appointing a representative, and often representatives who served on the
ICEF Board did so in conjunction with their service on other UN boards.
They attended the meetings of multiple organizations and were accountable
for reporting on UN activity to their individual national governments, jug-
gling hectic schedules in order to relay as much as possible about the activities of the new organization. This was certainly the case with the first U.S.

representative to the ICEF Executive Board, Eleanor Roosevelt, whom the United States eventually assigned to several UN committees.[49] Mrs. Roosevelt's notoriety as the former first lady, as well as her prior humanitarian work, made her a popular choice to represent the United States at the UN. Other representatives, like Adelaide Sinclair from Canada, appeared to have been selected specifically for their prior experience in maternal and child health and welfare administration. Her experiences reveal, however, that she may not have been chosen due to her credentials, and that the ICEF lived a tenuous existence at first, especially with regard to the difficulties in obtaining support for the organization from individual nations.

Born in Toronto, Adelaide Sinclair graduated from the University of Toronto in 1922 with a degree in political science. She obtained a master's degree in economics in 1925, and did post-graduate work at the London School of Economics from 1925 to 1926, then at the University of Berlin in 1929. Her educational credentials and professional experience parallel those of several of her ICEF counterparts from other countries, including many of the women who worked for the U.S. Children's Bureau. Sinclair lectured in both of her degree fields until 1930, when she married Donald Sinclair and ceased teaching. Then, in 1942, she picked up the threads of her professional life again and became an economist with the Wartime Prices and Trade Board in Ottawa, Canada. She joined the Women's Royal Canadian Naval Service in March 1943, and later became its director, retiring in 1946 with the rank of captain. Upon her retirement, she was asked to assume the position of executive assistant to the deputy minister of the National Department of Health and Welfare. According to *Who's Who in the UN* from November 1959, Sinclair's credentials had been a primary factor in her appointment to the ICEF Executive Board; she, however, recalled the process of her nomination as resulting from a lack of interest in the ICEF by the Canadian government coupled with the ability of her superiors to order her to go.[50]

Sinclair remembered that, in 1946, the Canadian government "didn't care a hoot [about who they sent to the ICEF]; just as long as they got a body that would take the thing off them. They weren't interested at all." The ICEF, she claimed, had received unanimous approval "by default because certain people weren't going to say they were against children, but they certainly weren't going to pull for this to happen." Once the resolution passed and Canada needed a representative, Sinclair quipped that "they tossed it over to George Davidson . . . my boss in the Department of Health and Welfare. . . . I came back from a weekend away . . . and George came into my office and he said, 'I'm afraid I've wished something on you while you were away, and I hope you don't mind.'" Upon finding out she would be Canada's delegate to the new UN organization, Sinclair responded, "All right, I'll be good. I'll go." Having no idea what to expect since "I had no instructions because nobody gave a hoot" Sinclair remembered that "it was really more fun that they didn't because I made up my own."[51]

Sinclair's lack of information about the task she was about to undertake did not prevent her from embracing it. She became a staunch supporter of the ICEF and its programs, eventually serving as chair of the Executive Board and remaining associated with the organization until 1967. Regardless of the overwhelming support it received from its individual board members, the ICEF, with its temporary permit to operate within the UN, its lack of support from powerful nations like the United States and Canada, and its meager funds, appeared to be off to a very shaky start. In addition, many UN delegates could not see the purpose in creating a fund whose functions could certainly be carried out by other UN organizations. It therefore became incumbent upon Pate in his role as executive director, as well as the members of the first Executive Board, to carve out a unique space for the ICEF while dispelling the idea that it might duplicate the efforts of other UN organizations.

According to Virginia Hazzard, a former UNICEF employee and historian, children had always been "the easily acceptable humanitarian target."[52] By reinforcing the ICEF's constituency as children and by including their mothers, Pate and the Executive Board made its efforts hard to oppose. In this way, as noted by Sinclair, the ICEF obtained unanimous approval from national governments, private charities, and individuals. The ICEF also relied on the traditions established by Save the Children and the U.S. Children's Bureau, both of which had amassed abundant information that appeared in pamphlets, reports, and appeals regarding the benefits of proper maternal and child care, and the cautions that emerged if these were ignored. In the words of the Executive Board, children made up the group on which "the hope of the world rests," the best hope for its future.[53] They reiterated the language in the resolution that created the ICEF, which declared that the "International Children's Emergency Fund [was] to be utilized for the benefit of children and adolescents of countries which were victims of aggression . . . [and] for child health purposes generally," since these children had been deprived "for several cruel years . . . [and] lived in a constant state of terror," and constituted one of the UN's most pressing problems—how to ensure their survival, thereby saving the world.[54] Only the ICEF, with its distinctive mandate, could salve the wounds of war and begin to remake the world by creating happy countenances of healthy, well-fed children cared for by competent, healthy mothers.

Upon closer examination, this resolution provides insight into the inevitability of ICEF program expansion and permanent status. It specifies a clearly defined demographic and a rather narrow range of functions that could be carried out to serve that demographic via the ICEF's programs. Limiting it to "assist[ing] in . . . rehabilitation" of children in countries affected by war, the resolution at the same time allows for unlimited expansion to these programs by charging the ICEF to intervene "for child health purposes generally."[55] This phrasing would eventually be used to modify or add programs as needs arose and to sanction moving into territories other than those identified as having been subject to a recent war. It also justified the inclusion of mothers, not specifically mentioned in the original resolution, who became an integral part of all of the ICEF's programs. Less obvious is that, through the vague phrasing, the ICEF often found itself perpetuating the U.S. post-war family ideal by maintaining the pivotal role of the dependent mother in the survival of her children.

The argument that dependent mothers had the greatest impact on the health and well-being of children had been a topic of study well before the creation of the ICEF, and became one of the most important factors in the ICEF's role in reinforcing the U.S. post-war family ideal through its programs. The multitude of studies produced by social welfare organizations in Europe and by the U.S. Children's Bureau attests to the pervasiveness of the image of the dependent mother, particularly evident in the number of Children's Bureau publications focusing on all aspects of motherhood, maternal health, and child-rearing. Mrs. Max West's "Prenatal Care," written for the bureau in 1913, was followed by a study published by Dr. Grace Meigs on maternal mortality in 1917, both of which indicate the mother as indispensable. In 1926, the bureau published a pamphlet titled "Public Aid to Mothers with Dependent Children: Extent and Fundamental Principles," which concluded that government funds should be provided in order to ensure that a mother could "maintain her children suitably in her own home" so that her children could receive "proper care and oversight."[56] These publications continued through the 1930s, emphasizing the critical role of the competent stay-at-home mother in ensuring that her children thrived. Once the United States entered World War II, special attention again focused on the role of the mother, this time in attempts to keep her out of the work force and at home with her children. With husbands away at war and with new opportunities for employment, women with children began to enter the workforce both to support the war effort and to provide financial support for their families. The Children's Bureau, however, repeatedly recommended that "although women are needed as an essential part of the defense program . . . it should be emphasized that mothers who remain at home to provide care for children are performing an essential patriotic service." It further stated: "Home life is essential to the best development for children," and that "plans must be made to preserve the important elements of the parent-child relationship" when mother's work outside the home became unavoidable. Part of a series of pamphlets simply titled "Children in Wartime," it concluded that "mothers of preschool children and especially of those under 2 year of ages *should not be encouraged* to seek employment; children of these ages should in general be cared for by their mothers in their homes."[57] Ample precedent therefore existed to support the ICEF's demographic definition, which, in keeping with the notion that the absence of mother endangered children, included children, pregnant women and lactating mothers, and mothers of children up to the age of eighteen, whether explicitly or implicitly named in the UN resolution.[58] Had the ICEF remained a rather small, unobtrusive, short-lived effort that would remain apolitical and would not deter the work of other UN organizations, its reliance on the notion of dependent mothers and children may have made little difference in its relief aid programs. However, based on its mandates and without addressing the incongruities its programs may have had with the UN declaration that all peoples were equal, Maurice Pate and the Executive Board began to plan for the ICEF's operations.

NOTES

1. U.S. Department of State, "Declaration Regarding the Defeat of Germany and the Assumption of Supreme Authority with Respect to Germany by the Governments of the United States of America, the Union of Soviet Socialist Republics, the United Kingdom and the Provisional Government of the French Republic," June 5, 1945, *Treaties and Other International Agreements of the United States of America*, Volume 3.

2. Mark Mazower, *Dark Continent: Europe's Twentieth Century* (New York: Vintage Books, 1998), 212–13.

3. Paul Kennedy, *The Parliament of Man: The Past, Present and Future of the United Nations* (New York: Random House, 2006), 7.

4. Kennedy, *The Parliament of Man*, 3, 5, 9.

5. Mazower, *Dark Continent*, 212–49.

6. *Charter of the United Nations*, "Preamble" (New York: United Nations Official Documents, 1945), and "The Charter of the United Nations," http://www.un.org/about/charter/introd.htm, accessed June 21, 2004.

7. *UN Charter*, Chapter 2, Article 3; "Membership."

8. *UN Charter*, Chapter 2, Article 4.

9. *Charter of the United Nations*, "Preamble."

10. *UN Charter*, Chapter 4, Article 10; Chapter 5, Article 24; Chapter 10, Article 62; Chapter 13, Article 87; Chapter 14, Article 92; Chapter 15, Article 97.

11. Paul Kennedy, *The Parliament of Man: The Past, Present and Future of the United Nations* (New York: Random House, 2006), 45–46.

12. The history of the headquarters of the United Nations can be found at the UN's website, http://www.un.org.

13. E/ICEF/160, *Final Report of the First Executive Board of the United Nations International Children's Emergency Fund 11 December 1946-31 December 1950*, 1.

14. Janet Pirkey, *A Gift from the Heart: Profile of Helenka Adamowska Pantaleoni, American Volunteer and Founding Spirit of UNICEF* (Franktown, Colorado: JP Enterprises, 1986), 97; and Pantaleoni interview, 6.

15. HIST/50, *The Contribution of UNICEF to the Peace Process*, 1.

16. "Our Greatest National Asset: Is It Well with the Child?" (London: Save the Children Fund, 1938).

17. Pantaleoni interview, 4.

18. Pirkey, *A Gift from the Heart*, 97.

19. Pirkey, *A Gift from the Heart*, 97.

20. Pirkey, *A Gift from the Heart*, 98.

21. Pantaleoni interview, 4.

22. Perrin Galpin to Maurice Pate, July 18, 1942; enclosed, letter from Secretary of State Cordell Hull to Herbert Hoover dated June 28, 1941. Maurice Pate Papers, Princeton University Library.

23. Maurice Pate, "Some Notes on Trip with the Hoover Mission," President's Famine Emergency Committee, Maurice Pate Papers, Princeton University Library, 2–5.

24. Pate, "Some Notes on Trip with the Hoover Mission," 8–21.

25. Pate, "Some Notes on Trip with the Hoover Mission," 21–88; and "The Children Are Hungry" (Washington, DC: U.S. Department of Agriculture, 1946), frontispiece.

26. Pate, "Some Notes on Trip with the Hoover Mission," 90–91.

27. Arthur C. Ringland, the President's War Relief Control Board, to Maurice Pate, May 17, 1946. Maurice Pate Papers, Princeton University Library.

28. Herbert Hoover to President Harry Truman, May 13, 1946, 3; UNRRA Estimate, June, 1946 (Washington, DC: U.S. Government Printing Office, 1946). Maurice Pate Papers, Princeton University Library; and UNRRA, *Report of the Director General to the Council for the Period 1 January 1946 to 31 March 1946* (Washington, DC: UNRRA, 1946), 78.

29. Pantaleoni interview, 5.

30. Maurice Pate, *Points for Discussion with Mr. Hoover, October 4, 1946*. Maurice Pate Papers, Princeton University Library, 1.

31. Pate, *Notes for Discussion with Hoover*, 4.

32. Henry Van Zile Hyde interviewed by Richard D. McKinzie for the Harry S. Truman Library, July 16, 1975, 16. Accessed at the UNICEF Archives.

33. Hyde interview, 18–19: "First Quarterly Report on UNRRA Expenditures and Operations" 78th Congress, 2nd Session, House Document No. 803, Message from the President of the United States transmitting the First Quarterly Report on UNRRA Expenditures and Operations in Accordance with the Act of March 28, 1944, Authorizing United States Participation in the Work of the United Nations Relief and Rehabilitation Administration, December 5, 1944— Referred to the Committee on Foreign Affairs and Ordered to be Printed with Illustrations (Washington: United States Government Printing Office, 1944), 42–43.

34. See Ludwik Rajchman, "Why Not? A United Nations Public Health Service," *Free World* 6, no. 3 (September 1943): 216–21.

35. Hyde interview, 67.

36. Hyde interview, 68.

37. Hyde interview, 69–70.

38. Pantaleoni interview, 10.

39. Mark Mazower, *Governing the World: The History of an Idea, 1815 to the Present* (New York: Penguin Books, 2012), 267

40. *TSOU*, 45.

41. Pantaleoni interview, 2; Pirkey, *A Gift from the Heart*, 98,

42. Maurice Pate to Hallam Tuck, December 17, 1946. Maurice Pate Papers, Princeton University Library, 1.

43. Pate to Tuck, December 17, 1946, 1.

44. Pate to Tuck, December 17, 1946, 2.

45. Maurice Pate to Trygvie Lie, January 27, 1947, and Maurice Pate's Letter of Appointment dated January 27, 1947. Maurice Pate Papers, Princeton University Library.

46. Pate, *Notes for Discussion with Hoover*, 3.

47. Adelaide Sinclair interviewed by John Charnow, November 17–18, 1982, 1. Accessed at UNICEF Archives.

48. Pantaleoni interview, 12.

49. E/ICEF/1, *Summary Record of the First Meeting Held at Lake Success New York 19 December 1946*, 27, 1.

50. *Who's Who in the UN, November, 1959*. Accessed at UNICEF Archives.

51. Sinclair interview, 1–2.

52. Virginia Hazzard, *UNICEF and Women, the Long Voyage: A Historical Perspective* (Geneva: United Nations Children's Fund, 1987), 1.

53. E/ICEF/160, 3.

54. E/ICEF/155, 33.

55. E/ICEF/160, 3.

56. U.S. Children's Bureau, "Prenatal Care," by Mrs. Max West, Care of Children Series No. 1, Bureau Publication No. 4 (Washington, DC: Government Printing Office, 1913); U.S. Children's Bureau, "Maternal Mortality from All Conditions Connected with Childbirth in the United States and Certain Other Countries," by Dr. Grace Meigs, Miscellaneous Series No. 6, Bureau Publication No. 10 (Washington, DC: Government Printing Office, 1917); U.S. Children's Bureau, "Public Aid to Mothers with Dependent Children: Extent and Fundamental Principles," by Emma O. Lundberg, Bureau Publication No. 162 (Washington, DC: Government Printing Office, 1926), 18.

57. U.S. Children's Bureau, "Children in Wartime No. 3," Bureau Publication No. 284 (Washington, DC: U.S. Government Printing Office, 1943), vii.

58. UNICEF's report to the Economic and Social Council in 1950 made it clear that children and adolescents, as well as pregnant and lactating mothers, had been the focus of most of its programs. In addition, since feeding programs were most often operated through schools, adolescents to the age of eighteen would have been included along with their younger counterparts. Virginia Hazzard also notes that though children and adolescents remained UNICEF's focus, women as mothers were included from the beginning given their association with the survival of the child. E/ICEF/160, 3–6; and Hazzard, *UNICEF and Women, The Long Voyage*, 1.

Chapter Three

A Plan of Work

On December 19, 1946, Chairman Rajchman asked the Executive Board to address a second issue after resolving the issue of Maurice Pate's nomination to serve as the ICEF's executive director. He urged the Executive Board to action, stating that "now the International Children's Emergency Fund [is] a legal entity, and it [is] therefore essential to take action immediately."[1] The second meeting of the Executive Board focused on establishing the priority tasks on which the ICEF would concentrate, stressing the gravity of the world food shortage and noting that 1947 would be a difficult year for food supplies in Europe. The Executive Board agreed that it had to obtain "the requirements of children and adolescents in 1947," a task they felt would be "simple and speedy." The ICEF could then "implement a three-part plan of action" in order to provide much needed relief aid.[2]

This plan of action included "A. Nutrition; B. Relief (including questions related to equipment and miscellaneous institutions): C. Training of staff (medical and welfare staff and social workers) to be placed at the disposal of the countries to be assisted" in no particular order of priority.[3] Among the countless questions to be answered in addition to how programs would be funded were how children had been affected by rationing systems, and how the ICEF's food supply would be incorporated into national supply pro-grams. The ICEF would need to familiarize itself with food programs such as canteens and school feeding, and "tackle the milk question in the various countries, a very serious problem."[4] Due to the destruction of agriculture and infrastructures, milk, for many decades touted as one of the best foods for infants and children, was in short supply. It is therefore not surprising that the ICEF chose to focus on procuring and distributing milk—a task for which it would become globally famous—since milk had been included in most food aid programs for children since the nineteenth century. This trend continued in the twentieth century as evidenced in a report by the Milk Committee. It had provided then U.S. Food Administrator, Herbert Hoover, with its conclusion that "milk is the best single kind of food for the proper development of growing children" in 1918, and the U.S. Children's Bureau, too, had often provided recommendations to mothers regarding where they could buy safe milk to provide to their children.[5] The Save the Children Fund also held up milk as one of the essential foods for children, having placed tinned milk as the first item on in its list of rations to be supplied to children in occupied regions of Europe in 1942.[6]

In order to determine just how much milk would be needed to supply the children it hoped to feed, the ICEF hired Dr. Martha May Eliot to conduct a survey that would assess the need in Europe. Eliot, a pediatrician and employee of the U.S. Children's Bureau, had received her undergraduate degree from Radcliffe College in 1913 and her medical degree from Johns Hopkins University in 1918, and from the start of her career had been interested in maternal and child health. After completing her residency, she became a member of the pediatric staff at the Yale University School of Medicine in 1921. When in 1924 she moved to Washington, DC, to direct the division of maternal and child health for the U.S. Children's Bureau, she remained on staff at Yale until 1935—a year after she had been appointed assistant chief of the bureau, which she eventually headed in 1951.[7]

While at the bureau, Eliot remained involved in multiple tasks. She went to Geneva in 1936 as the U.S. delegate to a meeting on nutrition sponsored by the health section of the League of Nations. As part of her duties as delegate, she visited seven countries to study their maternal and child health care practices. This trip, she claimed, "was really invaluable to me because it gave me background with respect to children's programs in these countries long prior to the war and before there were any major international UN activities."[8] She administered federal grants-in-aid in Washington; then, in 1946, she became vice-chair of the delegation to the international conference in Geneva that drafted the constitution of the World Health Organization. "By the way," she recounted, "you may be interested to know that I was the only woman delegate at this conference to sign this report. And I was the only woman signing the Constitution of the World Health Organization (WHO)."[9]

Even prior to the WHO Geneva Conference, Eliot had become more directly involved with the UN. She had attended the first International Health Conference in June 1946, which she recalled "had been recommended to the United Nations International Conference for the Organization of International Activities in San Francisco in April 1945 . . . that original conference laid the ground for the development of both WHO and UNICEF, the two organizations with which I have the greatest contact."[10] Then, while working with the committee that would establish the WHO, Eliot received an offer in the spring of 1947 to work for the ICEF as well, carrying on both her tradition of taking on multiple jobs and the tradition of assigning multiple duties to delegates to the UN.

According to Eliot, Maurice Pate approached her and asked whether she "would make this study of the needs of children in war-torn countries." She found it humorous that Pate "interviewed me for this job. It was the first time I had ever been interviewed in my life . . . for any new job that I was to have. That in itself interested me and amused me very much. I can see it now," she remembered, "in an F Street house where UNICEF was having headquarters—two or three rooms, that was all." She further claimed that "apparently, what I knew about the countries of Europe, as a result of that earlier trip I had made in 1936 and my experiences in England in 1941, interested Mr. Pate." Another of her assets included the fact that "[h]e also knew that at the time I was associate chief of the Children's Bureau, and that I knew the kind of work that was done for children, both voluntary and governmental."[11] Pate offered her the job, and she accepted; she did not give up her position at the Children's Bureau, however, having been granted a leave of absence by its chief, Katharine Lenroot, her long-time friend and colleague, and the U.S. delegate to the ICEF's Executive Board.

After enumerating the supplies she would need to conduct the study, including an assistant who spoke the European languages Eliot did not, she left for Europe on April 28, 1947, accompanied by ICEF chairman, Ludwik Rajchman, her assistant and interpreter, Susannah Mirick, and Dr. William Schmidt, professor of public health at Harvard University and medical advisor for the Joint Distribution Committee of the UN. They landed in Paris then took a train to Warsaw, where Eliot "was shocked beyond belief by the destruction of the city." The group traveled to the area where the ghetto had been, and Eliot recalled: "It was completely wiped out." She found hope, however, in the "energy and zeal the Polish people were putting in to rebuilding . . . their own capital."[12] Her trip, which included visiting France, Czechoslovakia, Austria, Yugoslavia, Greece, Montenegro, and Italy, concluded in time for her to return to the United States and submit her report at the Executive Board meeting at the end of June 1947.

Eliot's report covered both the general condition of children in war-stricken countries of Europe, and a section on the general principles of child nutrition, which was broken down into specific categories. These included pregnant and nursing mothers, infants, school age children, and adolescents. The results of the report were subsequently incorporated into the Report of FAO/WHO/IO Committee on Child Nutrition presented at the ICEF's meeting in July 1947, and illustrated the devastating conditions the ICEF programs would need to address. It concluded with the statement that the doctors and nutrition experts who had compiled the report strongly supported the aim of the ICEF: "Children are suffering from the effects of prolonged undernutrition . . . they need more and better food for satisfactory mental and physical development."[13]

Eliot's trip to Europe for the ICEF only confirmed the importance of its first official work item—providing food. Once it had been determined how much food aid would be required and how it would be provided, other challenges remained, among them how the ICEF would report on its activities to the Economic and Social Council. These discussions began almost immediately after the Executive Board was seated, and Katharine Lenroot opened the discussion regarding the best way to give and receive information. She requested that any reports from the ICEF should contain "numerical data in addition to the general plan of procedure," basing her contributions on the relationship the U.S. Children's Bureau had with the U.S. Department of Labor. She hoped that, by reporting in this manner, the Economic and Social Council could "afford general guidance to the Executive Board in order to expedite its activity." Rajchman's response, that the ICEF would only seek guidance "when guidance . . . had to be sought," seems to indicate that, as chairman, he had no interest in being led.[14]

Regardless, Lenroot pushed Rajchman and the other members of the Executive Board to adopt her suggestions. Not having been a part of creating the organization and therefore left outside its inner circle, she relied heavily on her experience with the U.S. Children's Bureau, either unaware or unconcerned that her suggestions may have seemed threatening. It is important to understand the considerable skill and status Lenroot brought with her to the Executive Board in order to put her attitude about her participation in the ICEF into its proper context. Years in the field of social work, maternal and child care and public policy had made her a seasoned bureaucrat and maternal and child welfare expert, and she displayed these qualities confidently when, in its early meetings, the ICEF established its work plan.

Born in Superior, Wisconsin, in 1891, Lenroot modeled herself after her activist politician father, Senator Irvine L. Lenroot. Senator Lenroot, a Progressive Republican who began his political career in the State House of Wisconsin, wrote much of the legislation that earned Wisconsin its reputation as a leading Progressive state. Katharine, who grew up among her father's political friends in Wisconsin and Washington, DC, became inspired by his career in service to the public. She began her career with the U.S. government at the age of twenty-four when she took a position with the U.S. Children's Bureau in 1915.[15]

Lenroot's work at the Children's Bureau led her to attend New York School of Social Work, after which she returned to Washington and was appointed assistant director of the Social Service Division of the bureau. In this capacity, Lenroot's work included participating in international relief aid programs. She provided information to the League of Nations on matters of international maternal and child health, and participated in Hoover's

American Child Health Association, a subdivision of his American Relief Administration.[16] She became assistant chief of the bureau in 1922, turning her focus to the causes and prevention of juvenile delinquency. Lenroot coauthored an extensive report with her colleague Emma Lundberg, which concluded that, when the normal life of children broke down and their needs were neglected by the community, both the children and the community paid a price. They published their study, "Juvenile Courts at Work: A Study of the Organization and Methods of Ten Courts," in 1925. It meticulously detailed the entire court process, and included a section called "Study of the Child."[17] This section concerned itself primarily with the underlying causes of delinquency and how to prevent the resulting cost of child crime. The study asserted that "when all the facts that a social investigator can gain about the child, his family, his home, his school, his recreation, and his companionships . . . the court is still far from knowing the kind of child it has to deal with." Claiming that courts often had little to no information on what caused the delinquency, she recommended studying the child—"his physical condition, his mental capacities, his personality, and the driving forces of his conduct." The report recommended remedial education and strict discipline as prescriptions for dealing with juvenile delinquency, and led to conferences that established juvenile court standards, gaining Lenroot a new level of recognition for her work with children and families.[18]

By 1934, Lenroot had worked for the bureau for nineteen years. She had traveled extensively both in and outside the United States, all the while advancing the bureau's notion that children should be provided with some type of assistance, whether directly or through their mothers, in order to assure their proper development. She became chief that year, and would oversee the next phase in the life of the bureau, during which it began to lose oversight of several of its programs. The first to go, Aid for Dependent Children (ADC), marked a trend that continued to shrink the bureau. Historian Kriste Lindenmeyer claims that by 1940, Lenroot found herself "resigned" to accepting that the bureau would share responsibility for child welfare with "several federal agencies."[19]

The ADC, originally established to provide grants to states in order to fund their mothers' aid programs, helped move relief aid away from what historian Linda Gordon and Attorney Felice Batlan identify as the "masculinist assumptions" imbedded in the Social Security Act to "provide aid to children whose mothers lacked the support of a male breadwinner."[20] It evolved to include strict guidelines for eligibility that did not rely on economic status alone, the new standards taking it beyond early Children's Bureau literature that offered simple suggestions for helping mothers obtain the necessary education for achieving competence in home and childcare in order to receive help. Social historian Ruth Sidel commented on this change in standards, noting that even though support for "some kind of public aid to mothers and children" existed in the United States, state and local officials eventually "had the right to conduct an investigation into the character of the mother" before she could qualify for aid.[21] European relief aid programs such as the ones that provided milk to mothers during the late nineteenth century had also used investigations and home visits in distributing aid. These, however, determined whether or not the aid was being properly distributed by the provider in addition to educating mothers rather than using the visits as a means for disqualifying individuals from receiving aid.

Other differences in United States and European programs existed as well. While European programs often provided assistance to mothers, particularly when a father was absent, an absent father was not always a requirement for families to request assistance. The U.S. version, however, frequently required the absence of a father, whether physically or economically, in order for mothers and children to obtain assistance. This notion, which coincides with Lenroot's own conclusions about the place of mother and father within the family, continued to be a provision of ADC programs for three decades. And, as Sidel points out, once the ADC no longer resided with the Children's Bureau, its standards influenced U.S. social policy much more widely both at home and abroad. Frances Fox Piven and Richard A. Cloward claim this type of social policy began to be used to regulate the behavior of the poor more generally.[22] They assert that relief policies tended to be cyclical, "liberal or restrictive depending on the problems of regulation in the larger society with which the government must contend."[23] These policies not only regulated the poor, but reinforced the gender definitions imbedded in those policies as well. This ensured that by the mid-1940s, the definition of relief aid recipients based on sex and age were clearly defined and consistently reinforced, and eventually became the model for the ICEF.

With its national programs undergoing a reduction after 1940, Lenroot and the bureau turned their attentions to children living in the United States and abroad whose lives were being affected by the war in Europe. This effort breathed new life into the bureau, and it began 1940 by issuing the results of its White House Conference on Children in a Democracy held in January. Under the heading *The Family as the Threshold of Democracy*, it declared "self-respect and self-reliance, as well as respect for others and a cooperative attitude" essential to all families. More specifically, the "health of all the members of their families" directly correlated to the "health and well-being of children," which indicated that the bureau's policy of upholding the ideal family with father as provider and mother at home would remain intact, regardless of the war.[24] The bureau turned its efforts elsewhere in 1941, providing guidelines for dealing with children evacuated from European war zones who would be arriving in the United States. Citing the order issued by the attorney general in July 1940, the publication listed the "Departments of State, Justice, [and] Labor" as collaborators in dealing with child evacuees.

These children required sponsorship by an individual or a group to guarantee the child would not become a ward of the state upon arrival in the United States, and sponsors were provided with fifty dollars to defray the child's expenses. The document noted that applications were to be sent directly to Children's Bureau chief, Katharine Lenroot, for review.[25]

Once the United States entered the war, the bureau began publishing its "Children in Wartime" series, providing instruction for a variety of situations parents might encounter. Managing a child's fears about war, the best ways for a mother to travel alone with her infant, and how to plan a menu for children in group care were among the topics covered.[26] The bureau also issued its *A Children's Charter in Wartime* in 1942, which committed to "guard children from injury; protect children from neglect, exploitation, and undue strain in defense areas" and offered to "strengthen the home life of children whose parents are mobilized for war or war production." It concluded with the promise to "conserve, equip, and free children of every race and creed to take their part in democracy."[27]

It can be concluded therefore that Lenroot, who had provided data and support for the child relief aid activities of the ARA, served as an advisor to the League of Nations on child welfare issues, participated in several Pan-American conferences on children and adolescents, and managed the U.S. Children's Bureau during World War II, would be a logical choice to represent the United States on the Executive Board of the ICEF. In 1947 at the age of fifty-six, she attended her first ICEF meetings, and her experiences with the bureau became evident immediately in her responses to proposed ICEF programs. By the time the Executive Board met on January 13 with Katharine Lenroot as the U.S. representative, Maurice Pate presided alongside Rajchman in his new capacity as executive director. Only nine members attended this meeting and they convened this time in Washington, DC, at the offices of the U.S. Children's Bureau. Pate had unofficially established his office in Washington as well, having been given space on Connecticut Avenue and a part-time secretary.[28] Rajchman called the meeting to order and presented a provisional agenda. It included further discussion of the ICEF's work plan, as well as an increasingly pressing issue: how and where the ICEF would obtain enough funds to operate.

Minutes from this meeting give more detail to the ICEF's initial attempts to create a plan of work, advising: "There should be a strict order of priority; the first, child feeding, and the second, medical care, and the third other subjects, such as fellowships and training of personnel."[29] Other delegates, most likely assuming that this brief list of duties implied malleability in establishing the work plan, suggested adding other responsibilities that would further widen its scope. The delegate from the Soviet Union, Mr. Fenov, quickly suggested that clothing should be one of the principle items provided by the ICEF. He stated that "the proportion, for instance, for food

$400 million and clothing $40 million to me is not quite appropriate. It may be good for southern countries like Greece or Italy, but for countries with severe winters, clothing and footwear are very important indeed."[30] Pate and Rajchman both responded, noting that overcoats had been of great value after World War I, and that any clothing supplied by the ICEF would vary from country to country according to its need. The ICEF did provide clothing and sewing materials as part of its initial relief aid supplies, but these never became a major portion of its programs or expenditures.

The delegate from the United Kingdom, Mr. Alexander, then brought another new item to the discussion. He began by saying, "I wouldn't want to indulge an argument, but there are countries with terrific pressure of population which might be glad to see that pressure eased. Emigration of adults is a ticklish problem, but of young people might be something which could be undertaken to the advantage of everyone concerned." He went on to say that one way of solving the problem of hungry children residing in orphanages would be to "encourage these orphans to be adopted by countries where conditions of life would, in fact, be considerably easier. . . . I feel sure there would be people in a number of countries who would be quite prepared to adopt children on a very large scale." Lenroot, who had overseen the U.S. program for accepting child evacuees from Europe during the early years of the war, also supported this type of program. Chairman Rajchman tabled the discussion rather swiftly, however, relegating "any suggestions of this type" as ones "welcome for study." No other discussions regarding migration or adoption programs ensued, and these did not become part of the ICEF's original or subsequent work plans.[31]

What bothered all of them the most, however, was not the kind of work the ICEF would do; that, they understood, and the many types of relief aid they could provide for children could all be weighed on their merits. More troubling was how they would fund any programs they wished to undertake, as well as how they could establish a system of funding that would ensure their long-term visions. Discussing funding took up most of the third meeting as they considered how the ICEF, now with only a meager sum from UNRRA instead of the much larger amount initially promised, would be able to help the thousands of children in Europe and elsewhere they knew needed immediate assistance.

From the start, the UN made it clear that it would not make any monetary appropriations for the ICEF, stating: "The effective operation of the Fund is dependent upon the financial resources which are put at its disposal." The ICEF would, it reasoned, given a generous donation from UNRRA; further, it did not truly qualify for UN funds due to its temporary and emergency status. Therefore, the General Assembly expressed "the earnest hope that governments, voluntary agencies, and private individuals will give the Fund generous support."[32] The General Assembly made an appeal to governments for support, and the Office of the Secretariat sent out a boilerplate fundraising letter on behalf of the ICEF. That letter asked that "all Governments would contribute, taking account of their particular circumstances" and included a description of the "Fund and its proposed method of operations." It closed with the appeal that each nation would "find the description helpful in its deliberation concerning contributions to the Fund."[33]

The delegate from the United Kingdom, Mr. Alexander, vociferously expressed his disappointment in the progress being made toward obtaining funds, and especially with the General Assembly's requirement that the ICEF collect the UNRRA funds first, then obtain donations from governments, then from other sources including voluntary contributions in that order. "I am sorry if, on the first occasion I speak . . . I appear to be a little lukewarm and throw some cold water," he began, "but I am afraid it is cold water I have brought here with me . . . my government feels . . . the second source of funds which can be obtained would be voluntary contributions, and the third source—and I do put it third—is governmental assistance."[34] Many believed, as did Alexander, that governments would not or could not commit funds to the ICEF's cause, and the Executive Board, in desperate need of cash, probably had little intention of following the General Assembly guidelines for collecting funds anyway. Indeed, Martha Eliot recalled that Chairman Rajchman had his own plan for funding the ICEF modeled on the one used to obtain donations for the Rockefeller Foundation. "Dr. Rajchman . . . did not want the money at the disposal of UNICEF [the ICEF] to be collected on a [UN] formula from all the countries," she claimed.[35] If funding could successfully be arranged avoiding the General Assembly's rules, then the ICEF could do two things. It could collect funds in any way it saw fit and from any source available to it, and could remain outside the UN budget altogether, allowing the ICEF to exert total control over its funds. It therefore became crucial from the start for the ICEF to obtain donations from wherever it could, regardless of the General Assembly's mandate.

Rajchman and Pate relied on their past experiences and determined that donations could be obtained in two ways. First, they reasoned that any government, organization, or individual could donate money or supplies directly to the ICEF. These contributions would be placed into a general fund, and would support the organization's operations. Second, the ICEF would require that governments applying for assistance commit to making a contribution to their own aid programs whether through providing money, supplies, or staff. Any country that had the capability to contribute and did not would find its application for assistance denied by the Executive Board.

The CRB and the ARA had both used this pay-for-aid model. It ensured the solvency of relief aid programs and upheld the idea that governments were committed to assuming at least some responsibility for their own relief aid programs by providing money, staff, and facilities. Historian Bertrand

Patenaude provides an example of this system, pointing to the ARA's efforts to provide corn to Soviet Russia during the famine it experienced during the early 1920s. Patenaude observed that, in addition to requiring that all participants make a contribution, the ARA managed the funds for its operations on a business model that appealed to individual donors and others contributing to the cause in the United States: "So much the better if a humanitarian operation abroad made good economic sense at home."[36] According to historian H. H. Fisher, governments receiving relief-aid made contributions to the ARA operations in the amount of "$11,357,325.13" and obtained another "$4,374,893.28" from the "sales in Russia to Affiliated Relief and Other Organizations." Hoover associates Frank Surface and Raymond Bland also recorded that "subsidies" to the ARA from governments receiving aid included "donations of commodities for the child-feeding programs in their own countries" as well as "services and facilities" though the latter had not been included in the final total of $14,652,432.21 collected from a dozen Central European countries.[37] The Executive Board reasoned that if this approach could be implemented, then it could keep the ICEF from going broke; however, when the ICEF staff began to seek contributions in 1947, they found that although many supported their cause, few would help to fund it.

Executive Director Pate made finding funding a priority when he began work in January 1947, and he wrote a letter to U.S. secretary of state, George Marshall, on January 23 to plead his case for a U.S. contribution. Noting that the ICEF intended to aid "twenty million infants, children and nursing mothers" at six cents a day, he asked for Marshall's "earnest consideration" for the project, which had a budget of four hundred fifty million dollars for the year.[38] By March, he noted in a letter to Hoover that he had received no word from the State Department regarding his request, and faced the second quarter of the year with insufficient funds to truly begin operations.[39]

A few days prior to his correspondence with Hoover, a proposal had been made to the Economic and Social Council to collect donations from individuals through a program called One Day's Pay. It enumerated the work about to be undertaken by the ICEF including "an absolute minimum supplementary food program for approximately 20 million infants, children and nursing mothers" that would require a budget of "450 million dollars," then claimed that by giving "common people everywhere the opportunity to play their part" by donating a day's pay to the ICEF, "it could bring in as much as 175 million dollars."[40] The Executive Board heard the initial proposal at its meeting on Friday, February 7, 1947, in Lake Success. A delegate from Norway, Mr. Ording, suggested that every individual could contribute the equivalent of one day's wages for relief purposes. It would then be placed in a "world community chest" with a large portion assigned to the ICEF.[41] Helenka Pantaleoni remembered Ording's visit to the ICEF Board meeting. He "got up . . . and made a speech. He thought that every single day laborer, or everybody who earned a salary all over the world, would be delighted to give one day of his efforts . . . it was enthusiastically received in one of those rare occasions when the whole meeting broke out into applause." Unfortunately, the enthusiasm for Ording's plan ended when the meeting did. "It was too difficult to implement. I suppose," remembered Pantaleoni. "There's always a 'how to' angle."[42] And, even though this program was reintroduced a year later by Eleanor Roosevelt, it did little to raise funds and never became a primary portion of the ICEF's donations.[43]

By June, Pate recorded that the meeting of the Executive Board, which had "welcome[d] an arrangement" such as the One Day's Pay campaign, still faced serious budget shortfalls. Notes from the meeting minutes evidence that contributions appeared early in the agenda, with Pate's notation that "During his recent visit to Europe, Dr. Ludwik Rajchman, your Chairman, conferred with several governments, and it is expected that at least five or six . . . will make contributions."[44] When the Executive Board met again in October of that year, funding again remained one of its most pressing items for discussion. Submitted again by Pate, the report notes that an "initial contribution of $15,000,000 from the United States, the $5,000,000 contribution of Canada" seemed virtually inevitable.[45] He went on to list several more governments that had at least pledged funds, including Luxembourg and Australia, and wrote that the Norwegian government "which has already contributed cod liver oil," might be counted on as well.[46] And, in November and December, Denmark and Belgium also seemed on the brink of contributing, but had not finalized plans to do so.[47]

Maurice Pate had noted a year earlier that, after having been at work "only four days . . . it seems to me in getting this work underway that the most important and large support that we should look for is a contribution from the American Government."[48] He knew that the U.S. government had not reallocated its UNRRA budget elsewhere, and hoped he could persuade Congress to give a sizeable portion of it to the ICEF. He requested a grant of 40 million dollars through formal channels, firmly convinced it was a fair and reasonable amount. Members of Congress, officials at the State Department, and the Bureau of the Budget thought otherwise, however, and began to raise questions, putting the request in jeopardy.

Martha Eliot, who had worked closely with members of the staff of the Bureau of the Budget while administering grants-in-aid for the Children's Bureau, discovered in April 1947

> that the Bureau of the Budget was really making trouble about any kind of
> appropriation [for the ICEF]. I knew we had to have it. So the first task I took
> on for UNICEF was getting the money for them from Congress. I remember
> one day . . . a warm day in April in Washington . . . sitting on the bench

somewhere outside the State Department, which was housed in the Executive
Office Building, and talking with two men from the Bureau of the Budget,
both of whom I knew.

Eliot could only recall one of their names—Geoffrey May—who had worked
with her on a project for the War Department in 1941.[49]

The two men argued with Eliot about the appropriation. She then told
them about her upcoming trip to Europe for the ICEF, and that it needed
money. "I told them the United States really had to put some money up—that
was all there was to it! And how much would they go for. We finally agreed
that if UNICEF would reduce its request to $15 million, unmatched, they
would go along." The discussion then turned to the rest of the initial request
for $40 million, and the issue of matching contributions arose. Eliot, who
wanted to be sure the ICEF received its full appropriation, pushed for as
lenient a matching formula as possible.

> I said . . . let us suppose that initially other countries put up only 250 dollars. Is
> that all I'm going to get out of the United States? . . . Finally, they agreed that
> the first $15 million would be granted to UNICEF without any conditions
> whatsoever. But thereafter for any additional monies UNICEF would have to
> show that a certain ratio had been contributed by other countries.[50]

Eliot, who had been told the ICEF would receive all of UNRRA's residual funds, left for Europe satisfied she had done well; she would not find out
until much later that "that was not correct . . . from the very beginning . . .
UNICEF was very troubled because they got their money from UNRRA in
dribbles and drabbles . . . they had to struggle continually to get from UNR-
RA what they felt was their right according to the arrangements for the
creation of UNICEF. But UNRRA was also giving money to WHO."[51]

And indeed, two incidents early in 1947 support Eliot's contentions. First,
UNRRA general counsel, Alfred Davidson, had notified the Executive Board
on January 31 that "The United States has laid before the Central Committee
of UNRRA a proposal which will involve a change in our program and
which would, in effect, increase the financial burdens of UNRRA, with the
result that the possibility of transferring UNRRA funds will be substantially
diminished."[52] Adelaide Sinclair later described the scene. "I remember at
one of the first Board meetings . . . a young man with a rather sharp face
came in and walked over to Rajchman and bent over the back of his chair and
whispered something in his ear and Rajchman said, 'Well, you'll have to tell
them.' . . . Well, this was the legal counsel of UNRRA whose name happened
to be Al Davidson."[53] Second, Director General Lowell Rooks, noted in his
report to the UNRRA Council for the first quarter 1947: "By the end of 1946,
no government has yet contributed to the Fund and no UNRRA financial
assets had been made available to it"; and it had only collected "$550,000"

from a private fund for its operations.[54] The report hints that UNRRA had not completely abandoned the transfer of its assets to the ICEF, and had heard proposals from Pate regarding a "tentative program based in part on studies of needs and costs prepared by UNRRA." Based on these, UNRRA had "agreed to lend the Fund up to 15 or 20 members of its staff until 20 June," but noted that "the transfer of residual UNRRA funds to the International Children's Fund should be the subject of a discussion between the Administration and the individual contributing governments."[55] UNRRA's reluctance to transfer its funds is clear; however, the basis for this reluctance is not. Pate, in a letter to Hoover written in March of 1947, indicated that his proposed ICEF policies had aligned with UNRRA's, ensuring that "title in relief supplies is vested with the Fund, and not with any Government." Conformity to UNRRA's operational principles, however, did little to speed the transfer of its funds to the ICEF.

Eliot also claimed that the UNRRA funds may have found another home with WHO, and Dr. Hyde's recollections reveal that not only was this the case, but that it caused some very real disagreements between the ICEF and WHO. UNRRA had, according to Hyde, funds in the amount of "twenty-five million or something," and that a proposal had been made to give the bulk of the funds to the ICEF; the WHO would receive only "about a million five hundred thousand." Hyde noted that, even though the ICEF was to receive the bulk of the funds, many agreed that the WHO should be in charge of the "professional and technical aspects of the [ICEF] programs" which led to the "issue of who was going to pay for that." According to Hyde, the WHO did assume responsibility for those programs, and that payment came from the WHO's budget, causing "some difficulty" between the ICEF and the WHO.[56]

The struggle to obtain funding for the ICEF had at least been initially resolved, thanks primarily to Eliot's efforts. Official histories regarding the U.S. contribution to the ICEF credit Herbert Hoover with persuading the U.S. Congress to grant an appropriation and make no mention of Eliot's involvement. It is clear, however, that without Eliot's efforts, the ICEF would likely never have been granted its first 15 million dollars.

With the U.S. commitment in hand, the ICEF began wooing other governments knowing that their contributions would be matched by U.S. funds. Meanwhile, additional alternate methods for funding the ICEF emerged. Pantaleoni remembered a suggestion made by Linn Sheffey, an early member of Pantaleoni's American Committee for UNICEF. Sheffey suggested that "returning passengers from foreign countries put their foreign coins into a special envelope, mail it to UNICEF, whereupon UNICEF would change the currency into dollars." Sheffey had calculated that the ICEF could collect millions of dollars a year that way, but her idea, too, was initially rejected. "Millions of ideas, and so far, few have worked out," remembered Pantaleoni; it only took a decade or two for most international flights to provide UNICEF donation envelopes to their passengers.[57]

The ICEF had drafted a report in February on its projected expenses, which would, once approved by the board, be submitted to the Fourth Session of the Economic and Social Council for review. It stated that "the Executive Board has considered the urgent needs of children in Europe and the Far East . . . [and] estimates that some 30,000,000 children in Europe alone and an equal, if not greater, number in the Far East are today in urgent need of supplementary aid." It first recommended providing a "supplementary mid-day meal of approximately 700 calories" at a cost of "6 cents a day or \$20.00 a year." In addition to this meal, the ICEF would provide "clothing, medical supplies or equipment for children's institutions." The report also included a "Tentative Breakdown of Expenditures by ICEF per \$1,000,000 contributed to its Funds," allocating the largest portion, \$678,000, to "[m]ilk and supplementary fats." The ICEF estimated that it could provide assistance to 85,000 children for that amount.

In addition to the financial information it provided, the report made clear that the ICEF had received very little funding to date in spite of historian Akira Iriye's claim that "in 1946, American donors are said to have given \$200 million to UNICEF." Iriye's information is gleaned from UNICEF historian Maggie Black's book *The Children and the Nations*, published in 1987; however, it is clear that in spite of Black's reporting, the ICEF's records indicate that no such amount had been contributed by 1946 or even by 1947.[58] The ICEF therefore reminded the Economic and Social Council that "in the discussions leading to the establishment of the fund, it was constantly emphasized that it would be both derogatory to the prestige of the United Nations and also a waste of effort and administrative money to let the Fund start operating with too small a sum to allow an effective contribution to the problem." It declared: "The Executive Board has decided that it would not be proper to start the Fund's operations until assurances are obtained of sufficient financial support."[59]

This statement sent a clear signal to the Economic and Social Council to intercede on the ICEF's behalf and to help it obtain funds. The threat for not doing so was clear—the ICEF would not operate until its finances were in order, leaving a blot on the UN's record. Sinclair also recalled that by that time, the ICEF board understood it could not comfortably rely on any further funds from the United States and UNRRA, and that it would need to establish other reliable sources of income.[60] "There were a lot of other campaigns because conditions were pretty bad for a long time . . . we got some good people on our Committee [Canadian Committee for UNICEF]" but she noted that competition from other philanthropic organizations often turned fierce, recounting an incident between fundraisers for the ICEF and the Save the Children Fund.[61] "The Save the Children had their headquarters in Europe and they'd been active long before UNICEF was ever thought of. The best people entered the Save the Children's Fund and did things in style." She went on to say that "they [Save the Children] were simply horrified when they got a letter from the head saying that you must put this UNICEF fund-raising out of business—it will be a great threat to us . . . nothing about doing more for children or anything like that."[62]

Helenka Pantaleoni recalled similar incidents in the United States "when steps were taken to organize the Children's Fund, the various private organizations, national organizations, started piling down to Washington. . . . The hundreds of organizations in this country, the church ones, for example, collecting for their beneficiaries . . . felt threatened. They were afraid [the ICEF] would cut across their efforts and spoil their own fund-raising."[63] Charles Taft, brother of Senator Robert Taft, was at that time in charge of coordinating all voluntary fundraising in the United States, and had to arrive at a solution that would satisfy each of the organizations. In the end, a campaign known as the American Overseas Aid—United Nations Appeal for Children (AOA-UNAC) collected funds, then divided them among the ICEF and various other organizations. Pantaleoni recalled that "the campaign was not a success in this country."[64]

The lack of funds was compounded by the stress of knowing much-needed aid was not yet being provided. By February, for example, Austria, Czechoslovakia, Finland, Greece, and Poland had already requested aid from the ICEF, whose total expenditures to date had been $4,000 spent on administrative costs for the board.[65] The ICEF had also heard a report from Dr. A. P. Meiklejohn on the deteriorating conditions he had witnessed on a recent trip to Europe, warning that although life in Europe appeared normal on the surface, "in many places civilization is now worn very thin."[66] He went on to caution: "In this setting a new generation of European children is growing up. They need desperately now, food, clothing, the means to learn, and proper care from adequately trained personnel."[67] If these were not received, claimed Meiklejohn: "My own belief is that unless standards of child life in Europe improve very soon the outlook for Europe and ultimately the world in general, is dreadful."[68] By March, Pate and the Executive Board worried that "UNRRA activities in European countries [will] soon come to an end and there [will] be an immediate need for food stuff in these countries . . . in [my] opinion, help from governments should be asked and voluntary organizations should be contacted."[69] Help finally arrived in June, when Secretary-General Lie stepped in and issued a formal appeal for funds.

In his address which was presented to the seventh meeting of the Executive Board "on his behalf," Lie proclaimed "a most important and welcome event has occurred. The Congress of the United States has authorized a contribution of Fifteen Million Dollars to the Fund with a promise of a further Twenty-five Million Dollars if the Fund raises about Thirty Million

Dollars from other Governments."[70] He then noted that he hoped other contributions would "shortly be forthcoming," as he would be "transmitting a renewed appeal" for cooperation that day.[71] That U.S. grant-in-aid to the ICEF, negotiated by Eliot, formally requested through House Joint Resolution 153 and voted on by the House of Representatives and the Senate on May 21, became official when signed by President Harry Truman on May 31.[72] Pate spelled out the conditions for receiving the funds, which followed exactly the agreements Eliot had made in April. The ICEF would receive an initial $15,000,000, but would have to obtain $43.00 or its equivalent for every successive $57.00 provided by the United States.[73] Pate's report, like the official histories, never mentioned Eliot's contribution.

Now, the ICEF could actually begin its operations. Never mind that the funds had not yet been delivered; with the promise of 15 million dollars, the ICEF could use the promise "for the procurement of milk," which for decades had been seen as a perfect food for children from the United States.[74] Pate's excitement at the prospect of being able to begin the work of providing aid is apparent, and he notes that "this would be the opportune time for procurement [since] the United States provides the main source of milk products, and the present is the height of the flush production period of milk in the United States."[75] He had already drawn up an agreement "in the form of a contract" to be signed by the ICEF and assisted countries, and noted that additional grants from "Canada, Australia and New Zealand . . . are shortly expected."[76]

Pate's report ends with the statement, "Since the last meeting of the Executive Board, the Central Committee of UNRRA has made a grant of $100,000 to the funds of the ICEF, which will be adequate to cover all our administration expenses until the first Government contribution becomes available."[77] Despite a much smaller contribution than the 25 million that had originally been expected from UNRRA, the ICEF plowed forward with the first priority of its plan of work—to provide food aid to the children of Europe and Asia.

NOTES

1. E/ICEF/1, 4.
2. E/ICEF/2, 2.
3. E/ICEF/2, 2.
4. E/ICEF/2, 2.
5. The Milk Committee, "The Production, Distribution and Food Value of Milk: A Report to Herbert C. Hoover, United States Food Administrator" (Washington, DC: Government Printing Office, 1918), 28: U.S. Children's Bureau, "Food for Young Children in Group Care," Children in Wartime No. 4, Bureau Publication No. 285 (Washington, DC: U.S. Government Printing Office, 1942), 4–5: U.S. Children's Bureau, "Children's Health Centers," Children's Year Leaflet No. 5, Bureau Publication No. 45 (Washington, DC: Government Printing Office, 1918), 5–6.

6. *Children in Bondage: A Survey of Child Life in the Occupied Countries of Europe and Finland Conducted by the Save the Children Fund* (London: Longmans, Green and Col., 1942), 11–122.

7. See Lillian Faderman, *To Believe in Women: What Lesbians Have Done For America—A History* (Boston: Houghton Mifflin Company, 1999), 229–305; Regina Markell Morant-Sanchez, *Sympathy and Science: Women Physicians in American Medicine* (New York: Oxford University Press, 1985), 123–24, 303, 335.

8. Martha May Eliot interviewed by Jeanette Cheek for the Schlesinger-Rockefeller Oral History Project, November 1973–May 1974, 181. Accessed at UNICEF Archives.

9. Eliot interview, 186.

10. Eliot interview, 181–82.

11. Eliot interview, 190–91.

12. Eliot interview, 192–93.

13. E/ICEF/23, *Programme Committee's Report to the Executive Board on Meetings Held in Hotel Majestic, Avenue Kleber, Paris, between 18th and 23rd August Inclusive, 1947*, 45.

14. E/ICEF/2, 5.

15. Katharine Lenroot's father appears to have changed the course of his educational ambitions, but not those for his career after the birth of Katharine and her sister. For example, instead of attending university as he had originally planned, he obtained his law credentials by studying on his own while working to support his family, providing a strong role model for Katharine. Herbert F. Margulies, *Senator Lenroot of Wisconsin: A Political Biography, 1900-1929* (Columbia: University of Missouri Press, 1977), 15, vi–x, 87–88, 91, 196.

16. *Encyclopedia of Social Work*, 18th edition, vol. 2, 932.

17. Note that this portion of the report provides detailed information including charts. See Katharine F. Lenroot and Emma O. Lundberg, *Juvenile Courts at Work: A Study of the Organization and Methods of Ten Courts* (Washington, DC: Government Printing Office, 1925), 94–108.

18. Lenroot and Lundberg reported on several U.S. cities, including Denver, St. Louis, Buffalo, San Francisco, New Orleans, and Boston. In a section titled "Methods of Dealing with Problem Children" they note that "maladjustment or misconduct varied greatly" and that various methods were used to deal with this behavior, including assigning "special officers" to conduct "special work" with the children (234); making "regular and frequent visits to schools" (235); holding "conferences with the children and their parents" (237); and establishing "special schools" (238). See Lenroot and Lundberg, *Juvenile Courts at Work*, 94, 216–23.

19. Kriste Lindenmeyer, *"A Right to Childhood": The U.S. Children's Bureau and Child Welfare, 1912-1946* (Urbana: University of Illinois Press, 1997), 182, 208.

20. Linda Gordon and Felice Batlan, "Aid to Dependent Children: The Legal History," at http://www.socialwelfarehistory.com, accessed September 2014.

21. Ruth Sidel, *Women and Children Last: The Plight of Poor Women in Affluent America* (New York: Penguin Books, 1992), 82–83.

22. Sidel, *Women and Children Last*, 84.

23. See Piven and Cloward, *Regulating the Poor*, xvii, 80–177, 123–45.

24. U.S. Children's Bureau, *Recommendations of the White House Conference on Children in a Democracy, January 18-20, 1940* (Washington, DC: Children's Bureau, 1940), 1, 4–5.

25. U.S. Children's Bureau, "Care of Children Coming to the United States for Safety Under the Attorney General's Order of July 13, 1940, Standards Prescribed by the Children's Bureau," Bureau Publication No. 268 (Washington, DC: United States Government Printing Office, 1941), v–vi.

26. See U.S. Children's Bureau, "To Parents in Wartime, Children in Wartime No. 1," Bureau Publication No. 282 (Washington, DC: U.S. Government Printing Office, 1942); U.S. Children's Bureau, "If Your Baby Must Travel in Wartime," Children in Wartime No. 6, Bureau Publication 307 (Washington, DC: U.S. Government Printing Office, 1944); and U.S. Children's Bureau, "Food for Young Children in Group Care," Children in Wartime No. 4, Bureau Publication No. 285 (Washington, DC: U.S. Government Printing Office, 1942).

27. U.S. Children's Bureau, "A Children's Charter in Wartime," Children in Wartime No. 2, Bureau Publication No. 283 (Washington, DC: U.S. Children's Bureau, 1942).

28. Pantaleoni interview, 6.

29. E/ICEF/5, *Summary Record of the Third Meeting Held in Washington, D.C. (Children's Bureau) 13 January 1947*, 2.

30. E/ICEF/5, 21.

31. E/ICEF/5, 25–26.

32. E/ICEF/5, 3.

33. Letter from the Executive Offices of the Secretary-General 23 January 1947, Reference 601–2–4/AD. Maurice Pate Papers, Princeton University Library.

34. J.A.C.C. Alexander as quoted in E/ICEF/5, 5–6.

35. Eliot interview, 189.

36. Bertrand M. Patenaude, "Herbert Hoover's Brush with Bolshevism" (Washington, DC: The Kennan Institute for Advanced Russian Studies at the Woodrow Wilson International Center for Scholars, 1992), 4.

37. Bertrand M. Patenaude and H. H. Fisher have both written about Hoover's years with the ARA and the ways in which Hoover funded his relief organizations. In addition, two of Hoover's associates, Frank Surface and Raymond Bland, published an extensive compilation of the work of Hoover's various aid organizations from 1914 to 1924, including financial reports. See Patenaude, "Herbert Hoover's Brush with Bolshevism"; H. H. Fisher, *The Famine in Soviet Russia, 1919-1923: The Operations of the American Relief Administration* (New York: The MacMillan Company, 1927), especially chapters 6, 13, and 14; and Frank M. Surface and Raymond L. Bland, *American Food in the World War and Reconstruction Period: Operations of the Organizations under the Direction of Herbert Hoover, 1914-1924* (Stanford: Stanford University Press, 1931), appendix B, 553. .

38. Letter from Maurice Pate to the Honorable George C. Marshall, Secretary of State, January 23, 1946. Maurice Pate Papers.

39. Maurice Pate, letter to Herbert Hoover, March 4, 1947. Maurice Pate Papers.

40. *Resolution on Relief Needs after the Termination of UNRRA Adopted by the General Assembly, Paragraph 8 (a) and (b) Report by the Secretary-General* (Lake Success, NY: Economic and Social Council, 1947), 3–4.

41. E/ICEF/7, *Summary Record of the Third Meeting Lake Success New York 7 February 1947*, 4, 6.

42. Pantaleoni interview, 130.

43. *Relief for Children: Selected Statements, United Nations Resolutions, September 21-December 12, 1948, Office of Public Affairs, The Department of State* (Washington, DC: U.S. Government Printing Office, 1949).

44. E/ICEF/17, *Director's Report to the Seventh Meeting of the Executive Board*, 3.

45. E/ICEF/25, *Report of the Executive Director to the 10th Meeting of the Executive Board held at Lake Success, New York 29 September-1 October 1947*, 4.

46. E/ICEF/25, 4.

47. Cable from Davidson, ICEF to Koch, Ministry Social Affairs, Copenhagen, 9 November 1947, and Memorandum from T. L. Peers de Nieuwburgh to Mr. A. E. Davidson: Subject, Contribution of the Belgian Government to UNICEF, December 16, 1947. Maurice Pate Papers.

48. E/ICEF/5, 15.

49. Eliot interview, 214.

50. Eliot interview, 214–15.

51. Eliot interview, 215.

52. E/ICEF/5, 9.

53. Sinclair interview, 3–4.

54. Report of the Director General to the Council for the Period 1 October 1946 to 31 December 1946 (Washington, DC: UNRRA, 1947), 10–11.

55. Report of the Director General to the Council for the Period 1 January 1947 to 31 March 1947 (Washington, DC: UNRRA, 1947), 3, 90.

56. Hyde interview, 69–70.

57. Pantaleoni interview, 130–31.

58. Akira Iriye, *Global Community: The Role of International Organizations in the Making of the Contemporary World* (Berkeley: University of California Press, 2002), 50.

59. E/ICEF/10, *Provisional Report of Programme and Estimate of Expenses 1947 to be Submitted to the Fourth Session of the Economic and Social Council*, 4.

60. Sinclair interview, 4.

61. Sinclair interview, 5.

62. Sinclair interview, 6.

63. Pantaleoni interview, 7.

64. Pantaleoni interview, 7.

65. E/ICEF/10, 6.

66. E/ICEF/12, *Statement Made Before the Fourth Meeting of the Executive Board of the International Children's Emergency Fund by Dr. A. P. Meiklejohn, Senior Consultant in Nutrition, European Office, UNRRA, Lake Success, New York, 24 February 1947*, 5.

67. E/ICEF/12, 12.

68. E/ICEF/12, 12.

69. E/ICEF/16, *Summary Report of the Fourth Meeting*, 2.

70. E/ICEF/18, *Statement of the Secretary-General of the United Nations Delivered on His Behalf at the Seventh Meeting of the Executive Board of the ICEF 17 June 1947*, 1.

71. E/ICEF/18, 1.

72. E/ICEF/17, 1.

73. E/ICEF/17, 2.

74. E/ICEF/17, 2.

75. E/ICEF/17, 2.

76. E/ICEF/17, 3.

77. E/ICEF/17, 5.

Maurice Pate's CRB photo identity card, February 2, 1916.

UNICEF Executive Committee holds a special meeting to pay tribute to Maurice Pate, 1965.

Maurice Pate, UNICEF Executive Director.

Maurice Pate with children assisted by UNICEF.

Maurice Pate, UNICEF Executive Director.

Pate with UNICEF Goodwill Ambassador Danny Kaye and UN Secretary-General Dag Hammerskjold.

UNICEF Goodwill Ambassador Danny Kaye with a child in Thailand.

Information pamphlet provided by the ICEF, circa 1946.

UNICEF public informational pamphlet "For All the World's Children."

Pate's pamphlet for the U.S. Famine Emergency Committee, "The Children Are Hungry," published by the U.S. Department of Agriculture.

UNICEF's *Compendium*, 1953–1954.

Dr. Martha Eliot (left) and Miss Katherine Lenroot.

El Sharrat UNRRA Refugee Camp.

Heroic Women of France
toiling to produce food

"Does it lie within the heart of the American people to hold to every convenience of our life and thus add an additional burden to the women of France?"
—*Alonzo Taylor*

"If we produce all we can, if we eat no more than our health demands, and if we waste nothing we will greatly lighten the load these noble women are carrying."
—*Herbert Hoover*

"It means (food conservation) the utmost economy, even to the point where the pinch comes. It means the kind of concentration and self-sacrifice which is involved in the field of battle itself, where the object always looms greater than the individual."
—*Woodrow Wilson*

Are you doing your part?
UNITED STATES FOOD ADMINISTRATION

WYNKOOP HALLENBECK CRAWFORD CO., NEW YORK

A publicity poster for the U.S. Food Administration directed by Herbert Hoover.

Chapter Four

Feeding Children

By the time the ICEF received Pate's news about the grant from the U.S. government in the summer of 1947, the UN had added Afghanistan, Iceland, Sweden, and Siam to its membership, bringing its total number of members to fifty-five.[1] It operated primarily out of Lake Success, New York, and listed the ICEF as a special body under the supervision of the Economic and Social Council.[2] The ICEF was identified as "the only special body thus far established" whose programs would officially "be utilized for the benefit of children and adolescents of countries which were victims of aggression . . . for child health purposes generally; and to safeguard the health of expectant and nursing mothers."[3] Pate and the others were anxious to begin living up to these expectations, and focused on the first of its priorities, to establish a food aid program.

The first order of business had to be ensuring no gaps occurred in the food and medical assistance provided to children in Europe after UNRRA made its last shipments in the spring of 1947.[4] The director general of UNRRA provided information to the UN secretary general on "The Transfer of Certain UNRRA Functions and the Continuation by other International Agencies" in June, which included a report from the secretary-general on "the Advisory Social Welfare Functions of UNRRA Transferred to the United Nations." The secretary-general's report listed countries that had requested assistance, as well as the types of assistance required. Several countries listed "child welfare" in their requests, including Albania, Austria, and Greece. Hungary asked for a "child psychologist," and the secretary-general noted that "United Nations experts" would serve as "temporary representatives of the Children's Fund" so the requests could be fulfilled, requiring: "The close cooperation with specialized agencies."[5]

That close cooperation, in addition to overlapping missions, brought the ICEF into an immediate working relationship with another UN agency. The Food and Agriculture Organization of the United Nations (FAO), established during the war as part of Roosevelt's vision for a post-war international organization, had also committed to ensuring that a period of acute food shortage did not exist between the end of UNRRA's shipments and the resumption of normal food production in Europe. Historian Gove Hambidge's *The Story of FAO* claims the organization was "born out of the idea of freedom from want" and the "need for peace," which he asserts are "interdependent" in ensuring the "welfare of producers and the welfare of consumers." Any gap in the availability of food would result in overwhelming starvation and, according to Hambidge, a surplus in food supply. The FAO began its operations under the auspices that agricultural production "deeply concerns the well-being of men and nations," yet Herbert Hoover, former U.S. food administrator and experienced food aid distributor, was not invited to be a part of these discussions.[6]

It was F. L. McDougall who first proposed a global food organization in 1942. According to Hambidge, McDougall envisioned agriculture as critical in achieving full employment and in raising the standard of living throughout the world, claiming that "at least 60 percent of the world's workers are engaged in farming." His version of the organization would have three broad functions. First, it would collect, compile, and interpret statistical data relating to food consumption; second, it would organize a world service around the sciences affecting agriculture; and third, it would provide technical guidance and help to less industrialized countries by employing agriculture experts to promote agriculture education. It would not function as a relief organization, but would determine existing needs then provide scientific and technical assistance to local people so that they could resolve the issues themselves. His ideas appeared in his "Draft Memorandum on a United Nations Program for Freedom from Want of Food" in October 1942, which eventually made its way into the hands of First Lady Eleanor Roosevelt. Mrs. Roosevelt invited McDougall to lunch and expressed her interest in sharing his plans with the president.[7]

McDougall presented his ideas to Franklin Roosevelt during an informal dinner at the White House that included discussion of Roosevelt's desire to establish an organization to succeed the League of Nations, which provides an explanation for the absence of Hoover, who became persona non grata in the Roosevelt administration. McDougall, Hambidge claims, told Roosevelt that food would be the first major issue his organization would face after the war, suggesting his idea as a logical starting point. Hambidge's account of the meeting states that Roosevelt listened politely, but "gave no indication that he favored the proposals." Hambidge also claims that no one from the Roosevelt administration contacted McDougall after their initial meeting to discuss his plan further. After meeting with Roosevelt, McDougall published "International Aspects of Postwar Food and Agriculture" in *The Annals of the American Academy of Political and Social Science* both to continue to publicize his plan and hoping it be enacted once the war ended. Plans for such an organization went on without McDougall, however. Roosevelt convened a conference in Hot Springs, Virginia, in May 1943, to discuss global food and agriculture issues and excluded the plan's originator.[8]

The Hot Springs conference "dealt with the most basic of the biological, social and economic problems of mankind—the provision of food for life and health." Forty-five countries sent delegates to the conference, an event of "unusual significance," and discussed all aspects of food production and consumption. Disagreements arose primarily over issues of supply and demand, especially when a proposal had the potential to raise prices for the food importing industrialized countries. They focused primarily on actual food consumption, nutrition requirements, how to increase production to meet these demands, and how to better distribute available food. The conference resulted in thirty-three recommendations and three reports on production, consumption, and distribution, and much of what it established echoed the prior work of the League of Nations.[9]

The group, headquartered in a private house in Washington, DC, "carefully and painstakingly prepared" a work plan. Motivated by the feeling that nations must work together to "prevent future conflicts" and by the belief that science could lead humanity to a new era of abundance, they drafted a constitution that would eventually create the FAO. The constitution's preamble stated that this food organization would "promote the common welfare by . . . raising levels of nutrition . . . [improving] the efficiency of the production and distribution of all food and agricultural products . . . [and] bettering the conditions of rural populations." The committee decided the organization—as McDougall had suggested—would act primarily in an advisory capacity, and would act only as necessary to promote its stated plan of work. The United States would be the largest contributor to the annual budget, providing 25 percent of the $5 million required to run the organization, with other member nations contributing smaller percentages based on their capabilities.[10]

With its plan of work and budget established, the committee decided that the original membership of the organization should consist of the forty-five nations that attended the Hot Springs conference. New members could be added by a two-thirds vote, and the organization would meet at least once a year to determine policy, approve the budget, and appoint a director-general. The first formal report, produced in 1945, included the constitution and was circulated to governments for their consideration and approval. Called *The Work of FAO*, the report stated that the first step, establishing the organization, required approval from twenty countries before any other work could be begun.[11]

Once it received the twenty required acceptances, the group scheduled the first conference of the Food and Agriculture Organization for October 16, 1945. Forty-four governments participated in this new co-operative, which had the distinction of being the first of the new United Nations agencies. They accepted the constitution as well as the plan of work, and established headquarters in Washington, DC. It was there they began to consider recommendations from experts in the fields of "agriculture, forestry, fishery, nutrition, and economics," again without consulting the former U.S. food administrator. The conference ended with a speech by L. B. Pearson, who had been elected conference chairman. He stated that "if we should . . . bring social progress in line with scientific development . . . then the work we have done . . . will have made a worthy and permanent contribution to man's long effort to move upward from the jungle of hatred, suspicion, and death." McDougall, who had been hired as special adviser to the director-general, had seen his vision realized after all. He would, over the course of the next few months, compile the first *World Food Survey* for the FAO. Published on July 5, 1946, it became a crucial source of information not only for the FAO, but for the ICEF as well.[12]

The FAO's *World Food Survey* consisted of a mere thirty-nine pages, succinctly presenting its findings on the required levels of nutrition to ensure good individual health. It also established the projected increases in percentage changes required in the world food supply needed to meet nutritional targets by 1950, and then predicted the additional increases that would be required by 1960.[13] Noting that "there is much starvation . . . in the world," the survey claimed that "facts and figures are needed if the nations are to attempt to do away with famine and malnutrition—an attempt to which they are pledged through the Food and Agriculture Organization of the United Nations."[14] Of interest to the ICEF was its caution that "poor nutrition is associated with high death rates and a low expectation of life, high mortality in infancy and early childhood and among women during the childbearing years" since this also "increased susceptibility to many diseases such as tuberculosis."[15] The solution to the problem, according to the survey, would be to increase individual productivity of subsistence farmers, a task they believed could be greatly affected by the help and guidance of the FAO. The ICEF's immediate contribution to solving this problem, however, would be to distribute food aid while agriculture infrastructures recovered. The survey concluded with the statement that ensuring an adequate world food supply "requires a kind of planning and organization . . . which neither producers nor nations acting by themselves can carry out," and recommended establishing a World Food Board to handle these tasks. Political scientist and anthropologist James C. Scott argues that there are inherent limitations to this type of program, since it relies on the "cyclopean shortsightedness of high-modernist agriculture" that pays "rigorous attention to productionist goals" and "casts into relative obscurity all the outcomes lying outside the immediate relationship between farm inputs and yields." Scott goes on to posit that by ignoring "agricultural practices that are not assimilatable" into more modern techniques, any program not willing to adapt will be "sharply limited in its utility to many cultivators."[16] Like the ICEF had relied on the groundwork already laid by its predecessors, the FAO, using McDougall's plan, had compiled and interpreted data for its operations. Even with its inherent limitations, this allowed the FAO to proceed to its next two steps, organizing a world service for improving agriculture and providing technical assistance to countries in need.[17] The FAO would also use this data specifically to help the ICEF in planning its food aid programs for Europe in 1947.

Both the FAO and the ICEF had indicated their organizations would fill the void left by the cessation of UNRRA food aid programs, which quickly led to questions and concerns regarding duplication of efforts despite their different modes of operation.[18] Members of the Economic and Social Council raised these concerns early in 1947, which lead to the presence of FAO representatives at the ICEF's Executive Board Meetings to ensure no overlaps in planning or programs occurred.[19] Both organizations realized the importance of fashioning a complementary relationship and, during the fifth meeting of the Executive Board held in February 1947, they set their collaboration in motion.

The minutes from the fifth meeting reflect that Chairman Rajchman called upon Mr. Ezekiel, the FAO representative, to make a statement concerning collaboration between the ICEF and the FAO. Ezekiel expressed "sympathy and desire to cooperate to the fullest possible extent with the ICEF," acknowledging that "the Fund's objective was closely connected with FAO's basic interest in higher nutrition levels, the promotion of food programs for underprivileged groups, and the development of the agricultural production of food." He also stated that the FAO's *World Food Survey*, conducted the previous summer, had made suggestions on how to increase levels of agricultural production to meet post-war levels, and that the FAO could send missions to various countries to study agricultural issues.[20] The other FAO representative present at the meeting, Miss Ritchie, stated that "the Nutrition Division of the FAO was particularly interested in the work of the ICEF" and "would cooperate in establishing an international technical advisory group for children's meals."[21]

The relationship between the ICEF and the FAO began cordially and only improved over time. This can be directly attributed to two factors: one, that the ICEF and the FAO were not competing for funds, having established very different bases for their operations; and two, that the ICEF's goals complemented those of the FAO, making cooperation easier because of the absence of competition. Since the FAO had never been envisioned as a distributor of relief aid, preferring instead to be an advisory body, it willingly shared its information with the ICEF. This allowed the ICEF to be the distribution arm of food aid for children and mothers, and the organizations combined their efforts to create effective child-feeding programs using the information and personnel they had at their disposal.

One month prior to the publication of the FAO's food survey, Martha Eliot had completed her report and had disclosed the results of her ICEF food survey in June 1947. Events such as these heightened concerns regarding duplication of efforts within the UN as is reflected in the U.S. Congressional Record concerning approvals for ICEF funding. It was probably fortunate for the ICEF, then, that its U.S. grant-in-aid had already been approved before the FAO's survey appeared; the likelihood of further protracted and negative debate coupled with the inevitable delays would surely have kept funding from being issued in a timely manner, and perhaps altogether. Luckily for Pate and the others, all of the food surveys, including one jointly prepared by the FAO and the United Nations World Health Organization Interim Commission on the state of Child Nutrition, failed to restrict U.S. funding and ultimately assisted the ICEF with its own food aid programs. The joint survey had focused on "[w]ar-stricken Countries of Europe and in China" in 1947 and had been created "[t]o advise ICEF," including detailed summaries of the FAO's study of child and maternal nutrition. It concluded that a lack of protein and calories constituted the "primary nutritional deficiency" and prescribed the means for providing adequate supplements to specialized groups by offering a variety of foods. The report segregated aid recipients into specific groups in order to take into account the often vastly different nutritional needs of pregnant and lactating mothers, infants, toddlers, school-age children, and adolescents. It also noted the differences found in the needs of adolescent girls and boys.[22] The report concluded by stating that

> [t]here can be no more important objective than the salvaging of damaged child life and the building of strong and healthy men and women who can play a full part in the reconstruction of a devastated world. The world cannot hope for a better future unless it looks after its children . . . [and] international action to promote the well-being of mothers and children will, moreover, foster a spirit of friendship and cooperation between nations.[23]

Clearly, the ICEF's objectives complemented those of the FAO. Its operations in no way overlapped the efforts of the FAO, and the two organizations seemed to be in complete agreement over their respective roles in combating world hunger. Each had an interest in supporting "higher nutrition levels, the promotion of food programmes for under-privileged groups, and the development of agricultural production of food" and they could achieve these goals without duplicating work. The FAO also noted that it would help to set up an international advisory group "for children's meals" in conjunction with both the ICEF and WHO.[24] These were of great importance to the ICEF, whose still precarious budget status made any assistance that would help it launch its global feeding programs for children welcome.

With the support of the FAO, its *World Food Survey*, and its study of the nutritional needs of children and mothers, the ICEF continued to reinforce the critical need for food aid. Questions remained, however, as to the actual number of children and mothers requiring assistance, how the aid would be most efficiently distributed, and what type of food aid would be immediately available for distribution. The ICEF turned first to data collected by UNRRA to try and discern an initial number of recipients. This helped only in part, since by the end of 1946, UNRRA had created an estimate of the number of children, nursing mothers, and pregnant women requiring aid in urban areas only. The ICEF therefore continued to focus on the urban in favor of the rural, presumably due to the ability to utilize any remaining infrastructures to set up feeding stations. A report by Dr. Meiklejohn provides justification for this position by assuming that agricultural production had been less disrupted than had urban life. He stated that "the total child population up to eighteen years, is about forty million with one and a half million pregnant mothers. Naturally not all of these are now in need of relief, because a substantial portion live in self-sufficient farming communities," implying that rural areas that had engaged in farming prior to the war had experienced little disruption, and needed less help than urban communities.[25] This attitude persisted despite the fact that the FAO's food survey had indicated a "destruction of dairy herds during the war . . . [and a current] shortage of feedstuffs for livestock." In addition, the FAO projected that "the 1947 crop, expected to be poor, would affect the feeding of livestock" as well as the human population.[26] The ICEF's aid recipient, however, remained identified mostly as urban.

Additional information provided by the U.S. Office of Foreign Relief and Rehabilitation Operations, or OFFRO, also countered the idea that urban populations were more needy. It identified "250,000 vagabond children reported to be moving about in Yugoslavia," as well as statistical information on Norway, Holland, Belgium, Luxembourg, France, Czechoslovakia, and Poland, none of which were enjoying the presumed bounty in rural areas or were comfortably situated in an urban area where a feeding station could be established.[27] These reports also separated mothers and child populations into specific groups, including children aged 0–4, 5–9, and 10–14, children under one, and pregnant women. The introduction to the tables for each nation noted that "children under one year are listed instead of the number of nursing mothers as it is generally assumed in census work that children of this age are nursing."[28]

This phrasing regarding the assumption that children under the age of one relied exclusively on their mothers for nourishment illustrates the emphasis of a mother's importance to the well-being of her children. Her good health and competence ensured she could perform her almost exclusive role in ensuring the survival of her children, and the ICEF based its programs on this long-held belief. When during the nineteenth century studies began to focus on pregnancy, childbirth, and child care in both the United States and countries in Europe, the data collected, compiled, and analyzed made it clear that mothers and children could not be uncoupled; to do so would have negative effects on the child and could, in some cases, be fatal. Mother, then, must be provided for and prepared to perform her necessary functions.

The work of social welfare historian Deborah Dwork illustrates the complex and longstanding history of this perception and helps establish its legacy in later aid programs including those of the CRB and the ICEF. Her examination of infant-feeding programs in England during the late nineteenth and early twentieth centuries posits that experts had proclaimed milk other than that provided by a mother was likely to be contaminated, reinforcing the link between breastfeeding and infant survival. She points to an article published in *The Journal of Hygiene* in 1903, which claims that infants fed with substances other than breast milk were "much more likely to suffer [and die] from diarrhea than those who receive the food nature intended for them."[29] Another study conducted in England from 1899 to 1911 on infant mortality linked it directly to improper infant feeding—any method other than breast-feeding—again placing sole responsibility for the survival of infants on their mothers.[30] In contrast, Dwork notes, programs begun in France at the same time provided sterilized milk to supplement breastfeeding, and the "results were truly wonderful."[31] Instead of the higher-than-usual death rate found among bottle-fed infants in England, babies in France fed through these *gouttes de lait*, or milk depots, gained weight and thrived. Set up partially in response to France's depopulation concerns, this practice became widely used in both urban and rural areas, and received funding from both government and private sources. The practice of establishing milk depots eventually spread to Belgium, as reported by Maurice Pate in his chronicling of his work with the CRB. He commented on a visit to a "Goutte de Lait" that "furnishes fresh milk each morning for 300 babies of the poorer class," observing that "the care and provision for children now is even better than before the war."[32] What is missing from these reports is the mention of mothers, who remained crucial to the survival of their children but were statistically invisible. The number of healthy mothers, rarely mentioned in studies regarding infant health, was overshadowed by the number of thriving infants who, surviving their first few years of life, illustrated the success of the programs and served to mitigate fears about the health of the nation.[33]

The U.S. Children's Bureau had, by the early twentieth century, also begun to investigate and publish study results regarding maternal health and welfare as illustrated in its report on maternal mortality in 1917. It compiled statistics on the causes of death during pregnancy and childbirth in the United States and six European countries, concluding that childbirth had caused more deaths among women aged fifteen to forty-four during 1913 than any other factor except tuberculosis. The report also claimed that "15,000 women died while pregnant from childbed fever and other diseases seen as most curable" and called for higher standards of care for women in pregnancy and childbirth.[34] The ICEF could therefore rely on the notion that mothers and children comprised an inextricably linked and therefore homogenous group and that mothers needed a provider—in this case, the ICEF—to support them in their role as the primary source of nutrition and guardian of the health of children. In order to serve its children and mothers, the ICEF eventually found it could not rely on UNRRA's data. Needing more accurate, up-to-date numbers in order to make the best use of its resources, the ICEF came to rely on reports from individual governments making applications for aid to allocate its resources. Having already received its initial spate of applications, the ICEF began to make plans for the distribution of food aid.

Food aid efforts enacted by the ICEF would be based "on the old Hoover model" according to Pantaleoni, and initially included a variety of non-food items such as clothing as had the earlier programs administered by the CRB and the ARA.[35] The difficulties in clothing distribution had been discussed early on by the Executive Board, and though the ICEF eventually committed to including clothing distribution as part of its relief aid, this never became a major focus of its programs. The reasons for this are illustrated by ARA historian H. H. Fisher, who confirmed that in 1922, the ARA had also faced challenges in its attempts to provide clothing packages to Soviet institutions and individuals. "Clothing packages had to be adaptable," so the ARA provided the components to make clothing, including woolen cloth, muslin, needles, thread, and buttons, and it sold each package for $27.50 US, instead of providing actual clothing. This type of aid relied on the assumption that someone possessed the skills to make clothing once they had the package, which was not always the case, leading Fisher to conclude that "though in no way comparable with the food remittance operation, the Clothing Remittances were a useful supplement to the other departments of relief." Food, on the other hand, posed no such challenges given its acceptability "to both sexes of all ages and sizes," and it became the primary component of the ARA's distribution focus as well as that of the ICEF.[36]

Food distribution for the CRB and the ARA, and the ICEF after them, relied heavily on creating districts based on a country's already-existing infrastructure of roads, rail lines, and public facilities. Each district had several food remittance delivery stations that took advantage of sites such as schools and post offices, and supplemental meals for children were most often provided through a school feeding program, "the teacher serving as kitchen manager."[37] Pate recorded his visit to one such "Soupe Scolaire" in Tournai, where "two immense boilers of food [were] presided over by a stout and good-natured Belgian cook." Five hundred children received a mid-day meal of rice and sugar or boiled potatoes, the distribution of which produced "shouts of joy."[38]

Distributing food assistance to children through schools had been in existence in the early 1900s, and early school meal programs, which grew out of the infant health movement studied by Dwork and others, were never designed to relieve mothers of the primary responsibility of caring for their children. Indeed, Maurice Pate's observations of children receiving meals from the CRB reflect this. He wrote to his parents that "The younger ones are accompanied by their parents (usually the mother) who does the feeding."[39] According to Dwork, many programs even expanded the role of women in public health by providing employment in women-identified occupations such as "school nurses, infant health visitors, and general health visitors." They claimed to focus more on "education and the maintenance of health itself" rather than on usurping the mother's role in the life of her child, and included frequent home visits from health workers designed to ensure mothers provided proper care for their children, whether in school or not.[40] Later programs, however, tended to redefine the role of mothers in distributing aid by leaving mothers out.[41] For example, Pat Thane writes that the provision of meals through school feeding programs was formalized in England via the Education (Provision of Meals) Act of 1906, which, though financed through voluntary contributions, did not penalize poor children whose parents could not afford to make a contribution. This act, according to Thane, was the first time schools became an instrument of public welfare. It was followed by a second act in 1914, which was funded by a subsidy from the Exchequer. This subsequent act provided meals based on an assessment of a child's health and also was not contingent on parental income. It provided aid directly to children and occasionally to mothers who did not give the aid to their children, which ensured the receipt of aid by the children and eliminated the need for home visits to check on the quality of care provided by mothers.[42]

Under the ICEF's programs that commonly used the school feeding model, mothers most frequently found themselves eligible to receive aid instead of retaining primary responsibility for distributing it. The mother's role, therefore, received less consideration under the ICEF's programs, which had begun to mirror state-run social welfare programs in both Europe and the United States. Historian Pat Thane argues that a change began during the 1870s when the notion that children were the responsibility of their families expanded to include the belief that children should also receive assistance outside the family. This assistance, Thane claims, came primarily from educators and morally good adults other than their parents.[43] Historian Susan Pederson argues that these expanded spheres, including social welfare programs, became "deeply structured along gender lines, distributing rights-based entitlements to men for both themselves and for their wives and children and providing lesser, means-tested assistance to women only in the absence of men."[44] What resulted was an increasingly dependent role for mothers, which historian Elaine Tyler May regards as an integral part of the U.S. post-war family ideal in which the idea of the "breadwinner and home-maker were not abandoned; they were embraced."[45] By relieving mothers of the full responsibility to ensure children received assistance, the ICEF did two things. It created a critical role for itself in supporting the well-being of children, and perpetuated a subordinate and dependent role for mothers in its programs.

Having established its preferred method for distributing food aid despite its implications for the role of mothers, the ICEF faced its next hurdle: deciding what type of food aid it would be able to obtain and provide. The FAO's study recommended providing an increased number of calories and a variety of foods, and it hoped the ICEF's food aid could prevent a crisis in maternal and child health in Europe by "perpetuating feeding schemes."[46] The FAO declared "consumption of any available foods containing carbohydrates, fats and proteins" could quickly restore the health of a nursing mother, while "cereals [and] potatoes" could serve as an economical source of calories in an emergency. Since relatively cheap foods could satisfy fat and carbohydrate requirements, it proposed that "the more expensive foods which are of value chiefly as a source of protein" should be provided so the body would not use its precious protein stores for energy instead of for repairing tissues.[47] Its list of acceptable proteins included skim milk, dried and canned fish, and canned meat. Minerals and vitamins, too, constituted a critical part of the supplemental diet to be provided and Martha Eliot remembered that "the countries all wanted this, and we worked out the plans as to how the vitamins would be provided in cod liver oil. Cod liver oil became a staple article for UNICEF to send."[48] The FAO endorsed the ICEF's plan for providing cod liver oil as well as whole milk products, calcium salts, green vegetables, and tomatoes to both mothers and children to ensure they received the required vitamins.

Faced with the challenge of having far less financial capacity than necessary to provide such a variety of foods, the ICEF began to search for the most efficient means of providing the fats, proteins, carbohydrates, vitamins, and minerals deemed necessary to sustain life. The FAO had concluded that in lieu of providing a variety of foods, "much can be achieved by the careful and well-organized expenditure of money and effort on the feeding and care of necessitous mothers and children."[49] In notes on his conversation with "Miss Lenroot and Mr. Schwartz of the Children's Bureau" on January 27,

1947, Pate recounted that they discussed providing "milk, pulses, and meat" in addition to "bread, margarine and hot chocolate early in the day." This would cost the ICEF ten dollars per child and cost more than 85 million dollars—money the ICEF did not have to spend in 1947.[50] What food product, the ICEF staff mused, could meet the most needs and be efficiently distributed? They found their answer in milk.

Cow's milk, according to the FAO, met at least some of the nutritional needs of mothers and children of all ages. It provided protein, vitamins, and fats, and contributed substantially to an individual's calorie intake in its whole form. Despite earlier concerns over its safe use in feeding young children, developments in sterilizing milk for human consumption had erased virtually all concerns over its potability as evidenced in a memorandum regarding rations for infants, children, and pregnant and nursing mothers. Written by William M. Schmidt, MD, of OFFRO in 1943, it recommended that one can of condensed milk be provided each week to "infants (other than those breast-fed)" in relief programs, and that "older children and pregnant and nursing mothers should be allowed sufficient quantities of food (other than milk) from the general stock."[51] This sentiment echoed an earlier pronouncement by the U.S. Children's Bureau, which had proclaimed the milk supply to be safe and recommended that mothers rely on "regular milk companies" for their supply.[52]

A U.S. National Research Council study titled "The Role of Milk in American Culture," conducted in 1943, helps to illustrate why the ICEF willingly embraced milk as its primary food aid product.[53] It reinforced the findings of a report provided to Hoover during his tenure as the food administrator conducted in 1918 by the Milk Committee that not only assured the "superlative value of milk in the dietary," but also recommended "that increased production of milk be encouraged . . . the future being bound up in the welfare of children."[54] The 1943 report, in addition to dispelling any worries about using milk as a dietary supplement for infants, also endeavored to uncover a general pattern in milk consumption among children, women, and men in the United States that would provide clues for changing any prevailing negative attitudes.[55] It included a cultural history of milk consumption, and reveals how the U.S. post-war family ideal could be reinforced through the ICEF's food program, which had placed milk as its primary form of aid.

Natalie A. Joffe, a technical assistant for the Committee on Food Habits at the National Research Council, recorded her findings regarding the deep social and emotional connections between women, children, and milk. She researched and wrote part A of the study, beginning by tracing the origins of milk to central Asia or the Near East. She chronicled milk's arrival in the colonial United States in the form of dairying when a diverse group of animals had provided their milk for human consumption. Eventually, she noted, most other milking animals had been eliminated in favor of the cow and, by 1943, she proclaimed dairy farming to be a practice "entrenched in our economy." So entrenched, in fact, that the term *milk*, which Joffe noted could be applied to "any mammary secretion," had by the 1940s taken on a "very definite connotation in . . . [U.S.] culture. Specifically, it is whole cow's milk, fresh, pasteurized, white, fluid and cold."[56]

The information presented in the report explains a great deal about programs such as the ICEF's that provided milk as their principle form of food relief. In particular, her treatise regarding the changing perceptions of women's breasts—a part of the body that, according to Joffe, belonged either to infants or husbands—explains an overall decline in breastfeeding by American women, allowing cow's milk to supplant breast milk as an ideal food for infants. She wrote,

> Milk is now regarded by a great many people as the perfect infant food. . . . However, this emphasis has arisen gradually and is a shift in affect (emotional response) from human milk to cow's milk. Until comparatively recent times all babies in this country were nursed, and when the child could not be fed in this way, it often was regarded as a real tragedy. Because of this emphasis, the breasts of an adult woman had little sexual connotation.[57]

She noted that, by the 1940s, first-generation immigrant mothers still breast-fed more than their counterparts born in the United States; however, as an immigrant woman had more children and lived longer in the United States, she became less inclined to breastfeed. Joffe attributed this shift to both the availability of a safe milk supply as well as the changing role of the female breast, claiming that in "societies where the human breast is outside the realm of consideration as a love object for the adult male" women used no other feeding methods for infants. However, she was quick to point out that "[q]uite the contrary is now true in most strata of American society," which had experienced "the quickening changes in the tempo of American life and the widening opportunities for women's activities." The female breast was "no longer considered primarily an organ of nutrition, 'child's property.' The desirability of a firm, full bosom has become of great importance in this society. . . . The female breast has become more and more an object of sexual adoration, 'man's property.'"[58] Joffe illustrates what Elaine Tyler May identifies as a trend in the United States, namely that sexuality, though contained in marriage, proliferated. Evident everywhere from song lyrics to civil defense, the idea that a woman's traditional role included being sexually available to her husband prodded women away from long-term breastfeeding and toward "increasing sexual . . . emancipation" that was widely encouraged when contained within marriage.[59]

The idea that women should forgo breastfeeding in order to use their breasts for another function had its flaws, and Joffe pointed out that despite the changing role of women's breasts, nutritional authorities did not consider cow's milk a perfect food for babies. It lacked vitamin C, they said, and did not contain the necessary nutrients in proper balance to ensure a baby thrived. Joffe also presented other reasons why, despite the advice and counsel of experts, many persisted in the belief that cow's milk constituted a perfect food for infants and children. These included milk's color, which many believed indicated its purity, and its connection with the word "pasteurization," which endowed milk with the fundamental premise of being germ free and thus more healthy. Less good for babies and only partially required for the health of most other groups, she concluded ironically that "the pregnant woman or nursing mother benefits by a high intake of milk as part of her regular diet . . . [and make up a group] for whom milk is considered essential."[60]

Having established milk facts in part A, part B of the study correlated the results of surveys taken by a broad group of individuals in order to find out how they felt about milk, especially their attitudes toward a possible milk shortage. Children mentioned milk as a snack, and some claimed it had "almost magical properties"; one respondent stated: "If less milk were available, I think a good deal of people would be sick and die. Also if milk was harder to get those children would die, and if all children grew up sickly or died, what kind of world would this be?"[61] Historian Donna Alvah's work on children who grew up during the Cold War indicates that these comments would not have been out of the norm for children living in the United States during this period. Even though there is often little historical evidence to evaluate directly from children, these survey results reinforce Alvah's claims that learning about current events through their classrooms, from their parents, and in the media, children were bombarded with images meant to reinforce themes and agendas. Her analysis of the effects of Cold War images of nuclear war and the ever-present Communist threat, which often included hungry children, concludes that children in the United States, along with their parents, believed deprived children could be easily persuaded to give up their liberties in exchange for a meal.[62] The results of the milk survey indicate that, like images of the Communist threat, images of milk as a perfect food reinforced themes and agendas regarding proper nutrition that assisted the ICEF in its attempts to isolate and obtain a commodity for distribution that would cause little controversy in the United States.

These attitudes about milk and its effects on health and the community prevailed among children and adults. The researchers found adults hard pressed to come up with a substitute for milk in the case of a shortage, as they did not know what foods could take its place. Teachers, they found, had overwhelmingly used their role as an adult authority figure to stress the importance of milk consumption to their students, and, in the end, it became apparent that milk had achieved the status of "a perfect food" among U.S.

children and adults; "there is no substitute for milk and we can't get along with less."[63]

The ICEF immediately embraced providing milk for children, and it became the one food item that defined ICEF food aid during its early years. It not only seemed to enjoy almost universal appeal in public opinion, but also was available in abundant supply in the United States. Helenka Pantaleoni remembered that "masses of milk was sent over [to Europe]."[64] Martha Eliot recalled that early on, countries requested hundreds of tons of milk and fats from the ICEF; Rumania alone requested "117 tons of whole milk . . . [and] 352 tons of . . . dried milk." The process of drying milk for shipment included spraying it onto large, heated rollers that removed the liquid and pulverized the resulting solid in a simultaneous process, creating a powder. This skim milk powder contained the necessary proteins and vitamins required by children and mothers, did not spoil in the transportation process, and could be immediately reconstituted with a minimal amount of water. Conveniently, the United States possessed an abundant supply of powdered milk, which had been produced in mass quantities for use during the war for the Allied troops. Since powdered milk seemed to provide an almost-perfect solution for everyone involved, it fell to Eliot to raise cautions regarding its limitations. "Skimmed milk carried all the calcium from milk which was needed, but it didn't have the fats, and therefore the vitamin A which ordinarily comes in milk was limited."[65] The ICEF addressed these concerns and provided both lard and butter to replace the fats absent in skim milk. Also considered was the process of mixing whole milk with the reconstituted milk, a process called "toning," in order to increase its nutritional value.[66] Hardly a perfect solution but one that was affordable on the ICEF's limited budget, the milk program moved rapidly forward.

Unsurprisingly, the United States provided the largest contributions of milk to the ICEF's programs, and Pantaleoni remembered that, despite its rather unenthusiastic position on the ICEF, the U.S. government made sure to let all concerned know that it had provided the powdered milk being distributed by the ICEF. "When we sent the dried skimmed milk, there were big letters all over those drums saying 'Gift of the United States People,' so this did make propaganda for the United States . . . except it gave a little bit unbalanced picture of the situation."[67] This ICEF food program, then, clearly offered publicity to the U.S. government, whose desire to be well-regarded in Europe in the years directly following World War II cannot be understated. Its foreign policies, focused on combatting the spread of Communism, took advantage of any occasion to combat what historian Tony Judt calls "Communist rhetorical violence." Not "widely popular in Western Europe" due to fears of "loss of national autonomy and initiative," the United States faced a daunting battle in the "Cultural Cold War."[68] Anxious to portray itself positively, the United States swiftly provided powdered milk to the ICEF and distribution began in September 1947, to supply eight European countries through ICEF plans of operation.[69]

The Executive Board established a Programme Committee late in 1947 to oversee the administration of individual national food aid programs, and this committee quickly reported that in order to meet its objectives: "In general, assistance was to be given through group feeding . . . whole milk was to be furnished only to children up to 1 year old. . . . The assistance furnished would be increased to the extent that shipping costs were borne by the recipient country."[70] The ICEF therefore maintained its work plan, adhered to the recommendation of the FAO regarding infants, and remained true to its commitment of supplying food aid to children and mothers only. By October, its overall operating budget had increased with the addition of funds from Canada, France, and Norway, and by March 1948, the Executive Board had decided to establish permanent missions to China, the Southwest Pacific, and South America in order to establish and oversee programs in these areas as well.[71] Establishing the missions to China and to the Southwest Pacific fell within the scope of the ICEF's charge to provide relief to countries and regions directly affected by World War II, but the mission to South America illustrates the ICEF's intent to pursue its charge more broadly—and, no one protested. The initial *Report of the Survey Mission to the Far East (Other than China)* resulted in recommendations for programs in eleven additional countries and, by the following year, recommendations had been made for both China and for nations in Latin America.[72]

After disbursing its initial milk shipments, the ICEF conducted its own survey of children, parents, and teachers in Europe regarding their opinions concerning extra milk and other rations to school children in order to ascertain the effectiveness of its programs. The actual survey results do not survive, but a summary of its results are contained in a report to the Medical Sub-Committee. That the ICEF conducted the survey at all demonstrates the primary importance of milk in the ICEF's food programs. It was reported to the Executive Board in August 1948, and included questions for children as had Joffe's survey for the Dairyman's Council five years before.

The first three questions directed at children required that their answers be recorded by an adult, presumably a mother or a teacher. These asked the child to provide its age, its sex, and the "[p]rofession of the father."[73] The child then answered a series of queries regarding the number of brothers and sisters living in the home, how much they liked milk as a snack, and why they thought milk was good for their health. Several assumptions inherent in the survey included the notion that children in Europe viewed milk in the same way as children in the United States, and, more importantly, that the mother, not mentioned but implied, remained at home to care for her children and ensure they received their daily portion of milk. By assuming that the father had a profession and the mother did not, this survey illustrates how the

ICEF, whether knowingly or not, reinforced the U.S. post-war family ideal as well as U.S. foreign policy regarding Communism, conforming to what May describes as a "domestic ideology [that] emerged as a buffer against those disturbing [communist] tendencies."[74] Vigilantly containing Communism by reinforcing the importance of its family ideal, U.S. foreign policy propaganda relied heavily on pitting the image of women who nurtured and remained at home with their children against women who worked outside the home for a wage. This is reflected in the survey provided to parents that asked the profession of the father, the ages of all children living in the home, and the number of rooms in the house. It went on to inquire about what "parents"— essentially, the mother—thought about milk as a snack, how much milk a child should drink, and who should pay for any supplemental snacks or meals provided by a school feeding program, alluding to the pay-for-aid practice. The part of the survey intended for teachers remained the most benign in terms of its gendered perceptions. It only asked six questions, most of them concerning how much time, if any, should be taken from the school day to feed children. While this survey helped the ICEF make better projections on the number of persons requiring its aid, it also maintained a strict adherence to U.S. ideas regarding family and politics that would eventually face challenges as the ICEF expanded its operations outside Europe.

Armed with the results of its survey by December 1948, the Programme Committee began to study "Factors Affecting the General Milk Situation" and had summarized the plans for updating its feeding operations in at least twelve European countries by the following February.[75] The Executive Board also produced a report titled "Summarized Plans of Feeding Operations in Europe" that noted that "UNICEF supplies are matched" and provided statistical information on the "principal categories of beneficiaries in the . . . feeding plans."[76] By March, reports noted that a "child food unit . . . [which] consists of 240 calories daily for a period of six months of milk, and fats and cocoa" could be reallocated as necessary to ensure the proper feeding of the child, pregnant mother, and nursing mother population.[77] This reallocation could presumably apply to any part of the world in which children and mothers suffered deprivation due to a number of circumstances, and throughout 1949, the ICEF continued to expand its food aid programs, eventually installing them in regions of the world not affected by the war. By 1950, Pate reported that the ICEF had shipped "more than 30,000 tons of supplies valued at more than $9,000,000.00. . . . The bulk of the tonnage . . . resulted from the shipment of dried skim milk."[78]

For decades afterward, the ICEF became identified almost exclusively as the organization that provided milk to poor children the world over.[79] Countless photographs pictured smiling children holding tin cups above their heads about to receive milk, the magic elixir of life, from the ICEF, their benevolent provider. Its dedication to eradicating child hunger earned the ICEF a reputation outside the United States for being one of the best-known and least controversial UN operations, and it kept U.S. criticisms at bay for a time by preserving the Western ideal of the family during its early operations in Europe as well as tacitly supporting U.S. foreign policy. Its food aid programs begun, the ICEF faced another of its priorities: how to establish medical aid programs for children and their mothers to ensure better maternal and child health and welfare throughout the world. What to treat and how to treat it became the primary questions concerning the Executive Board as enacting the plan of work continued.

NOTES

1. United Nations Publication Sales No.: 1947.112. *The Structure of the United Nations [1947]*. 1.
2. *The Structure of the United Nations [1947]*. 22.
3. *The Structure of the United Nations [1947]*. 23.
4. In its report to the Economic and Social Council concerning UNICEF operations from 1946 to 1950, the organization reported not only on its mission to provide for children and their mothers, but also the pressing need to act in 1946 as UNRRA would no longer be providing this type of aid. E/ICEF/160, 3.
5. E/458, *Progress Report of the Secretary General on Implementation of Resolution 58 of the General Assembly on the Advisory Social Welfare Functions of UNRRA Transferred to the United Nations* (Lake Success, NY: Economic and Social Council, 1947), 9, 28.
6. Gove Hambidge, *The Story of FAO* (New York: D. Van Nostrand Company, Inc., 1955), 54–55. 58.
7. Hambidge, *The Story of FAO*. 48–49.
8. Hambidge notes that McDougall wrote the article "late in 1942," implying that its publication came after his meeting with President and Mrs. Roosevelt. Hambidge, *The Story of FAO*. 48–49.
9. Hambidge, *The Story of FAO*. 50.
10. The United Kingdom was the next largest contributor at 15 percent, followed by the USSR. China, France, Canada, India, Brazil, and Australia. The remaining countries contributed much smaller percentages, some as little as one half of 1 percent. Hambidge, *The Story of FAO*. 52–53.
11. United Nations Interim Commission on Food and Agriculture, *The Work of FAO* (Washington, DC, August 20, 1945).
12. Hambidge, *The Story of FAO*. 59–62.
13. Food and Agriculture Organization of the United Nations, *World Food Survey* (Washington, DC, July 5, 1946).
14. FAO, *World Food Survey*, 5.
15. FAO, *World Food Survey*, 8.
16. James C. Scott, *Seeing Like a State: How Certain Schemes to Improve the Human Condition Have Failed* (New Haven and London: Yale University Press, 1998), 264.
17. *World Food Survey*, 30.
18. Early in 1947, the Economic and Social Council raised concerns over the duplication of efforts among UNICEF, FAO, and WHO but chose not to intervene. Because there is no evidence of further concern on the part of the council, it appears that the agencies reached acceptable compromises to continue to work together. See for example E/ICEF/14, *Summary Report of the Fifth Meeting, 28 February 1947*; E/ICEF/23, annex 3, *Report of FAO-WHO Committee on Child Nutrition (to advise ICEF), 23-26 July, 1947*; E/ICEF/129, *Report of the Executive Director to the 93rd Meeting of the Programme Committee to be held on 20 October 1949, New York City.*

19. Two representatives of the FAO attended the ICEF Executive Board meeting for the first time on February 24, 1947. E/ICEF/13, *Summary Record of the Fourth Meeting, Lake Success, New York 24 February 1947*, 1.

20. Statement made by FAO representative to the Executive Board of the ICEF on February 28, 1947. E/ICEF/14, 2.

21. E/ICEF/14, 3.

22. E/ICEF/23, 5–7, 34–42, annex 3, 31.

23. E/ICEF/23, 45.

24. E/ICEF/14, 2, 3.

25. E/ICEF/12, 1.

26. E/ICEF/14, 2.

27. J. H. Hildring, Major General, Chief, Civil Affairs Division, War Department, to the Honorable Herbert H. Lehman, Director, Office of Foreign Relief and Rehabilitation Operations, 27 August 1943; Memorandum and Report from David Weintraub to Mr. Lithgow Osborne, Department of State, Office of Foreign Relief and Rehabilitation Operations, May 21, 1943, National Archives, Maryland Facility, Office of Foreign Relief and Rehabilitation Operations, General Subject File 1942–1943, Record Group 169, File Location 169.5.

28. Weintraub Memorandum and Report, 2.

29. An early twentieth-century study concluded that infant feeding played a critical role in the survival of a child, and that breast milk was best, since much of the cow's milk and evaporated milk provided to infants contained bacteria and other contaminants that led to infant illness and death. Additional studies provided staggering statistics when correlating infant mortality rate and breastfeeding, one of which noted that infants fed with anything other than breast milk were those most at risk to die. Analysis by H. Meredith Richards, in the *Journal of Hygiene* (1903) in Deborah Dwork, *War is Good for Babies and Other Young Children: A History of the Infant and Child Welfare Movement in England, 1898-1918* (London: Tavistock Publications, 1987), 29.

30. Deborah Dwork writes that great concern existed over the fitness of British men for military service as well as the declining birth rate and high rates of infant mortality, all of which indicated in their nineteenth-century context that Britain could be facing national decline. This was an issue that led to closer examinations of the reasons for infant mortality. See Dwork, *War is Good for Babies and Other Young Children*, 20, 23, 26, 52.

31. Dwork, *War is Good for Babies and Other Young Children*, 98–99.

32. Maurice Pate, letter to his mother and father, September 22, 1916. Maurice Pate Papers, Princeton University Library.

33. Dwork points to the work of Pierre Budin during his tenure as chef de service at the Charité Hospital in Paris, where he established infant clinics. She notes that, even though he focused on breastfeeding as the primary food source, his program provided sterilized cow's milk as well, which often caused mothers who began his program as breastfeeders to cease breastfeeding in favor of the sterilized milk. His work caused an appreciable drop in infant death rates. Another practitioner, Dr. Leon Dufour, was the first to set up *gouttes de lait*, which Dwork notes became a popular term for places providing maternal and infant care as well as supplies of sterilized milk for infant feeding. The French also feared that the combination of a declining birth rate and an increasing infant mortality rate would relegate France to a lesser place in the hierarchy of nations. See Dwork, *War is Good for Babies and Other Young Children*, 94–95, 98–101.

34. U.S. Children's Bureau, "Maternal Mortality from All Conditions Connected with Childbirth in the United States and Certain Other Countries," by Grace L. Meigs, MD, Miscellaneous Series No. 6, Bureau Publication No. 10 (Washington, DC: Government Printing Office, 1917), 7.

35. Pantaleoni interview, 23.

36. H. H. Fisher, *The Famine in Soviet Russia, 1919-1923: The Operations of the American Relief Administration* (New York: The MacMillan Company, 1927), 424–425.

37. In Fisher, see especially chapter 7, "The Russian Transport Crisis"; chapter 9, "Distributing the Corn"; chapter 10, "Skirmishes on the Home Front"; and chapter 16, "The Last Days"; all of which provide information regarding aid distribution and the use of infrastructure:

101; see also 94, 306, as well as the RIGA agreement between the ARA and the Soviet Republic, which clarifies who will be fed through the ARA's programs, 507; and 556–57.

38. Maurice Pate, letter to his mother and father dated September 22, 1916. Maurice Pate Papers, Princeton University Library.

39. Maurice Pate, letter to his mother and father, September 22, 1916. Maurice Pate Papers, Princeton University Library.

40. Dwork, *War is Good for Babies and Other Young Children*, 204–6.

41. Pat Thane, *The Foundations of the Welfare State* (New York: Longman, 1982), 75–6.

42. Thane, *The Foundations of the Welfare State*, 75–6.

43. Thane writes that social investigation in the late nineteenth and early twentieth century led to a "greater understanding of the complex causes of poverty," among them temporary unemployment and chronic underemployment, leading to the conclusions that even the worst forms of poverty were "not self inflicted." Thane, *The Foundations of the Welfare State*, 38, 42.

44. Susan Pedersen, *Family, Dependence, and the Origins of the Welfare State, Britain and France, 1914-1945* (New York: Cambridge University Press, 1993), 10.

45. Elaine Tyler May, *Homeward Bound: American Families in the Cold War Era* (New York: Basic Books, Inc., Publishers, 1988), 3.

46. E/ICEF/23, 33.

47. E/ICEF/23, 34–35.

48. Eliot interview, 205.

49. E/ICEF/23, 45.

50. Maurice Pate, Conversation with Miss Lenroot and Mr. Schwartz of the Children's Bureau, 30 January 1947, 1–2. Maurice Pate Papers, Princeton University Library.

51. Memorandum from William M. Schmidt, MD, regarding the Rations for Infants, Children and Pregnant and Nursing Mothers in Relief Programs, September 10, 1943. National Archives, Maryland Facility, Office of Foreign Relief and Rehabilitation Operations, General Subject File 1942–1943, Record Group 169, File Location 169.5.

52. U.S. Children's Bureau, "Children's Health Centers," Children's Year Leaflet No. 5, Bureau Publication No. 45 (Washington, DC: Government Printing Office, 1918.), 5–6.

53. Patricia Woodward, Natalie F. Joffe, Marjorie Janis, and Eva Shippee, *The Role of Milk in American Culture* (Washington, DC: Committee on Food Habits, National Research Council, 1943).

54. "The Production, Distribution and Food Value of Milk: A Report to Hebert C. Hoover, United States Food Administrator by the Milk Committee" (Washington, DC: Government Printing Office, 1918), 28–32.

55. Woodward et al., *The Role of Milk in American Culture*, 1–2.

56. Woodward et al., *The Role of Milk in American Culture*, 3.

57. Woodward et al., *The Role of Milk in American Culture*, 9–10.

58. Woodward et al., *The Role of Milk in American Culture*, 9–10.

59. May, *Homeward Bound*, 92, 103–106, 109

60. Woodward et al., *The Role of Milk in American Culture*, 9–10, 14.

61. Woodward et al., *The Role of Milk in American Culture*, 14, 19.

62. Donna Alvah, "'I Am Too Young to Die': Children and the Cold War," *OAH Magazine of History*, October 2010, Volume 24, Issue 4, 25–28.

63. Woodward et al., *The Role of Milk in American Culture*, 19, 31.

64. Pantaleoni interview, 13.

65. Eliot interview, 204–5.

66. Eliot interview, 205; unpublished *History of UNICEF* written by John Charnow, 1964–1965 (New York: UNICEF), 75.

67. Pantaleoni interview, 17.

68. Tony Judt, *Postwar: A History of Europe Since 1945* (New York: The Penguin Press, 2005), 220.

69. These countries were Austria, Greece, Italy, Poland, Czechoslovakia, Finland, and Hungary. E/ICEF/23, 1.

70. E/ICEF/23, 5.

71. E/ICEF/25, 4–5.

72. E/ICEF/72, *Report of the Survey Mission to the Far East (Other Than China)*, 2.

73. E/ICEF/77, *Report of the Session of the Medical Sub-Committee Held at Paris UNICEF Headquarters 9-10 August 1948*, 22.

74. May, *Homeward Bound*, 10.

75. Countries included Albania, Austria, Bulgaria, Czechoslovakia, Finland, France, Greece, Italy, Poland, Rumania, and Yugoslavia. See E/ICEF/88, *Report and Recommendations of the UNICEF-FAO Panel of Dairy Experts*; E/ICEF/10A, *Summarized Plans of Feeding Operations in Europe,* 1.

76. E/ICEF/10A, 3, 20.

77. E/ICEF/107, *Compilation of Major UNICEF Policies*, 4.

78. E/ICEF/155, 9.

79. Ritchie Calder wrote in 1962 that an infant boy in Thailand whose mother had died in childbirth regained his health through "careful milk-dieting" administered by UNICEF. Ritchie Calder, "Growing up with UNICEF," *Public Affairs Pamphlet No. 330* (New York: Public Affairs Committee, 1962), 2.

Chapter Five

Medical Treatment for Children

While the ICEF's food programs got underway, another aspect of the ICEF's charge—to provide basic medical treatment to children and mothers—began to take shape. Milk programs would provide immediate food aid relief to millions of children and mothers, but they needed more. Maternal and child health, a pivotal portion of the activities of the U.S. Children's Bureau since its founding in 1913, had focused on prenatal care, infant mortality, and all aspects of child care, producing what it believed to be the most up-to-date information on preventing health issues and fatalities in the mother and child population. The ICEF would be faced with a momentous task in trying to provide this type of care in Europe, and Tara Zahra reinforces the gravity of the situation they faced, writing that UNRRA predicted there were tens of millions of displaced persons in Europe after World War II, most of these located in Eastern Europe.[1] These displaced persons not only faced severe food shortages and the aftereffects of psychological trauma resulting from the war, but also found themselves subject to the rapid spread of illness and contagious diseases due to the paucity of any kind of medical infrastructure, including the loss of thousands of doctors and other medical personnel to the war. The ICEF's limited resources made it unlikely that its medical aid programs could make a difference unless it collaborated with another organization. Fortunately for the ICEF, the UN had begun working toward establishing a health organization that could partner with the ICEF in its maternal and child health initiatives.

Talk of forming a United Nations health organization had begun during the summer of 1946, but Dr. Henry Van Zile Hyde recalled that up to "1945, there was very little interest in what was going on in health; it was a sideline." Health professionals, concerned about the omission of any reference to matters of health in the original draft of the UN charter, "got together and decided something should be included in the [UN] Charter on health." They introduced a resolution, found that it was too late for consideration by the time they got around to introducing it, but were allowed to introduce a declaration instead. This declaration led to the insertion of health "as one of the ways which there could be a specialized agency."[2] As a specialized agency, the proposed health organization would be subjected to the UN's lengthy approval process. This meant establishing an interim commission, drafting a resolution, receiving acceptance from a specified number of member nations, and then awaiting final approval from the General Assembly. Martha Eliot recalled that "ECOSOC [Economic and Social Committee], in a meeting on the 15th of February, 1946, did adopt a resolution recommending that an international conference be called [regarding a health organization] . . . they established a technical preparatory committee."[3] Though Eliot stated that she had "no specific relationship with this interim commission," Hyde claimed he had worked on the first draft of its constitution in his capacity as a member of the staff of the U.S. Surgeon General's office and with UNRRA, participating later as a member of the committee that convened in March. He served as secretary for the drafting committee, and recalled that his primary contribution to the document "was taking the 'whereas' out of it."[4]

While the ICEF worked to obtain funding and establish its programs, the document Hyde helped create that would form a health organization received unanimous approval. It only required slight revisions to make it final, and the delegates to the International Health Conference held in Flushing Meadows, New York, in June and July 1946, moved it to the next phase.[5] Martha Eliot, having returned from her ICEF survey of Europe, attended the conference as the vice-chairman of the delegation from the United States, one of sixty-four nations at the meeting.[6] The conference established the general outline of the plan of work for the health organization, and required that twenty-six nations accept the constitution before it could come into being and hold world health assemblies.[7]

Of special concern to Eliot was the inclusion of specific language regarding maternal and child health and welfare. This concern was based not only on her pediatric career and her work with the U.S. Children's Bureau, but also on her recent trip to Europe to view conditions there for the ICEF. She fought to have these included in the WHO constitution, remembering: "The draft constitution had a section in its preamble which drew attention to the importance of the 'healthy development of the child.'" For some reason, this item was objected to by some of the U.S. delegation, a problem she attributed to competing bureaucracies, specifically the "basic problem between the Children's Bureau and the Public Health Service." She noted that the final wording, presented in a speech made by Canadian delegate Dr. Brock Chisholm "at my urging," was changed to read "the ability to live harmoniously in a changing total environment is essential to the healthy development of the child. I accomplished through Dr. Chisholm what I wanted!"[8]

Eliot did not stop there. She and Chisholm collaborated again to insist that the statement of functions of the organization include reference to maternal and child health. The wording that resulted, "To promote maternal and child health and welfare," Eliot pointed out, included the reference to welfare because of her efforts. "It was I who put in 'and welfare.' . . . Because I knew that many countries thought of welfare as including health . . . [but] other countries, like the United States, separated them."[9] Having achieved her primary goals to include maternal and child health concerns in the constitution of WHO, Eliot had unknowingly succeeded in placing the ICEF and WHO in direct competition for control over matters of child health within the UN. Her personal involvement in both organizations did little to prevent the ensuing battle over funds from the waning UNRRA, and the two organizations were forced to establish a relationship that required all of the cooperation but had none of the cordiality that the ICEF and the FAO enjoyed. Eliot pointed out that providing funds to WHO caused UNRRA to limit its contribution to the ICEF, significantly reducing its original pledge. When asked whether or not a way could have been found to avoid the duplication in child health by the WHO and the ICEF, Eliot mused, "Well, if the language in the two constitutions . . . had been more specific or if there had been an explanation of the fact that each of these organizations was to be enabled to do child health, but that they should work it out together. . . . We should remind ourselves that the overlap in the field of child health was not extensive or serious. So it was a matter of finding a way to solve this problem."[10]

Unfortunately, the ICEF and WHO had great difficulty in resolving these issues. From their first meeting in 1947, friction existed between them. The former insisted that it had a special responsibility to provide medical care to children and mothers based on the resolution that created it, while the latter insisted that the ICEF had been created uniquely for supplying food in an emergency situation and lacked the competence to undertake medical programs. Chairman Rajchman, in an attempt to open a dialogue to address the tensions, raised several issues that concerned both organizations at the fourth meeting of the ICEF Executive Board. Attended by Dr. Calderon, the interim commissioner of WHO, Rajchman began the meeting neutrally. He declared that the correspondence between the ICEF and WHO concerning a study of milk available for children and adolescents, monographs regarding the condition of children in countries affected by the war, and the training of medical and public health personnel had begun. He also acknowledged that UNRRA had transferred "to WHO $1,500,000 to continue UNRRA medical activities, including the granting of study fellowships, in 1947" funds that the ICEF could no longer rely on to bolster its medical relief aid efforts.[11] While his statement established that the ICEF and WHO had a shared interest in cooperating to meet the needs of the maternal and child population, he also conveyed the bad news that the ICEF could no longer rely on the original amount promised by UNRRA to bolster its own medical relief aid efforts.

Dr. Calderon, too, addressed the meeting, stating that "in the absence of the Executive Secretary of his Organization, he was unable to make statements of detail" regarding the relationship between the ICEF and WHO. Instead, he announced that WHO was sympathetic to the purposes of the ICEF, and wished to support it, since "problems of children, especially of the youngest, were essentially problems of public health." He further stated that, at that time, he could not say what portion of a $500,000 grant for training fellowships could be allotted to the ICEF.[12] In complete contrast to the first presentation of the FAO at an Executive Board meeting, Calderon made clear that WHO would dictate to rather than cooperate with the ICEF. This is perhaps best illustrated in the *Report on Child Nutrition* that WHO prepared in conjunction with the FAO. WHO representatives considered their information a generous gift to the ICEF, but because of the way in which it was presented, it did little to warm relations between the two organizations. Perhaps in an attempt to signal to WHO that it did not constitute the only source of information and support for the ICEF's medical relief aid programs, Chairman Rajchman opened a discussion at the October 1947, Executive Board meeting regarding a recent proposal to establish a Children's Center in Paris. This center, he stated, would study all aspects of childhood, including children's medical issues. WHO delegates expressed worry that Rajchman was proposing an entirely new health organization, thereby encroaching on WHO's territory. The end result was the unleashing of a new wave of animosities in the struggle to control post-war medical relief aid for children and mothers.

Dr. Forrest, representing WHO at the October ICEF Executive Board meeting, "had some questions to put concerning the proposed Center." Co-sponsored by the French government, it was stated during the meeting that the main medical tasks of the Children's Center "would be international teaching and surveys, both of which are needed [to combat] the widespread shortage of medical personnel." The center would be international in character, and would not limit its activities to any particular territory. Dr. Forrest quickly expressed concern over the lack of precision in defining the center's fields of research, and noted that it did not seem to fit any category of international agency with which he was familiar. Would it be an international governmental agency or an international non-governmental agency? In an attempt to reinforce the importance of WHO's role in international medical programs, he announced that since the League of Nations had been concerned with the problems of child health before WHO was organized, and since WHO was taking over the functions formerly performed by the League of Nations, then "the problems of child health are within the scope of the WHO," not the Children's Center.[13]

Chairman Rajchman's response indicates that he must have viewed Dr. Forrest's remarks as defensive. Rajchman calmly stated that "the representatives of the ICEF would make a statement [regarding the role of the Children's Center] in reply after the representatives of the other agencies" present at the meeting—including the FAO, UNESCO, and UNRRA—"had presented their views." The other agencies, probably to Forrest's disappointment, unanimously declared that "the French Government should be commended for its efforts in the interest of the problems of children," and that the Children's Center could count on their cooperation. As a result of these early meetings, little trust had been forged between the personnel of the ICEF and WHO. They dealt with each other suspiciously for the rest of 1947, waiting to see who would make the next move, but neither had to wait for long. On January 29, 1948, WHO dealt a decisive blow to the ICEF in a meeting of its Committee on Relations. It presented its newest proposals regarding collaboration with the ICEF, specifically regarding the use of fellowship grants from France, Switzerland, and Denmark. These three countries had all made fellowship grants to the ICEF to train medical personnel, but WHO had been given control of their distribution. WHO took this opportunity to severely curtail the scope of the ICEF's medical relief aid work, stating it its report that the fellowships could only be used to train ICEF personnel "in BCG work to be held in Denmark." All other proposals in the field of fellowships, it concluded, were "under consideration." It clarified, albeit vaguely, that allocations would be made on the basis of "a number of factors," all at the discretion of WHO, including the allocations already made for food and the losses of medical personnel in the country concerned.[14]

To be fair, WHO may have taken this narrow position to offer training only in tuberculosis prevention partly due to the ICEF's insistence that maternal and child tuberculosis qualified as a post-war emergency. That meant that tuberculosis qualified as belonging to the ICEF, whose experts in maternal and child health care understood that it usually spread rapidly among a family's most vulnerable members—usually babies, small children, and the elderly.[15] Eliot's survey of Europe provided the ICEF with proof of the ubiquity of tuberculosis in the child population: "When I went into the hospitals, as I did in each place, I found many children with tuberculosis. I'd never seen so much, rows of infants and young children in hospital wards, emaciated, dull, lifeless." One of her primary concerns was that "many died of what was known as miliary tuberculosis that is scattered like seed throughout the body." She observed that immunization against tuberculosis had already been developed at the National Institute for the Study of Tuberculosis in Denmark, and that the Danish Red Cross, in conjunction with the Norwegian and Swedish branches, had already established groups of technical workers to go to war-devastated countries and set up clinics. [16]

Relying once more on the CRB and ARA model of utilizing these already existing programs and infrastructures and having been promised funds from Denmark and Belgium for medical relief aid, the ICEF began to plan a program for vaccination against tuberculosis. Correspondence generated by Chairman Rajchman in December 1947 as well as reports from the ICEF's medical sub-committee illustrate that the ICEF had already forged a relationship with the Danish Red Cross in attempts to join its campaign to distribute the recently created and more readily available Calmette-Guerin Bacillus, or BCG vaccine campaign. In a letter to Dr. Johannes Holm dated December 16, 1947, Chairman Rajchman indicated that the ICEF had received communication from the Danish Government "in connection with the BCG campaign conducted by the Danish Red Cross." He invited Holm to "direct, on behalf of the ICEF, the above BCG campaigns," and indicated he would be "very grateful if you would consider the matter in due time and give me the benefit of your observations." [17] A day later, Chairman Rajchman wrote to Dr. Madsen in Denmark that the ICEF, at its December 2 meeting, had established a sub-committee on medical projects, "in the first place the extension of the BCG." [18] By February 1948, the report of the Sub-Committee on Medical Projects confirms that the ICEF had already begun working with the existing movement to combat the spread of tuberculosis. Training facilities had been provided by both France and Switzerland for ICEF medical personnel, and "Dr. Holm . . . described the training program in tuberculosis work, which had been going forward in Denmark." [19] Holm offered the ICEF access to training facilities run by the Danish government to train "twenty-five students at one time for a three-months course," and went on to report to the sub-committee on Denmark's experience in testing for and treating tuberculosis. [20] This report also includes information on the treatment of "normal children" and "deficient children" with those in the deficient category possessing some physiological or mental deficiency, or being "illegitimate, delinquent, neglected or abandoned." [21] That the ICEF included these children in its treatment programs indicates that its commitment to providing aid to all children was being upheld. And, in keeping with its agreements with governments to participate alongside the ICEF in relief efforts, a report by Dr. H. F. Hemholz and Dr. J. M. Latsky notes that with the "emergency measure" of testing and treatment being carried out in conjunction with the Danish Red Cross acting for its Norwegian and Swiss associates, countries would be expected to "develop a comprehensive anti-tuberculosis programme" of their own. [22]

Rajchman's correspondence with Madsen clearly indicates that the ICEF's early medical relief aid programs answered to another authority in addition to WHO. The ICEF also gave consideration to the U.S. State Department "in view of the agreement concluded by the Fund [ICEF] with the Department of State in Washington, concerning the matching by the United States Treasury of funds contributed by governments to ICEF." Obtaining matching funds, he wrote, relied on two factors. The first included obtaining "formal title to the appropriation . . . even though that appropriation is immediately utilized for the purpose mutually agreed upon by the government and the Fund." The second, though not contained in Rajchman's correspondence, is the ICEF's requirement to continue to act in accordance with U.S. foreign policy as outlined by the State Department, evident in the four-page attachment included with his letter that outlined the required agreement between the ICEF and the Danish Red Cross and the actions to be taken to ensure receipt of those matching U.S. funds. It begins by proclaiming that the Danish Red Cross had undertaken a "remarkable initiative . . . on a scale never before attempted," and that this "lasting contribution for the welfare of European childhood and adolescence" fell "fully within the programmes and policies assigned to the International Children's Emergency Fund." The ICEF promised grants-in-aid would be issued from the United States to the Danish Red Cross, and expected the "proposed extension and intensification of tuberculosis work" would eventually include Norway and Sweden as collaborators. Distribution of supplies, staff, and salaries were also covered, and required "mutual consultation" to ensure uniformity in all countries participating in the program. All arrangements, it concluded, should be made with Dr. Johannes Holm, "to whom all BCG activities of the ICEF would be entrusted."[23]

Managing these multiple reporting relationships did not slow the pace if the ICEF's medical relief aid planning. Rajchman, ever vigilant in his efforts to move the medical relief aid programs forward, wrote a letter to Dr. Brock Chisholm, executive secretary of the interim commission of the World Health Organization, on December 18 to try and establish a more formal working relationship between the two organizations. He stated that the ICEF's Executive Board had "unanimously decided to make two recommendations" to WHO, the first that "frequent periodic meetings" take place between the experts from both organizations. These meetings would be primarily for the exchange of information, and would include "[t]echnical consultants and representatives of the [ICEF] Executive Board" as well. Convening a joint conference was his second recommendation "in order that all participating countries would be aware of the work that is going on and in order that uniformity be assured in the plans and their implementations."[24]

By the end of the first quarter of 1948, the ICEF and the Danish Red Cross had finalized their agreement to allow the ICEF to augment the tuberculosis vaccination programs already under way in Europe. WHO, because of its insistence that the ICEF could only provide medical relief aid with WHO's approval, subsequently found itself at odds with both the Red Cross and the ICEF, a situation further exacerbated by the fact that WHO did not truly have the authority it attempted to wield over the ICEF until it received its official status from the General Assembly. Interestingly, when WHO finally received its mandate in April 1948, it became more willing to discuss the matter, ostensibly because the concern over its approval had been lifted. Eliot recalled that both the ICEF and WHO planned a meeting in Geneva to be held in June 1948. The two organizations, she stated, had realized "it was a good time for the two organizations to find out how they could work together," and relations between them became more cordial in the following years.[25]

Internally, the ICEF Executive Board had little debate over choosing tuberculosis as one of its primary targets, or over how to manage the tuberculosis prevention program. Once it accepted a country's application for assistance, the ICEF would determine its need for the BCG vaccine, and then provide whatever the country needed to implement the program including the vaccine, medical supplies, and medical personnel. It may seem odd that the ICEF virtually ignored typhus, since it still constituted the worst epidemic both in Europe and throughout the world in the years directly following World War II; however, typhus had been dealt with through international cooperation prior to World War II, while little effort had been made to coordinate tuberculosis control. Therefore the ICEF's efforts toward curbing the spread of tuberculosis afforded the opportunity to establish international cooperation with new partners and to produce impressive results on a large scale, despite the fact that scientific and medical communities never firmly concluded that the BCG vaccine proved effective. In the end, the ICEF could justify its participation in the anti-tuberculosis program because tuberculosis had spread rapidly in the child and mother population during the war years, making it an important epidemic in its own right as well as one that was particularly harmful to children and their mothers, the latter of which had to remain healthy in order to ensure the health and safety of their children.

Providing this treatment for children and their mothers suffering from tuberculosis constituted only one-half of Rajchman's aggressive maternal and child health program. Treating children and mothers for syphilis would allow the ICEF to radically influence the disease's effects on mothers and children in Europe since syphilis could be effectively treated with a course of penicillin treatments—the first real syphilis cure.[26] As had been true of tuberculosis, the numbers of syphilis cases in Western Europe were far less than those in Eastern Europe. This resulted in fewer requests for aid from the ICEF in countries such as France and Finland, both of whose recoveries had benefitted from aid received in conjunction with the Marshall Plan.[27] Whether in the east or the west, however, the ICEF faced several cultural obstacles in taking on this second project.

One of these obstacles, that children and mothers with syphilis had long been deemed degenerates, had rendered them entirely unworthy of treatment in the past. The ICEF medical staff knew, however, that treatment for pregnant women with untreated, active syphilis could make a marked difference in overall maternal and child health in Europe. Advances had been made in understanding how diseases spread, and this led to a shift in the perceptions about syphilis patients. In particular, the discovery that men as well as women could transmit the disease to a sexual partner forced anti-syphilis campaigns of all sorts to emphasize that men, too, bore responsibility for the spread of the disease. Studies concluded that men could pass the disease on to women and to any children the couple produced. Moral responsibility for infecting children, now portrayed as innocent victims instead of degenerate offspring, rested equally on fathers and mothers.[28] This information regarding men's role in the spread of syphilis allowed for the image of syphilitic mothers and children to begin to change from one of disdain to one of pity for the first time.[29]

Physician Oscar Daniel Meyer emphasized the new image of syphilitic mothers and children in his 1952 publication titled *That Degenerate Spirochete* meant to educate the general public regarding the disease. He cautioned of the numerous complications that could occur in conception, pregnancy, and childbirth if "the father or mother gave a history of syphilis."[30] Treatment, he claimed, could keep the infection from being passed on to their unborn children, help to avoid "pitiable miscarriage," and prevent a child from "die[ing] after birth or within two years."[31] Meyer and others knew that, by the 1940s, penicillin had been proved to alleviate the symptoms of syphilis and could also render it dormant, resulting in the conclusion that infected individuals would no longer be contagious. This causal link, discovered first by Alexander Fleming in the 1920s, did not result in broad treatment programs until twenty years later when the technology to produce penicillin in mass quantities became available.[32] Therefore, when penicillin production increased, it combined with the other factors and resulted in the reexamination of the underlying assumptions that drove anti-syphilis campaigns. This led to changes in treating women and children in particular, and even called into question legislation regarding curfews, banning women from certain public places, and refusing service to women except during approved hours.[33] Dr. Harry Wilmer of the American Social Hygiene association had made a series of recommendations regarding syphilis treatment programs in 1945 that evidences these adjustments. Noting that penicillin, "latest of the wonder drugs," could "cure" early syphilis with a single injection, he recommended that should it be in short supply, mothers and children should be treated first. He reasoned that this would prevent the progression of the disease and even death, and should be combined with testing and treatment of "the mother during pregnancy," which would "assure the birth of a healthy baby in practically every instance."[34] Treating pregnant mothers, mothers, and children with syphilis upheld the ICEF's commitment to better maternal and child health care overall. Its programs might help to prevent myriad health issues including "handicaps both mental and physical," ulcers, rashes, fever, and a variety of physical deformities in mothers, infants, older children, and teenagers.[35] Defying prior cultural norms on such a large scale made the ICEF's ambition to "eradicate diseases, especially the fight against venereal diseases," without precedent.[36]

Another cultural issue the ICEF's anti-syphilis program challenged was that women, whether mothers or not, had been blamed throughout history for infecting men with syphilis, reinforcing gender biases against treatment for women. Mary Spongberg argues that as far back as the fifteenth century, communities identified syphilitic-spreading females as a means of controlling their ability to spread the infection. Whether literally identifying them by branding prostitutes on the cheek with a hot iron, as had been done in Aberdeen in 1497, or through the passage of the Contagious Diseases Acts in nineteenth-century England, women systematically received blame but not treatment.[37] Even in the twentieth century, these cultural attitudes persisted.[38] Mary Louise Roberts found that, when in 1944 the U.S. military established brothels in France because General Charles Gerhardt decided "his boys needed sex," the emergence of numerous cases of syphilis resulted in placing the blame squarely on the female sex workers. "Army officers ultimately blamed the French women for infecting U.S. soldiers with venereal disease," which resulted in managing "the health and mobility of French women."[39]

Roberts also hones in on another cultural aspect of syphilis, which is that men have historically been seen as victims rather than perpetrators of syphilis. Men, of whatever class afflicted with syphilis, almost always sought out and received treatment, and the ICEF's refusal to treat men constituted a marked divergence from past attitudes. Men's relationship to syphilis developed quite differently from that of women's, since virile, sexually aggressive males, even if physically satisfied through marriage, were assumed to seek sexual partners elsewhere.[40] Unable and not expected to restrain himself, a man could become the passive and unwitting victim of syphilis should he come into contact with an infected female, which would cause him great personal suffering and distress.[41] There is, of course, an inherent paradox in this assessment; surely men, so aggressive and virile, could not be victims as well. Nevertheless, this notion aligned with classic characterizations of manly men and loose women. A man, unable to resist his urges or the sexual advances of women, fell prey and always at great personal cost to himself. Women, on the other hand, paid a price for "illicit" sexual behavior and faced far more reprisals from society for that sexual behavior. The gendered nature of the medical profession, too, guaranteed that doctors providing treatment were overwhelmingly male, a fact that deterred many women, but not men, from seeking help. Finally, and most importantly, doctors provided cures to their male patients without passing judgment because of society's willingness to accept that males must express their sexuality to remain healthy and sexually satisfied.[42]

Though the ICEF did not refuse treatment of men in an overt attempt to overturn this cultural tradition, this part of its program often brought it into conflict with nations in the Soviet bloc. Their governments insisted on the premise that its male and female citizens were equal, and therefore deserved equal consideration and treatment in the ICEF's programs. With an enormous amount of cultural baggage to overcome for its alarmingly vast clientele, the ICEF went forward with plans to undertake a broad anti-syphilis program at the end of 1947.

Poland submitted the first application to participate in the ICEF's anti-syphilis campaign, and Chairman Rajchman acknowledged this in a lengthy letter to Executive Director Pate. There is little evidence that the ICEF and WHO experienced the same tensions over this campaign as they had in the anti-tuberculosis campaign, made clear in Rajchman's simple statement that "[t]he WHO VD panel meets about January 12 [1948] at Geneva when the Polish plan may be considered."[43] He had been notified of the meeting in a cable from Dr. Brock Chisholm on December 8, and had confirmed that at least one representative from Poland would be able to attend to "present the Polish plan."[44] Rajchman recorded that "The Polish VD programme is of considerable magnitude," including expenditures of around "1½ million dollars" of which about one quarter would need to be used to treat the "mothers, infants, children and adolescents to the age of 18" residing in Poland.[45] According to additional statistics gathered from various European nations, the 57,320 cases of endemic syphilis registered in Europe prior to 1941 had grown to over 200,000, including those individuals "infected during the war" but excluding new cases of congenital or acquired syphilis in children.[46] These initial estimates, which the ICEF noted included mothers under the classification of "women with fresh infections," made clear that "all other women and men are excluded" from its treatment programs.[47]

Another complication arose when it became apparent that no two countries viewed an anti-venereal-disease program in the same way. Applications from individual countries evidence a pronounced lack of standardization, with some following the ICEF's mandate that only children and mothers be included while others requested treatment for all cases. For example, the Polish government's original application included men in the number of individuals requiring treatment. After amending its original request, which had been denied by the Executive Board for including men, Poland asked to receive a penicillin allotment in 1948 sufficient to treat a total of approximately 32,000 cases of infant and maternal syphilis exclusively.[48] Obviously pleased with Poland's change of heart, a report by the ICEF's Programme Committee published in October of that year noted that

> [a]s regards Poland, the Expert Committee on V.D. of WHO noted with satisfaction that the UNICEF/WHO Joint Committee, the Programme Committee and the Executive Board of UNICEF took action on a request from the Polish Government for assistance on the pre-natal and infantile phase of the over-all anti-syphilis programme of that country. The Committee notes that the possibility of obtaining assistance represented a considerable stimulae in the preparation for, and the initiation of this campaign. [49]

Efforts to standardize applications for the anti-syphilis program reinforced the ICEF's goal to confine treatment to children and their mothers and are illustrated in a 1948 presentation by Dr. H. F. Helmholz and Dr. J. M. Latsky on "Nutritional and Health Aspects in Six UNICEF Countries in Europe." They wrote: "The interest of UNICEF is in particular the prevention of congenital syphilis by treatment of the pregnant mother, that forms a logical part of any campaign of eradication." During 1948 and 1949 applications increased, especially from Eastern European countries, which would make up the largest group enrolled in the ICEF's anti-syphilis programs. [50] In almost every instance, however, the applications of individual countries included men as a part of the total case population requiring treatment, placing them continually at odds with the ICEF's requirements. When wrestling with the applications from countries in Eastern Europe, all of which were heavily influenced by the newly established Communist governments under which they now operated, the ICEF most often decided to deny the request until the application conformed to the stated policy. Dealing with the scrutiny of the U.S. State Department as well as the need to remain focused on maternal and child health, the ICEF's policies collided with and ultimately overrode the desire of public health officials in Eastern Europe to treat syphilis more broadly than the ICEF prescribed.

Yugoslavia provides a clear example of the ways in which the ICEF's policies and intentions clashed. When it applied for assistance in 1947, Yugoslavia's report noted that cases of endemic syphilis totaled about 100,000. [51] Dr. P. Gregoric, president of Yugoslavia's Public Health Protection Committee, clearly included males in his total as a part of the overall plan to "[liquidate] endemic syphilis and to combat sporadic syphilis" by utilizing aid from the ICEF. [52] In order to receive assistance, however, Dr. Gregoric and his committee had to make modifications to their application and focus their efforts on the ICEF's intended population of children and mothers, which they must have done relatively quickly. In a 1951 report issued from Executive Director Pate, Yugoslavia was promised "$40,000 from the European area allocation for penicillin and laboratory supplies to aid the continuation of the Government's campaign against endemic syphilis."[53] This disbursement had been granted due to the fact that "the largest percentages of infected active cases were among children . . . [and] pregnant women," and Yugoslavia was congratulated for having tested "1,033,000" persons and for treating "nearly 72,000" by late August 1951.[54] Yugoslavia had treated children and mothers exclusively with the supplies it received from the ICEF, leading to the commendation that "The impact of this programme has gone beyond merely the finding and treatment of mothers and children infected with syphilis. . . . It is thus having immediate effect not only in terms of the disease itself, but also on the total health problems of the people."[55] Other countries, such as Hungary and Albania, also received instructions to concentrate their anti-venereal-disease campaigns on curing "expectant and nursing mothers and infants."[56] And, in order to prove its conformity with the ICEF's rules, Bulgaria even went so far as to provide painstaking detail regarding the precise dose of penicillin it would provide to children according to age and weight to receive its ICEF approval.[57]

The ICEF's insistence that supplies be used only to treat mothers and children as well as the ways in which this affected the overall goal to eradicate syphilis paints a rather unflattering picture of the anti-venereal-disease campaign. Worse yet, results of the ICEF's programs in 1949 showed little progress in combating the spread of syphilis, and a report from that year noted that "the development of programmes and projects have been subject to some delay . . . due to procurement difficulties." It predicted: "The year 1950 should consolidate the gains of the programme[s] launched in 1949: the requests in terms of penicillin and supplies are now being studied by WHO."[58] Penicillin, which had remained in short supply in the first five years following the end of the war, forced the ICEF to modify the exclusive use of penicillin. It provided instead "one course of penicillin treatment . . . [to be completed with] bismuth therapy," a treatment that had virtually no chance of curing the disease.[59] Limited personnel as well as the commitment to first serve the needs of children and mothers also provide a partial explanation for the program's lack of success, but this program often fell short of the ICEF's goal to deal with the "urgent problem . . . to ensure the survival of children . . . [and] millions of adults" who had emerged from the war "less fit to meet the grave problems of the day."[60] Flawed from the beginning because of lack of penicillin to treat the millions of syphilis cases and a focus that excluded others spreading the disease, the choice to undertake such an aggressive anti-syphilis campaign appears questionable. By contrast, the TB prevention program as a whole yielded much more dramatic results, since it could prevent children and mothers from contracting the disease. In the end, the anti-syphilis program failed to make even incremental changes to what Martha Eliot observed when she visited Europe in 1947. "There was so much venereal disease . . . some in the children, but the mothers—the pregnant and nursing mothers . . . many were infected." She inquired about the children as

well as the mothers, but noted that, in keeping with the image of the ideal
U.S. post-war family, "they [mothers] were the most critical members of the
family, if the family was going to be held together." Perhaps this is one of the
primary motivations for the ICEF's campaign—not only to treat children, but
also to treat mothers, whether expecting or not, so that they could continue to
perform their function, allowing the ICEF could play its role as provider.[61]

The ICEF's anti-syphilis program, despite its forward-looking position on
the treatment of children and mothers and challenges posed by physicians to
the prevailing moral and social ideas regarding syphilis, still advanced its
role as provider for dependent children and women, thereby reinforcing the
U.S. post-war family ideal. [62] By insisting that supplies be used only to treat
mothers and children, it remained perfectly in line with its mandate, but
counteracted its pledge to assist any person deemed necessary to the survival
and well-being of a child by excluding their fathers. The insistence on bringing attention to the plight of syphilitic mothers and children but excluding
men from treatment exposed the flaws in its own programs, which would
eventually require significant modifications in order to achieve their desired
results. It should also be noted that single and childless women over the age
of eighteen did not qualify for ICEF treatment, which helped perpetuate the
notion that these women remained a dangerous group as transmitters of syphilis. Reinforced in prescriptive literature produced in the middle of the twentieth century, these women, as had their predecessors, preyed on innocent
men. Pamphlets produced during the 1940s and 1950s were frequently directed toward young men in the military in particular. Away from home for
the first time and ill-prepared for encounters with "foreign" women, these
publications cautioned men about the dangers of having sexual intercourse
with seemingly "nice" girls they met, since one never knew where a single
girl had been before. How confusing it must have been, then, when the U.S.
military established brothels for its soldiers and sailors abroad, encouraging
them to take advantage of this perk.

The ICEF's anti-tuberculosis and anti-syphilis programs drew on all of
the past experiences of its staff as well as the most recent information from
science on health care. Myriad diseases, including typhus, polio, syphilis,
dysentery, and tuberculosis, had raced through Europe during the twentieth
century, and the ICEF had, by 1946, already faced daunting challenges in
efforts to curb their effects. Lack of supplies, war-devastated infrastructures,
and feuding national governments made combating the common enemy of
disease seem impossible, but, by the end of 1949, the ICEF had managed to
report that it had provided food and medical care to thousands of children
and mothers in Europe. As 1950 approached, the ICEF, by now referring to
itself as "UNICEF," faced yet another challenge as it prepared to extend its
programs and achieve permanent UN status. The individuals who had
worked tirelessly to provide aid to children and mothers hoped that, before

the end of 1950, the General Assembly would grant the ICEF status as an official UN organ and view it as more than a temporary effort, guaranteeing its programs could be continued and expanded. World political events would, however, force UNICEF into inaction as its fundamental policy of treating children and women only came under fire almost immediately in post-war Eastern European nations that had allied themselves with the Soviet Union.

NOTES

1. Tara Zahra, "The Psychological Marshall Plan: Displacement, Gender, and Human Rights after World War II," *Central European History* 44 (2011): 37–62.

2. Hyde interview, 15, 27.

3. Eliot interview, 182.

4. Eliot interview, 183; Hyde interview, 25.

5. Hyde interview, 31; Eliot interview, 182.

6. Eliot interview, 182-83.

7. Eliot interview, 183.

8. Eliot interview, 184–85.

9. Eliot interview, 185.

10. Eliot interview, 215–216.

11. E/ICEF/13, 12.

12. E/ICEF/13, 12.

13. E/ICEF/33, 2 3.

14. WHO.IC/R/44/Rev. 3, annexes 2 and 3, *Committee on Relations: Co-Operation with United Nations, Relations with UNICEF.*

15. Evolving descriptions of the symptoms of tuberculosis can be found in a wide range of publications as well as online. See for example: Addison Porter Dutcher, *Pulmonary Tuberculosis: Its Pathology, Nature, Symptoms, Diagnosis, Prognosis, Causes, Hygiene, and Medical Treatment* (Philadelphia: J. B. Lippincott & Co., 1875); Allen Kramer Kraus, *Environment and Resistance in Tuberculosis: A Presentation of the Environment and Resistance and Their Relation to the Pathology, Diagnosis, Symptoms and Treatment of Tuberculosis* (Baltimore: Williams & Wilkins Co., 1923); and L. Randol Barker, John R Burton Phillip D. Zieve, eds., and Thomas E. Finucane, assoc. ed., *Principles of Ambulatory Medicine* (Baltimore: Williams & Wilkins Co., 1998).

16. Eliot interview, 196.

17. Ludwik Rajchman, letter to Dr. Johannes Holm, December 16, 1947. Maurice Pate Papers, Princeton University Library.

18. Ludwik Rajchman, letter to Dr. Madsen, December 17, 1947. Maurice Pate Papers, Princeton University Library.

19. E/ICEF/43, *Report of the Sub-Committee on Medical Projects,* 19.

20. E/ICEF/43, 19.

21. E/ICEF/43, annex 10, 47.

22. E/ICEF/78, *Report on Nutrition and Health Aspects in Six UNICEF Countries in Europe by Dr. H. F. Helmholz and Dr. J.M. Latsky,* 17.

23. Ludwick Rajchman, letter to Dr. Madsen, C/14, December 17, 1947. Maurice Pate Papers, Princeton University Library.

24. Ludwick Rajchman, letter to Dr. Brock Chisolm, December 18, 1947. Maurice Pate Papers, Princeton University Library.

25. Eliot interview, 218.

26. J. D. Oriel, *The Scars of Venus: A History of Venereology* (London: Springer-Verlag, 1994), 98–9.

27. A report from the UNICEF Programme Committee in October 1949, noted that France and Finland had notified the Programme Committee that they would be removing themselves

from the roll of countries receiving food aid. E/ICEF/W.72, *Recommendation of Executive Director on Unutilized Portion of Hungarian UNICEF Allocation Following Closure of Hungarian Mission*, 1.

28. Mary Spongberg, *Feminizing Venereal Disease: The Body of the Prostitute in Nineteenth-Century Medical Discourse* (New York: New York University Press, 1997), chapters 8 and 9; Oriel, chapter 5.

29. Harry Wilmer, *Corky the Killer: A Story of Syphilis* (New York: American Social Hygiene Association, 1945), 42, 44, 46, 48; Edward B. Vedder, *Syphilis and Public Health* (Philadelphia: Lea and Febiger, 1918), 18–22, 72–75, 136, 202, 205–8.

30. Oscar Daniel Meyer, *That Degenerate Spirochete* (New York: Vantage Press, 1952), 77.

31. Meyer, *That Degenerate Spirochete*, 78.

32. Oriel, *The Scars of Venus*, 97–98.

33. Spongberg, *Feminizing Venereal Disease*, 177.

34. Wilmer, *Corky the Killer*, 42.

35. Wilmer, *Corky the Killer*, 84.

36. E/ICEF/33, *Consultation Concerning the Proposal of the French Government to Establish an International Children's Center in Paris. Summary Record of Consultation, Lake Success, New York, 26 September 1947*, 2.

37. Spongberg, *Feminizing Venereal Disease*, 1, 6–7; see also chapters 1, 2, and 3.

38. See, for example, Roger Davidson, "The Culture of Compulsion: Venereal Disease, Sexuality and the State in Twentieth-Century Scotland," in *Sexual Cultures in Europe: Themes in Sexuality*, Franz X. Eder, Lesley A. Hall and Gert Hekma, eds. (Manchester: Manchester University Press, 1999), 58–68.

39. Mary Louise Roberts, "The Price of Discretion: Prostitution, Venereal Disease, and the American Military in France, 1944-1946," in *AHR Forum, American Historical Review* (October 2010), 1002–30.

40. Spongberg, *Feminizing Venereal Disease*, 10.

41. See Spongberg, *Feminizing Venereal Disease*, 1–10; Davidson, 66–67.

42. Davidson, "The Culture of Compulsion," 67; see also Spongberg, *Feminizing Venereal Disease*, 63–65.

43. Ludwick Rajchman to Maurice Pate, December 18, 1947. Maurice Pate Papers, Princeton University Library.

44. Ludwick Rajchman to Dr. Brock Chisholm, December 1947. Maurice Pate Papers, Princeton University Library.

45. Ludwick Rajchman to Maurice Pate, December 18, 1947. Maurice Pate Papers, Princeton University Library.

46. E/ICEF/68 add. 2, *Number of Syphilis Cases to be Treated by Penicillin*.

47. E/ICEF/68 add. 2.

48. E/ICEF/W.3 annex K, *Poland: Summary of Needs*.

49. E/ICEF/W.31, *Statement on Anti-Syphilis Campaign*, 2.

50. E/ICEF/78, 18, and Yugoslavia, Romania, Poland, Bulgaria, Hungary, and Slovakia began to receive UNICEF aid after 1948. See E/ICEF/68 add. 2 annex IV, 6 July 1948, *Supplement to the National Plan to Combat Syphilis Among Pregnant Women and Children Under 18 Years of Age in Bulgaria; Romania; General Remarks and Conditions of the V.D. Campaign in Slovakia; Plans for a General V.D. Control Campaign in the Federative People's Republic of Yugoslavia; Memorandum from Dr. Tibor Bielek, Chief Public Health Inspector, to Dr. Pierre Descoeudres, Chief of UNICEF Mission to Hungary, 5 February 1948*; E/ICEF/W.3 annex K, *Poland: Summary of Needs*.

51. E/ICEF/68 Add. 2 annex IV, *Programme of the Campaign Against Endemic Syphilis in Yugoslavia*, 38.

52. E/ICEF/68 Add. 2 annex IV, *Letter from Dr. P. Gregoric to Dr. D. Adler, Chief of UNICEF Mission in Belgrade, 9 June 1948*.

53. E/ICEF/R.246, *Recommendation of Executive Director for an Allocation to Yugoslavia to Extend the Campaign Against Endemic Syphilis*, 1.

54. E/ICEF/R.246, 2–3.

55. E/ICEF/R.246, 3.

56. E/ICEF/68 Add. 2 annex IV, *Memorandum from Dr. Tibor Bielek, Chief Public Health Inspector, to Dr. Pierre Descoeudres, Chief of UNICEF Mission to Hungary, 5 February 1948.*

57. E/ICEF/68 Add. 2 annex IV, *Supplement to the National Plan to Combat Syphilis Among Pregnant Women and Children Under 18 Year of Age in Bulgaria.*

58. E/ICEF/W.76, *Recommendations of the Executive Director Regarding the Use of Anti-Syphilis Allocations*, 2.

59. E/ICEF/68 Add. 2 annex IV, *Treatment of Endemic Syphilis by Penicillin.*

60. E/ICEF/160, 3.

61. Eliot interview, 196.

62. Meyer, *That Degenerate Spirochete*, 31, 35.

Chapter Six

Continuing the Work for Children

UNICEF had accomplished a great deal by 1950. It had increased its annual operating budget from approximately $50 million US to over $150 million, receiving contributions from fifty-nine countries as well as from its own fundraising efforts. This had allowed it to provide relief aid to children and mothers in sixty-four countries on four continents through supplementary feeding, clothing distribution, tuberculosis vaccination, maternal and child health care programs, insect control, and anti-yaws, bejel, and syphilis treatment campaigns.[1] This year also marked the beginning of the end of UNICEF's reliance on the U.S. government for the bulk of its operating budget. It had established working relationships with six UN agencies and multiple non-governmental agencies as well as with many national governments.[2] The general progress report of the executive director on October 26, 1950, provided even more detail on how far UNICEF had come since 1946. The report noted that the estimated total number of beneficiaries from October to December of that year would be approximately "26,865,000" and that these individuals would receive "supplementary feeding, shoes and clothing, and vaccination and treatment of communicable diseases."[3] The relief aid remained in keeping with the ICEF's original mandate, and the population to whom it was distributed through "UNICEF-assisted programs" now included "Palestine Refugees" and "refugee mothers and children in India and Pakistan."[4] The report also included a request that the Economic and Social Council "give greater emphasis . . . for promoting the economic and social development of under-developed areas."[5] Regardless of its many achievements, UNICEF's staff, committees, and programs were scheduled to be dismantled at the end of 1950, the emergency of the post-war crisis having passed. Its dedicated personnel and volunteers agreed, however, that

UNICEF's work should continue to combat "under-nourishment and nutritional and social diseases . . . rampant among children and adolescents."[6]

"I think you couldn't do that work for a long time without reaching some conclusions about moving on to more action, if you had intelligence," remembered Adelaide Sinclair. "It was so obvious, in a sense, that although we would help solve an emergency it wasn't going to solve anything else if we'd just stopped at the end of that and left that country as it was before."[7] Helenka Pantaleoni suggested that the UNICEF's original mandate to run for three years "was undetermined," and that "Maurice Pate, who used to go to our government with a request for funds, [said during UNICEF's fourth year that] 'this is the last time.'" Eventually, however, "Maurice, with his large horizons . . . saw that it was extremely important to keep UNICEF going."[8] John Charnow and Julia Henderson, who also worked with UNICEF, remembered there being no question that the ICEF would continue its operations beyond 1950.[9]

As UNICEF made plans to appeal its temporary status, it relied more and more on the notion that "bringing relief to the continuing emergency needs for children" could be achieved by geographically and demographically broadening its scope.[10] UNICEF also continued its reliance on an elementary human desire to protect and cherish mother and child. Mr. E. D. Marris, assistant secretary, Ministry of Education, UK, eloquently voiced these sentiments regarding the hallowed place of children during an address to the Executive Committee. He praised UNICEF, claiming, "I am most deeply impressed with the initiative taken by the United Nations to help children. . . . This is a time for faith and I believe that despite all our troubles, the elementary human desire to protect and cherish mother and child is one of the greatest unities through which, God willing, we may build the new world."[11] But permanent status could not be achieved with expansion and appeal alone. Without strong partnerships with other organizations and agencies, the continued stream of funds from countries other than the United States, and the support of the members of the Security Council, UNICEF would not survive, and none of these seemed certain as tensions inside and outside the UN complicated UNICEF's appeal for a stay of execution.

Several of the UN agencies with which UNICEF had worked in the past posed some of the most viable threats to its efforts to continue providing relief aid for children. Amy Staples reveals some of the reasons for this turn of events, noting that several of the programs requiring collaboration with UNICEF had fallen victim to changing staff and administration. She cites the Milk Conservation Program, which, because of a change in leadership and an unwillingness to advance funds, was scaled back by its new director. She writes that the director "scaled back the FAO's participation . . . citing budgetary shortfalls even though the program provided a direct and relatively cost-efficient way to improve Third-World nutrition and health."[12] Julia

Henderson, former head of the UN's Social Welfare Division, claimed: "There was no doubt WHO was delighted with this position [to close down UNICEF]." Henderson, who had been "very protective of UNICEF," supported its efforts to obtain permanent status.[13] Margaret Gann, who worked in UNICEF's mission in Asia, also remembered the tensions between the various organizations as well as the combative atmosphere this uncertainty often created. She recalled that when WHO, FAO, or UNESCO representatives arrived to teach training courses for UNICEF employees and volunteers, they often came in "with a halo around their heads. What the agency people said was right and so many times UNICEF people weren't prepared or were too innocent to fight with them." She therefore "fought with technical agency representatives, and I won, too," emulating the attitude of her boss, Sam Keeny, whom Gann noted had dealt aggressively with detractors: "I heard Sam say to a WHO representative, 'I created your job and I can abolish it too.'"[14] UNICEF therefore found itself unable to count on FAO, WHO, UNESCO, and others to be its "natural allies and partners." Whether they simply remained silent or openly opposed permanent status, UNICEF continued its quest for permanent status knowing the other "agencies were no friends of ours."[15]

In addition to its internal enemies, UNICEF faced a formidable external foe as well. The U.S. government, from which UNICEF had never received resounding support, became more aggressive in its efforts to shutter UNICEF during 1950. This position was expressed at the UN during a meeting of the Social, Cultural, and Humanitarian Committee on October 6, 1950, by U.S. delegate Eleanor Roosevelt just weeks before UNICEF's scheduled termination. Mrs. Roosevelt, relaying the U.S. government's sentiment to the body gathered for the meeting, "proposed the dissolution of UNICEF as it was and reorienting it into a more technical body," and asked that UNICEF's activities for children be parceled out to WHO, FAO, and other UN agencies.[16] Mrs. Roosevelt's comments reflect UNICEF's continued scrutiny from "elements in the Department of State which frankly didn't want UNICEF to continue." Helenka Pantaleoni remembered that many individuals were "very—hostile is too strong a word, but [they] wanted the fund to close up early in its history." Indeed, Pantaleoni stated that "there were a great many elements in the State Department who couldn't understand why the World Health Organization didn't take over UNICEF's functions." These individuals had determined that the emergency in Europe had ended, and that "those countries should get back on their own feet."[17] And, when in 1950 the U.S. allocation for UNICEF was in danger of "being skipped," Pantaleoni claimed it was primarily because Congressional Committee members, having been influenced by the State Department and the newly formed House Un-American Activities Commission (HUAC), wanted to end UNICEF relief aid distribution in Communist countries. Funds from the U.S. government "depend[ed] on the whim of the State Department and Congress," neither of which had ever truly supported UNICEF.[18] Pantaleoni claimed, "I don't think they took it very seriously. . . . Then the isolationists and the crackpots, the rabid ones, started attacking UNICEF."[19] In the end, the U.S. State Department, combining its efforts with HUAC, not only jeopardized UNICEF's funding, but also placed several UNICEF personnel under scrutiny for their alleged association with the Communist party.

How, then, did UNICEF weather the storm from 1950 to 1953 and manage to achieve permanent status as a UN agency? One answer can be found in the way it shifted its focus to programs concerned with development. Development in the second half of the twentieth century, according to Amy Staples, constituted an "international obligation" that spawned an "international civil service" whose goal was to "promote the well-being of the earth's people as a whole."[20] These goals meshed will with UNICEF's already-existing programs as an overall shift in UN "priorities [that] were clearly in the health field," making UNICEF's continuing relationships with WHO crucial.[21] Martha Eliot therefore helped develop UNICEF/WHO training programs for midwives and health care workers providing maternal and child health care in developing nations. Eliot, a strong supporter of the UN's new emphasis on health, kept close watch over UNICEF's maternal and child health agenda during this transition. She hoped by partnering with WHO and providing training that "in the end, countries should, you see, do it themselves."[22] Henderson remembered that Pate, too, began to see the benefit of moving away from enacting programs that "were fuzzy long-term stuff which didn't have much bearing on the work of UNICEF."[23] By adopting new programs in new places, UNICEF continued to reinforce its relationships with UN organizations, national governments, and other agencies. This also allowed UNICEF's relief aid programs to produce easily quantifiable results, thereby demonstrating their undeniable success. The result was that, at the end of 1950, the General Assembly approved Resolution 417 (V) allowing UNICEF to continue its operations until 1953. Titled "Continuing Needs of Children: United Nations International Children's Emergency Fund," it recognized "the necessity for continued action to relieve the suffering of children, particularly in underdeveloped countries" and provided UNICEF with hope that by 1953, it would become a permanent UN organization.[24] Virginia Hazzard remarked that the resolution launched UNICEF on the next part of its journey. It officially expanded UNICEF's mandate, directing it to assist children in developing nations, which Hazzard notes "covered just about everything and did turn the spotlight on the Third World."[25]

With its extension in place and its mandate broadened, UNICEF proceeded into 1951 a very different organization in many ways. Adelaide Sinclair became the chair of the UNICEF Executive Board when Ludwick

Rajchman resigned that position in 1950. With Rajchman gone, Pate's role changed as well. He became a more visible, public figure while retaining his role as both the driving and stabilizing force of UNICEF. Pate's importance as a constant presence also increased as the Executive Board continued to experience other significant individual departures. Sinclair recalled the effect of these on both UNICEF and the Executive Board, reflecting that "we had these 'giants' on the Board who made such an important contribution in their own personal right [at first] . . . there were four or five or six of these giants. Then there seemed to be a gradual movement away from such people."[26] Their departures meant less notoriety for UNICEF, and often occurred when delegates moved on to other fledgling UN committees; however, it can also be argued that their governments may have decided having a notable representative on the Executive Board was no longer needed. After all, UNICEF had achieved widespread support around the world for its programs by the end of 1950, and would be ending its operations in 1953 regardless. With much uncertainty ahead, UNICEF entered into what Julia Henderson characterized in January 1951 as a "crisis about its future."[27]

In spite of the atmosphere of crisis, UNICEF continued expanding its relief aid programs in order to mitigate the effects of crises for children and mothers around the world. It moved into new locations and began to offer new types of relief aid in partnership with the FAO, WHO, and UNESCO as it had in the past. Expansion had originally begun in 1948 when the General Assembly passed Resolution 215 (III). This declared that the "widespread response to the United Nations Appeal for Children, the large number of countries which have co-operated . . . and the support . . . from non-governmental organizations" had revealed that, in addition to helping children in the aftermath of war, UNICEF's programs were needed to help distressed children elsewhere.[28] As a result, UNICEF added addressing "the age-old problem of poverty" in other nations to its goals.[29] The 1948 resolution charged the "United Nations International Emergency Children's Fund with special responsibility for meeting emergency needs of children in many parts of the world," meaning that UNICEF could now go beyond the bounds of the postwar arena. It established administrative offices and relief programs in new locations, using its mission in China to expand its operations in the region.[30] As a result, UNICEF had been able to establish a formidable presence in Southeast Asia.[31] Its new Regional Office for the Far East could more readily oversee the expanding operations, and it submitted information about morbidity rates, specific diseases, and recommendations for disease prevention and cure that became the *Report of the Survey Mission to the Far East (Other Than China)* for July 1948. UNICEF continued to expand there, adding ten new countries including India, Pakistan, the Philippines, and Singapore.[32] By August 1948, additional recommendations had been made for expansion into Lebanon, Syria, and Israel, and a request had been made on behalf of refugees in Palestine.[33] Then, when "[t]he winds of change were to blow away most of the remaining colonial order in Africa and the Caribbean," Latin American nations began their appeals for UNICEF relief aid. Programs established in Latin America in early 1949 mark an important shift in UNICEF's programs, as these were the first to officially assist with development as well.[34] "Adding development objectives to its humanitarian approach," UNICEF not only kept pace with shifts in UN policy, but also could become involved in planning for developing nations as a part of establishing its aid programs.[35]

Its focus on development and planning, rather than on specific populations and conditions of war, changed the way UNICEF approached the role of children in individual countries. Instead of needing help to recover from war to participate in the revival of their nations, children became vital to the development of new nations.[36] It established national health programs in newly independent areas supported by a network of local UNICEF auxiliaries, which conformed to UNICEF's new direction but maintained its institutional identity as a primary provider. In doing this, UNICEF perpetuated the U.S. post-war family ideal by continuing to insist that mothers and children remained dependent. It can be argued that this also forestalled the granting of full citizenship to women in many regions of the world after the war by reinforcing that citizenship—"long presumed to be male" and defined by the state—had always rested on providing support for family, home, and women.[37] Elaine Tyler May posits that "the self-contained home held out the promise of security in an insecure world" and kept women out of the realm of men.[38] UNICEF, despite its opportunity to focus on developing regions and to create vastly different programs than it had in Europe, did nothing to dispel this standard when it began providing assistance there. It would be several decades before UNICEF changed these basic assumptions in order to address inequality as well as cultural differences when carrying out its programs in developing regions.

Although it did little to advance the cause of gender equality and often ignored basic cultural differences between East and West, moving its programs into developing countries helped UNICEF make its case for permanent status by providing more quantifiable results on both its food aid and medical aid programs.[39] Combating new diseases in new regions, UNICEF expanded beyond its original anti-tuberculosis and anti-syphilis campaigns, concentrating on region-specific health concerns such as yaws. Pate's report on medical relief aid in the Philippines evidences this: "An estimated 8% of the rural population . . . suffers from yaws . . . [and] it has been reported that 70% of the yaws cases consist of children under 11 years of age."[40] Heart-wrenching photos of miserable infants covered in painful sores from yaws illustrated the need for these programs; photographed after receiving UNICEF medical relief aid, the same wretched children appeared happy and sore-free.[41] By using "quantitative targets" to make the results of UNICEF's work difficult to dispute, Gann pointed out that this helped UNICEF demonstrate the effects of its work and allowed for process improvements as well. She recalled that "hidden in that one figure . . . were so many variables that could have gone wrong, and if a target wasn't accomplished then we had to track down what they were, what had gone wrong . . . if you got that many children vaccinated or injected, or fed with milk, then all these other essential steps were being accomplished."[42] By providing numeric evidence of its effect on the child population, easily recorded over the short term, UNICEF could present a stronger case to the General Assembly for continuing its operations and make them more efficient and effective at the same time.

By redirecting its focus in maternal and child health to medical programs while continuing its feeding programs, UNICEF's message began to have more positive impacts everywhere but in the United States. The problem of spreading UNICEF's positive message more widely in the United States, as well as using it to convert detractors, fell primarily to Helenka Pantaleoni, who founded the U.S. Committee for UNICEF on December 23, 1947. Troubled that UNICEF had not been able to achieve the same level of positive sentiment within the United States as it had elsewhere, she began by embracing the U.S. Committee for UNICEF's responsibility for educating Americans about UNICEF. At a meeting in Paris attended by an international delegation, she realized that "UNICEF was [still] very dependent on the United States government contribution. The United States government contribution in a democracy was very dependent on the response of the people . . . if the people don't respond, the Congress won't respond. . . . So I thought it was extremely important to build a solid situation for UNICEF in the United States."[43] Her efforts focused mostly on obtaining funding for UNICEF, but expanded to include protecting UNICEF's reputation when it or a member of its staff faced accusations of complicity with Communism. Pantaleoni's recollections illuminate the extent to which U.S. government policy affected UNICEF during the early 1950s, especially its expectations of UNICEF's continued allegiance to U.S. foreign policy both at home and abroad.

Her mission clear, Pantaleoni returned to the United States after the Paris meeting and began to solicit other organizations to help her in her quest to gain support for UNICEF. One of UNICEF's most successful and long-standing fundraising campaigns, the sale of holiday greeting cards, began as a result of this type of collaboration. Pantaleoni recalled it began when Nora Edmunds of *House and Garden* magazine brought the idea to Pate. "She thought it would be nice to have a card for the benefit of UNICEF, done by a well-known artist." Pate took the idea to Gilbert Redfern, director of public information for UNICEF, who then presented it to the chair of the United States for UNICEF Committee, Mary Lord. Lord had taken over leadership from Pantaleoni, who had by then taken charge of Women United for the United Nations. Lord claimed she did not have the staff to handle the program as the U.S. Committee for UNICEF had been "put . . . in mothballs" due to its lackluster results, so Redfern, according to Pantaleoni, approached the Information Centre for the United Nations. "We, Women United for the United Nations, were in charge of this Information Centre," so Pantaleoni quickly seized the opportunity and set up an informational luncheon with some of her well-connected philanthropic contacts. Her attendees included Mrs. Thomas Lamont, Mrs. Lloyd Garrison, and Mrs. Oscar Reubhausen, whose support she hoped would launch the program.[44]

"Zelia Reubhausen represented the League of Women Voters," and Pantaleoni was thrilled when she offered her organization to take on the project. The League of Women Voters agreed to use its own facilities to publicize the sale and to collect orders and, according to Pantaleoni, became one of UNICEF's most powerful U.S. supporters as a result.[45] When planning began, the first card illustration chosen did not come from a famous artist, as had initially been proposed. Instead, it came from a young girl named Jitka Samkova from the Czech Republic. Her drawing, originally intended for use on UNICEF publicity posters, made its way to UNICEF's New York offices via Prague. It depicted five young girls dancing around a maypole under a smiling sun, and its use made her the first greeting card artist, 1949. At first, only a few thousand cards were published for purchase by UNICEF and UN employees. The cards received so much acclaim, though, that the UNICEF staff urged Pate to issue similar cards annually. Pate, concerned that such a venture might seem too commercial, agreed to print the cards but only if their sale did not result in a profit. He felt the cards would be better used to raise public awareness—"so UNICEF's name would become known."[46] Pantaleoni confirmed that the greeting card campaign served a twofold purpose. "If you get enough cards sold, is millions of dollars profit, so say nothing of the subtler-the propaganda value of it."[47] The Executive Board approved the project and it became one of UNICEF's most well-received fundraising activities. It did not avoid notice by those concerned about Communists inside the UN, however, and Pantaleoni recounted just how extreme anti-Communist sentiment in the United States had become when the color red was used for one series of cards.

"Bizarre things happen which are hard to believe," recalled Pantaleoni. "Some very conservative friend of Maurice Pate's called him up and asked why the cards were imprinted in red, when red was a Communist color?" Pate, concerned over the criticism, took it very seriously—he did not want to damage UNICEF's reputation, and made the decision to put the project on hold. "He'd rather almost scrap the whole thing than run the risk of having it considered Communist," said Pantaleoni. She remembered that the volunteers working on the project, reduced to tears and screaming, feared this one comment would end the entire campaign. "We finally had to say, 'Well, Maurice, Santa Claus's suit is red!' Absolutely bizarre."[48]

Despite this setback, the U.S. holiday card effort proved so successful that other countries eventually used its model to establish their own campaigns. The now-global campaigns received another boost in 1952 when artist Raoul Dufy agreed to create and donate an original design to UNICEF. Other artists followed, and eventually Henri Matisse, Marc Chagall, Pablo Picasso, Salvador Dali, Georgia O'Keefe, Joan Miro, Paul Klee, and Wassily Kandinsky all lent their talents to the holiday card campaign.[49] Pantaleoni lamented that the cost of the campaign was "terrific . . . in fact, so costly that we sometimes ask ourselves how long we can continue," but the publicity gained made the effort worthwhile. "[M]any people are tripped into interest, you know, just by getting a card. They will say, What is this organization? What does it do? Often, in a roundabout way, they become ardent fans of UNICEF just by getting a card."[50]

Public relations in the United States improved with the holiday card campaign, but private donations did not materialize as quickly as Pantaleoni and the others had hoped. UNICEF had since 1946 been forced to share any charitable donations received in the United States with various other organizations due to restrictions put in place on allowable charitable contributions by the U.S. State Department. Charles Taft, she claimed, "was the one then charged with co-ordinating all voluntary fund-raising," so he "eventually, after months and months, arrived at a formula where they could raise money."[51] UNICEF then turned to professional fund raisers, which resulted in spending "two million dollars to raise half a million dollars for UNICEF."[52] Global donations far exceeded those received from the United States, and, anxious to help maintain funding, the U.S.A. for UNICEF group embraced another fundraising campaign. This one involved children, and many in UNICEF hoped it would further educate the U.S. public. The U.S. Committee for UNICEF, having been brought "out of mothballs" by 1953, eventually took ownership of this project, which it hoped would appeal to U.S. citizens and would make them more sympathetic to UNICEF's causes.[53]

This second campaign originated in 1948 when the Reverend Clyde and his wife Mary Emma Allison asked children in their church to collect money instead of candy during Halloween. Their collections would be donated to help charities providing aid to countries "that had suffered from the war." The campaign proved a success and, by 1950, Reverend Allison had been appointed the editor for a Presbyterian publication aimed at junior-high school groups. Keen to find new ideas for the publication, he adapted his original fundraising program to focus on collecting money for UNICEF after his wife reported that she had seen a cow while walking through downtown Philadelphia. Pantaleoni retold the story, claiming that Mary Emma became "so intrigued with what a cow was doing in a big city that she followed it right over to Wannamaker's store." Elsie the cow, she discovered, had been collecting donations for UNICEF's milk-feeding programs with Gertrude Ely, one of the founders of the U.S. Committee for UNICEF. According to Pantaleoni, Reverend Allison agreed when Mary Emma suggested he encourage children to collect funds for UNICEF. He promoted the idea through his publication, and that Halloween, the Allisons' three children became the first to collect money for UNICEF. Pantaleoni claimed that some believed the Halloween collection had begun elsewhere, but she noted that "Clyde Allison—really, we give him the full credit" for having begun a new fundraising tradition.[54] Once the idea made its way to Pate and his staff, several of them including "Betty Jacob [and] Helen Matushek" encouraged him to provide UNICEF funds to Allison so he could publish his article more widely. Realizing UNICEF's budget could not be stretched to accommodate this request, Pate did what became a habit, Pantaleoni quipped: "He put his hand in his own pocket and gave . . . the money."[55]

Pate eventually assigned the Trick or Treat for UNICEF project to the U.S. Committee for UNICEF, to which Pantaleoni had by then returned. She remembered that she quickly extricated it from its "quasi-relationship" with the U.S. State Department, confirming that she had become increasingly uncomfortable that the U.S. State Department insisted on viewing UNICEF as an arm of U.S. foreign policy. Elaine Tyler May argues this type of arrangement was common, and typically used by the State Department to "spread a beacon to the free world" by insisting that its "family ideal [was] worth protecting against hostile outside forces," namely Communism. UNICEF's insistence on providing aid to Communist countries meant that, instead of upholding this ideal, it was reinforcing "those disturbing Communist tendencies" that might threaten the "Cold War consensus."[56] Pantaleoni's refusal to cooperate meant that the U.S. State Department and the government in general, with its decidedly anti-Communists component, ultimately made her job all the more difficult by continuing to jeopardize both UNICEF's funding and its staff.

One glaring example of how UNICEF's relationship to the U.S. State Department affected its funding appears in Congressional debates over approval for continued UNICEF allotments. Distressed over the possibility that UNICEF would go unfunded due to Cold War machinations, Pantaleoni asserted that she resorted to some Cold War politics of her own and went directly to members of the Congressional committee to plead UNICEF's case. During her visits, she produced a newspaper article regarding a conference being held in the Soviet Union for the benefit of childhood. Pantaleoni knew that the article would cause concern among the Committee members, as it "stated that the USSR had invited sixty governments, all of whom came, and it really looked as if they wanted to start another UNICEF." She "took that clipping . . . I can't remember who it was, Senator Wiley, some people like that in Washington—who sort of scratched their heads and said, oh my goodness. We were going to miss the boat. They promised to support a contribution."[57] As a result, the U.S. allotment to UNICEF was approved; not to ensure UNICEF could continue its work to aid children and mothers, but to ensure UNICEF continued to function as an arm of U.S. foreign policy with the expectation that if the U.S. government supplied the funds, then UNICEF would uphold U.S. efforts to defeat and eliminate any communist influence anywhere—even within the apolitical UN. U.S. funding became tenuous during the three years that followed, and while Pantaleoni disbanded her U.S. Committee for UNICEF due to its almost-complete failure to raise funds, she went on to form the Citizens Committee for UNICEF. This committee functioned as a lobbying group that "used to telephone people all over the country to have them express support for UNICEF." She and her colleagues spent the years between 1951 and 1953 engaged in these efforts, and by 1953 "things were enough solidified that we could dust off the U.S. Committee again."[58] Challenges still persisted, however, including Congressman John Bell Williams's attempt to eliminate UNICEF funding by excluding her committee from the Congressional hearings in an unusual way.

Pantaleoni remembered Williams as an isolationist who had always criticized UNICEF. In this instance, he used his position on the Appropriations Committee to try and quash any support for UNICEF's request for funding before Congress by keeping the Citizens for UNICEF Committee from presenting its case. "The Citizens Committee . . . were all set for hearings . . . in order to testify for UNICEF," she stated, "but Williams called [the] meeting at one a.m., when everybody was asleep, so the Citizens Committee wasn't represented." Williams, having eliminated any opposition, "really went to it, cutting out the UNICEF contribution completely." The contribution was eventually restored, but according to Pantaleoni, "there were very hazardous times" when it appeared the United States intended to abandon UNICEF altogether if it failed to perform its expected function.[59]

Popular sentiment regarding UNICEF clearly played a role in its perception within the U.S. Congress, evident not just in debates and Williams's maneuvering, but also in the efforts of private citizens like Lawrence Timbers. A decorated World War II veteran who ran a small printing business in Seattle, Washington, Pantaleoni stated that he attempted to associate UNICEF with Communism by taking up the cause of the House Un-American Activities Commission (HUAC). He focused his attentions in particular on exposing subversive elements among the UN's employees. "I think he sort of saw himself as a great patriot, who was going to save his country from these wicked foreigners . . . and he flooded the country with anti-UNICEF literature," recalled Pantaleoni. "[T]hey did us a great deal of harm."[60]

HUAC, created between 1946 and 1947, had originally been intended to continue the work begun by Harry Truman to uncover "fraud and profiteering on government military contracts."[61] Senator Patrick McCarran of Nevada, who had been critical of UNRRA's operations during World War II, became a key member of HUAC and subsequently threw his considerable support as chairman of the Judiciary Committee behind Senator Joseph McCarthy's anti-Communist efforts. McCarthy succeeded in shifting the committee away from Truman's original plan and toward searching out Communists in the United States.[62] He claimed this ideology posed a threat to democratic societies everywhere and could, if allowed to exist unchecked in the United States, bring about the downfall of the government and the nation.[63] Having the Soviet Union's 1949 nuclear tests to help him stir up hysteria, McCarthy claimed that Communism, on the rise around the world and in the United States, had not benefitted due to some superior strength possessed by the Soviet Union. Instead, this phenomenon had occurred because "of the traitorous actions of those who have been treated so well by this Nation . . . who have had the finest home, the finest college educations, and the finest jobs in Government we can give." McCarthy focused first on the U.S. Department of State, but cast the net wide to eventually include individuals working for the UN.[64]

Several UN staffers can be counted among the casualties of the HUAC's investigations. UNICEF most likely lost its chairman, Ludwick Rajchman, largely because he had been appointed to the UN by Poland's Communist government, and had refused to bend to the United States' demand that UNICEF deny relief aid to Communist China. Sinclair noted that during his time with UNICEF, Rajchman had remained committed to preventing the distress of children everywhere, and did whatever he had to do to achieve that end. "He was perfectly right about that, but not everybody was prepared to listen to him and to do the kind of thing he wanted."[65] In addition to Rajchman: "There are other women, several who were extremely able, who ran into this cloud of the McCarthy thing. As far as I can tell, very unjustly. Their departures were made easy, simply I think because of the insistence of the U.S. government." She claimed that the entire UN found itself in a "terribly hard position," noting that they "didn't want anything to reflect on the integrity of their organization."[66] One of these women, UNICEF press aide Ruth Elizabeth Crawford, was fired in 1953 when she admitted to membership in the Communist Party. *Evening American* covered the story on January 22, 1953, under the headline "UN Fires Woman Press Aide, Self-Admitted Red." It reported that Crawford had been "the only American UN employee to admit membership in the Communist Party," and that her dismissal had come directly from Secretary-General Lie, "who said he acted on the recommendation of Maurice Pate, director of the UN Children's Fund."[67]

The U.S. government clearly attempted to exert its influence over the UN in general and UNICEF in particular into the 1950s, but this influence did not go unchallenged by non-U.S. members of both organizations, many of whom hailed from countries that were now providing funding for UNICEF's programs. In one such instance, Eleanor Roosevelt faced censure and rebuke from Pakistan's delegate, Ahmed Bokhari, after she made her proposal to disband UNICEF in 1950. Pantaleoni, in attendance at the meeting, called the events of that day "unforgettable."

Bokhari, who served as vice-chairman of the Social, Cultural and Humanitarian Committee, listened intently as Mrs. Roosevelt spoke about the future of UNICEF. After she was seated, Pantaleoni noticed that Bokhari rose. He announced that he was stepping down from his role as chairman to address the group as the delegate from Pakistan, and began by stating, "I have the greatest respect for my distinguished colleague, Mrs. Roosevelt, but listening to her, I felt as though I was at the funeral of the International Children's Emergency Fund." Shocked by photos of emaciated European children, he claimed he and his Asian colleagues had been no less shocked to realize the children in their countries were no better off. "You were willing to help postwar needy children in Europe, but now you're not willing to come through for the equally needy children of the developing world?"[68] "There was great silence in the hall," recalled Pantaleoni. "Mrs. Roosevelt blanched, the blood ran out of her face." Pantaleoni called Bokhari's action brilliant and eloquently delivered, noting that in put the United States "on the mat." He made it clear that while the emergency in Europe may have been over by 1950, children in Asia lived in a state of continual emergency. "This is what happened that famous day at Lake Success. Interesting."[69]

Bokhari's speech, in addition to its masterful positioning of developing countries as places to be courted as part of the U.S. State Department's Cold War agenda, must have also been viewed by UNICEF staffers as a clear signal that they should continue with their efforts to make UNICEF a permanent UN body. Expansion in the developing world had been more well received by the U.S. government than had its efforts to provide relief aid to Communist countries, making these efforts more likely to win public support than providing milk to children in Red China. Its greeting card campaign and Halloween collections had succeeded in increasing awareness of and interest in UNICEF in the United States; but, UNICEF still lacked the widespread name recognition and support necessary to ensure continued funding to support its programs. A chance meeting in 1953 between Maurice Pate and actor Danny Kaye would, however, provide an innovative solution to UNICEF's publicity problem.

While aboard a plane in danger of crashing into the ocean, Pate and Kaye struck up a conversation that would result in the creation of the position of UNICEF goodwill ambassador. This position forged the first public relations relationship between celebrities and international organizations when Kaye, an international film star, endowed UNICEF with a new visibility by using the medium of film to publicize UNICEF's global efforts on behalf of children and mothers both in the United States and elsewhere.

Judith Spiegelman writes that Kaye recalled that meeting Pate as an event "could easily make a Hollywood movie." He had boarded a flight from London to the United States, and the plane took off without incident. Kaye recalled he had fallen asleep, but was awakened suddenly by a crew member saying, "[Y]ou'd better wake up Mr. Kaye, we may have to ditch!" The plane's propeller had ceased to operate, and Kaye remembered "asking everybody to take off his shoes and to tie the life raft to his wrist in case we had to plunge into the water." The plane eventually landed safely in Ireland at Shannon Airport, where the passengers deplaned. [70] Pantaleoni, who heard the story from Pate, said he recalled "there was a terrible moment [on the flight]. Maurice told me he saw Danny and asked him to sing. I don't think Danny sang, but those were sort of the first words that Maurice [exchanged with Kaye.]"[71]

Kaye remembered that after re-boarding: "Sitting next to me on that second plane was a man named Maurice Pate. . . . Maurice Pate was tall and stately, an imposing figure with silver hair and a quiet yet warm manner. He had spent half his life helping the world's unfortunate children, and he began explaining to me what UNICEF's work was." Six months later, Pate invited Kaye to lunch at the UN when he read that Kaye was about to take a trip around the world. "You know," Pate began, "people are having a lot of trouble identifying UNICEF. If you would stop at some of our installations and then come back and go on the radio or write a magazine article, it would help us a great deal." Kaye promised to do more than that—he promised to make a documentary. [72]

Kaye kept his promise. He obtained the necessary equipment and a pledge from Paramount pictures to underwrite his expenses. All proceeds from the film, he assured, would be donated to UNICEF. The UN appointed Kaye ambassador-at-large, and charged him with "making known the needs of children throughout the world." The resulting film, called "Assignment: Children," opened in theaters in 1955 and was eventually translated into nineteen languages. [73] Pantaleoni claimed that Kaye, whom she called "a Pan-like figure," found himself followed by children everywhere, and this appeal, captured on film, made a lasting impression on the General Assembly and many others who viewed the film. Pantaleoni served as mistress of ceremonies for the UN screening, which afforded her the opportunity to meet Kaye for the first time. She recalled: "He deeply cares. He's wonderful with children. He just has a special language with them, and they respond to him. He's extraordinary."[74] Kaye became the first of many ambassadors, including Peter Ustinov, Liv Ullman, Tetsuko Kuroyanagi, Audrey Hepburn, and eventually Helenka Pantaleoni's granddaughter, Tea Leoni, all of whom gave their time and energy to bring attention to the cause of maintaining and increasing UNICEF's visibility.[75]

Greeting cards and goodwill ambassadors helped to further UNICEF's cause to achieve permanent UN status, and, due to its increasing visibility, UNICEF found it necessary to publish informational pamphlets. These publications covered UNICEF's new work in Africa, Asia, and Latin America, describing its efforts to help "those children [who], generally speaking, have far less than their fair chance from the very outset of life."[76] These publications often included more photographs than text, and depicted everything from rows of smiling children about to drink their daily UNICEF cup of milk to the contents of a midwifery kit. Mothers and children lined up for medical care were depicted with female volunteers serving supplementary meals to school children over captions claiming "powdered milk from UNICEF has provided the incentive for establishing school-feeding programs." Often, maps were included to illustrate UNICEF's work as a "world cooperative."[77]

Through its various publicity endeavors, UNICEF began to appear more like an organization engaged in serious philanthropic and fundraising by 1953. Within the UN, reports on its progress began to be presented in a more formal manner, and included the all-important quantifiable result. Also by 1953, the Executive Board had adopted a strict protocol for its meetings. Pate had truly become the chief administrator of UNICEF, and provided his progress reports to the Board complete with a table of contents and page numbers. These reports, instead of including transcripts of lively and often-caustic discussions between delegates such as those that had taken place when UNICEF had been attempting to establish itself as an organization in 1946, now presented charts and graphs and synopses. Though little had changed regarding its institutional image, the way it went about its work had changed drastically. It still relied on needy children and mothers for its purpose, as well as on the CRB's and ARA's distribution model to expand its programs, which now produced quantifiable numbers in order to demonstrate successful results. That these programs had been carried out in developing countries created a close alliance between UNICEF and its recipients, and by 1953, they became UNICEF's most vocal supporters.

In March 1953, the Executive Board met to discuss the future of UNICEF, stressing several features of the organization that would be especially significant to its continuation when presented to the General Assembly in support of UNICEF's permanent status. First, UNICEF constituted the only organization in the UN primarily concerned with children. Second, its programs had proved to be successful in both the short and long term and—notably—at no cost to the UN. Third, UNICEF had established an effective constitutional structure and an economic administration. Fourth, it attracted resources that would have otherwise been unavailable if no special agency for children existed. Finally, UNICEF's activities provided one of the best vehicles for promoting the UN as a whole. These points, eventually discussed by the Economic and Social Council and in the General Assembly during that same year, proved persuasive. By October, the General Assembly unanimously decided to grant UNICEF permanent UN status, and approved Resolution 802 (VII). At the same time, it reaffirmed the broader operating terms under which UNICEF had been granted an extension in 1950, and dropped "International Emergency" from its name.[78]

1953 marked a new beginning for UNICEF. Government contributions increased, and programming changes reflected its commitment to long-range measures, noting that "the Board favours aid for programmes which give results on the basis of low per capita costs, which are within the capabilities of the country to continue after the initial period of international aid, and with set local organizational patterns capable of being duplicated and extended elsewhere in the country."[79] Having achieved permanent status, UNICEF could move forward with the knowledge that its programs, no longer based on the need to react to an emergency, could establish maternal and child health and welfare services that would perpetuate. Virginia Hazzard wrote that "it seems unbelievable now that anyone could have doubted the need to keep alive and nurture a UN agency devoted to helping governments preserve in good condition their most valuable investment for the future—children"; but, until 1953, this was the case.[80] What is even more unbelievable is the story of how this agency created itself, crafted its image, and managed to survive despite the odds. Based on the idea that children and their mothers require the care of a primary provider and bolstered by the U.S. post-war family ideal, UNICEF came to life as the father to the world's children, and every individual who participated in its functions supported and perpetuated that image in order to obtain funding, establish programs, and ensure its approval as a permanent UN agency. As UNICEF moved into the next decades, it would find that its image, while useful in developed countries for obtaining funding and maintaining support, did not always fit the developing nations it tried to assist.

NOTES

1. E/ICEF/160, 32, 34–37.

2. UNICEF had relationships with the United Nations Department of Social Affairs, the Division of Technical Assistance, the WHO, the FAO, the ILO, and UNESCO. It also worked with the Red Cross in several countries, the Don Suisse pour les Victimes de la Guerre, and Aide Suisse à l'Europe in addition to other voluntary agencies. E/ICEF/160, 24–25.

3. E/ICEF/155, *General Progress Report of Executive Director [UNICEF] 26 October 1950*, 7.

4. E/ICEF/155, 7.

5. E/ICEF/155, 34.

6. E/ICEF/160, 3.

7. Sinclair interview, 9.
8. Pantaleoni interview, 12.
9. Julia Henderson interview by John Charnow, July 30–31, 1983, 3–5. Accessed at UNICEF Archives.
10. General Assembly Resolution 214 (III). In E/ICEF/160, 29.
11. E/ICEF/22, *Statement Made to the 9th Meeting of the Executive Board of the ICEF by Mr. E. D. Marris, Assistant Secretary, Ministry of Education, U.K., on 19 June 1947*, 10.
12. Amy L. S. Staples, *The Birth of Development: How the World Bank, Food and Agriculture Administration and World Health Organization Changed the World, 1945-1965* (Kent: The Kent State University Press, 2006), 103.
13. Henderson interview, 4–5.
14. Margaret Gann interview by John Charnow, November 21, 1983. Accessed at UNICEF Archives, 9.
15. Henderson interview, 4–5.
16. Pantaleoni interview, 16–17.
17. Pantaleoni interview, 15–16
18. Pantaleoni interview, 8.
19. Pantaleoni interview, 8.
20. Staples, *The Birth of Development*, 2.
21. Henderson interview, 5.
22. Eliot interview, 206.
23. Henderson interview, 5.
24. E/ICEF/160, 30–31.
25. Virginia Hazzard, *UNICEF and Women, the Long Voyage: A Historical Perspective* (Geneva: United Nations Children's Fund, 1987), 4.
26. Sinclair interview, 12.
27. Henderson interview, 3.
28. E/ICEF/160, 29–30.
29. "Fifty Years For Children," www.unicef.org/sow96/50years.htm, accessed 21 September 1998.
30. General Assembly Resolution 215 (III) titled "Extension during 1949 of the United Nations Appeal for Children," submitted 8 December 1948 to ensure UNICEF's continued funding, and General Assembly Resolution 318 (IV) titled "United Nations International Children's Emergency Fund," submitted 2 December 1949, both state that the need to continue providing relief for children is urgent. E/ICEF/160, 29–30.
31. See Maggie Black, *Children First: The Story of UNICEF, Past and Present* (New York: Oxford University Press, 1996), xiii, 7, 8–9.
32. E/ICEF/72, 1–2.
33. See E/ICEF/74, *Statement of Needs of Refugee Children and Mothers in the Middle East*, annex 1, annex 2, annex 4.
34. "Fifty Years For Children," 2, and E/ICEF/89, *Report of the Executive Director to the 71st Meeting of the Programme Committee to be Held at Lake Success, 20 January 1949*, 1.
35. CF/HST/MON/1989-002, 3.
36. CF/HST/MON/1989-002, 3.
37. Jan Jindy Pettman, "Globalization and the Gendered Politics of Citizenship," in *Women, Citizenship and Difference,* Nira Yuval-Davis and Pnina Werbner, eds. (New York: Zed Books, 1999), 207.
38. Elaine Tyler May, *Homeward Bound: American Families in the Cold War Era* (New York: Basic Books, Inc., Publishers, 1988), 3, 19.
39. CF/HST/MON/1989-002, 44.
40. E/ICEF/R.130, *Recommendation of the Executive Director for an Additional Apportionment to the Philippines*, 1.
41. *UNICEF Pictorial Record*, 25.
42. Gann interview, 4.
43. Pantaleoni interview, 21–22, 25–26.
44. Pantaleoni interview, 25–26, 28–29.

45. Pantaleoni interview, 28.
46. Spiegelman and UNICEF, 136–37.
47. Pantaleoni interview, 109.
48. Pantaleoni interview, 30.
49. Spiegelman and UNICEF, 136–45.
50. Pantaleoni interview, 31.
51. Pantaleoni interview, 7.
52. Pantaleoni interview, 7.
53. Pantaleoni interview, 26.
54. Pantaleoni interview, 27.
55. Pantaleoni interview, 26–27; and Spiegelman and UNICEF, 113–15.
56. May, *Homeward Bound*, 10, 161.
57. Pantaleoni interview, 19.
58. Pantaleoni interview, 22.
59. Pantaleoni interview, 22–23.
60. Pantaleoni interview, 63.
61. Arthur Herman, *Joseph McCarthy: Reexamining the Life and Legacy of America's Most Hated Senator* (New York: The Free Press, 2000), 44.
62. Ellen Schrecker, *The Age of McCarthyism: A Brief History with Documents* (New York: Bedford Books, 1994), 47.
63. Schrecker, *The Age of McCarthyism*, 96–99.
64. Schrecker, *The Age of McCarthyism*, 97, and McCarthy as quoted in Herman, *Joseph McCarthy*, 99.
65. Sinclair interview, 1.
66. Pantaleoni interview, 94.
67. *Evening America*, Thursday, January 22, 1953, 6. Maurice Pate Papers, Princeton University Library.
68. Ahmed Shah Bokhari as quoted in Spiegelman and UNICEF, 66.
69. Pantaleoni interview, 17.
70. Spiegelman and UNICEF, 86.
71. Pantaleoni interview, 81.
72. Spiegelman and UNICEF, 86.
73. Spiegelman and UNICEF, 86–87.
74. Pantaleoni interview, 82.
75. Spiegelman and UNICEF, 92–107.
76. *UNICEF, A Pictorial Record: For All the World's Children* (New York: United Nations International Children's Emergency Fund, August 1952), 4.
77. *UNICEF Pictorial Record*, 13, 6–17.
78. Charnow, *History of UNICEF* (Unpublished), 25.
79. Charnow, *History of UNICEF* (unpublished), excerpt from E/ICEF/226, 25.
80. Hazzard, *UNICEF and Women, the Long Voyage*, 4.

Conclusion

Beyond 1953: The Future of Children

UNICEF's commitment to becoming a permanent part of the UN is most obvious in the changes evident in its formal reports of the proceedings of its various committees as well as in its year-end status reports. UNICEF had adopted formal rules of procedure in 1947 shortly after its founding, but these were not always successful at producing clear and concise statements regarding UNICEF's outcomes. The rules underwent revisions in 1948 in an attempt to make meetings and minutes more straightforward and organized, since the 1947 protocols had failed to filter out the individual voices that had become part of the permanent record. These rules of procedure did not, however, succeed in formalizing reports from the Executive Board for several years. Until 1950, UNICEF's reports continued to reflect lively debate between delegates, including colorful exchanges regarding everything from providing toys to facilitating the adoption of orphaned children. A pronounced change in the official records of UNICEF became evident in 1950, however, when the written records UNICEF produced to provide information on the work of the Executive Board reveal a deliberate evolution. Gone was the banter between Executive Board members, replaced now by sterile, columnar, statistical reports filled with results instead of the individual voices of UNICEF's administrators. The more formal tone and format make clear the organization's intent to appear as official and businesslike as possible, most likely to support the notion that UNICEF, with its excellent and easily readable program results, deserved to be elevated to permanent status. By 1953, only Maurice Pate remained a visible presence in UNICEF's records in his role as executive director. Pate had guided UNICEF through its first phase as an emergency relief aid organization, and forward into its second, when UNICEF's focus shifted to development along with the rest of the UN.

UNICEF's new focus on development allowed Pate to emphasize children as the best hope of the future by highlighting their pivotal role in development instead of their need to survive in the wake of a war. This new direction also allowed UNICEF to include substantially more countries around the world in its programs, which in turn allowed UNICEF to provide relief aid to more and more people, thereby reinforcing its indispensability. In a series of letters during the years between 1953 and 1954, Pate chronicled his visits to Spain to discuss establishing programs in Morocco, to Paris to finalize yaws, bejel, and syphilis treatment programs in French West Africa, and his junkets to African nations where UNICEF programs could help combat the spread of malaria. Pate also visited Jerusalem, Beirut, Damascus, and several small cities in the Middle East, all of which he summarized for the UNICEF Staff News publication in January 1954.[1] Pate had visited "14 countries in Africa, Europe, and the Eastern Mid-Region," which had given him "a stronger feeling of confidence in the value of UNICEF work," and he reported that "the overall picture" indicated that UNICEF continued to display "outstanding team work and great zeal and devotion by people in the field in obtaining maximum value out of the funds entrusted to them."[2] UNICEF would now begin to focus on "investment in children" in nations that were both "behind" and "just getting used to their newfound independence."[3]

Concurrent with this new policy direction, another, perhaps unintended, transformation in UNICEF's policy language occurred. Regardless of UNICEF's purported continued focus on maternal and child health and welfare, reports produced as early as March 1949, began to exclude mothers as a separate category of relief aid recipients, providing verbiage primarily on the effects of its programs on children only. The *Report of the Meeting of the Subcommittee on Medical Projects* held in Paris, for example, provided information on the BCG vaccines being distributed, on the anti-VD and anti-Malaria campaigns, and on training for staff and local personnel, but it makes no mention of mothers as a separate group of aid recipients.[4] The programs being planned for Palestine and China, too, focused exclusively on children, with breakdown of the "main study periods, each of them related to one special aspect of child care" that existed in a child's life. It enumerated specific medical skills required in order to ensure their proper management of these periods, including the pre-natal, neo-natal, and post-natal periods, but had fused mothers and children together by 1949 by categorizing pregnancy and childbirth as functions of child care rather than as functions of pregnancy experienced by the mother.[5]

In addition to their exclusion from program reports, mentions of women as mothers began to disappear in other rather significant ways as well. In a

1961 statement, Pate omitted any mention at all of mothers as a factor in UNICEF's ongoing programs for development. UNICEF's adherence to the U.S. post-war family ideal seems to have persisted, then, allowing women to fade from the text given their inextricable link to their children and their obvious distance from any significant role in development. Amy Staples notes that early programs on development relied heavily on a "top-down" approach that required the intervention of experts. Their "sense of social purpose," found in "the concept of welfare economics," relied on "the notion . . . that economic analysis must supply policy makers with the tools and information needed to improve the lot of humankind."[6] Women in developing regions, existing only in relation to their reproductive role and all but subsumed into the category of "child," had little to do with what Staples identifies as the "economists and their professional cousins in banking" who often guided both foreign and economic policy.[7] UNICEF's official documents, evidence the persistence of these images of women solely as mothers. And, though there is some variation, the roles of women remained closely tied to the ideals and expectations created in the West rather than realistically embracing the vastness of women's experience and responsibilities elsewhere in the world. Several decades would pass before dissonant voices that had raised questions regarding the chasm between UNICEF's prescription and the reality of people's lives resulted in the inclusion of women both as mothers and in their other capacities. However, as is clear in UNICEF's programs, women remained encapsulated in women-identified roles and professions during the initial period that focused on development.

Regardless of its new focus on development, during the 1950s and into the 1960s, reports on UNICEF's policies and programs continued to fail to mention mothers as a category separate from their children. A 1951 summary of UNICEF policies and practices seems to have established this standard, reporting that UNICEF would, if necessary, seek advice from other sources regarding "child and family" welfare, not maternal and child welfare as had been the case in the past. While mentions of "child health" and "child welfare programs" abound, the mention of mothers is rare—a conspicuous absence given the statements made in UNICEF's charter.[8] Programs became intently focused on the child, including all emergency aid, self-help programs, and long-term health programs in developing nations. This can be seen clearly in UNICEF's 1957 announcement to provide aid to Africa, for when UNICEF unveiled its program plans, mothers as a category of aid recipients received no mention.[9] Even Katharine Lenroot, a career-long champion of maternal and child health and welfare programs, fell into step. She prepared a report in 1961 titled *United Nations Aid to the Developing Countries for Extending and Improving Their Services for Children and Youth*.[10] While she mentions that "[i]n 1960, over 56 million children and mothers benefited from the principal UNICEF-aided projects," she quickly moved to concerns over the "gaps and weaknesses in the whole range of United Nations programs for children," and only mentions mothers once more, this time as a group in need of proper prenatal care to ensure the birth of healthy children.[11] During the mid-1960s when it became clear that UNICEF's programs in developing nations, as well as those of the UN as a whole, could not thrive without the assistance of properly trained indigenous workers to put them into action, this began to restore women's presence in UNICEF. This time, it would be as health care providers in woman-identified roles such as midwife and teacher instead of in the more traditional role of mother.

Nitza Berkovitch writes that during the 1960s, the UN as a body began to discuss ways to "mobilz[e] nation-states to take action against the various types of discrimination that women suffer in their respective countries."[12] Thus, its new policy direction, as well as the need to train local workers, seems to have influenced UNICEF's move toward including women more readily in its programs as well as recognizing them in a wider variety of roles. Indeed, Maurice Pate stated in 1965 that "the welfare of children and the advancement of women are inextricably bound together," and UNICEF had therefore become deeply involved in the advancement of women. "Women play a dual role in UNICEF-assisted projects," Pate claimed, noting that their education and cooperation would be essential if UNICEF's projects were to have their long-range impact. UNICEF would give young women "a new outlook for a career in a socially useful occupation," and would provide them with training that would "inevitably carry over into their own family life." While Pate's statement makes it clear UNICEF had realized its programs were not working as anticipated in several regions of the developing world, these failures were attributed not to differences in culture, but to the lack of proper education and training of women according to the traditional Western model.[13]

This statement regarding women's roles in UNICEF would be one of Pate's last as executive director. He succumbed to complications from heart disease in January 1965, after battling ill health for several years prior to his death at the age of seventy. A special communication with "the UNICEF family" titled "Notes on Maurice Pate's Last Illness" stated that, on the evening of January 18, Pate and his wife had left a meeting of the Board of the Recording for the Blind Foundation. While walking to the apartment of a friend, Pate had collapsed on the street. A doctor had been called, and Pate had been transported to Bellevue Hospital's cardiac unit, where he never regained consciousness. The note ended by claiming that "the result of the autopsy indicated that he would not have had any hope of doing so."[14] His passing left many at both UNICEF and the UN in shock, and UNICEF with a gaping vacancy at the helm. For many months afterward his death was commemorated at the UN, in the U.S. Congress, in his hometown of Denver, Colorado, and by his many friends, colleagues, and family around the country and around the world. Later that year, UNICEF, whose global status and reputation as the most successful child relief aid organization in the world was due largely to Pate's efforts, would be awarded the Nobel Peace Prize.

Helenka Pantaleoni attended the Nobel award ceremonies in Oslo, Norway, and heralded the event as "the highest honour accorded to mankind." During the ceremony, Pate's contributions to UNICEF were remembered when Mr. Henry Labouisse, who became UNICEF's executive director after Pate, claimed on behalf of UNICEF that Pate was "UNICEF's architect and builder," while another speaker proclaimed him an "unassuming person, but on the road that leads to peace, and where politicians are still groping their way in the dark, Maurice Pate has lit many a candle."[15] Pate had overseen UNICEF through its formative phase, directing every aspect of the organization's operations as it began and augmented its operations. Using his vast experience and connections within the U.S. government, he only acceded that UNICEF's direction needed alteration when, as a full-fledged UN agency, UNICEF became involved with development.

Blanche Bernstein, too, chronicled the shifts in UNICEF's policy direction under Pate's leadership in a report written for the U.S. Department of State in 1966 titled *UNICEF—The United Nations Children's Fund*. Bernstein, writing in her capacity as the officer in charge of international education and social affairs in the Bureau of International Affairs, introduced her findings by claiming the report had been written to "describe the evolution of UNICEF's policies and programs and the role the United States has played in helping to shape them." She noted that "UNICEF has not always rested on universal consensus," and that "[t]he reason for recurring ambivalence about UNICEF" rests on the fact that it did not "fit logically into the pattern of U.N. bodies designed to promote social progress."[16]

Bernstein boldly asserted that, given these confusions over UNICEF's functions, it could be argued that no need existed for an organization like UNICEF; however, she concluded, "the justification is easy and can be made on practical grounds"; the needs of children could not be overlooked. The "[e]motional appeal of the organization," she claimed, steered its policy until 1953, when UNICEF "favor[ed] action projects over research projects." To that end, UNICEF devoted its resources to "basic maternal and child welfare services . . . disease control . . . [and] nutrition."[17] It was not until 1961, however, that UNICEF changed direction, adopting a "New Look" that included helping governments "draft national plans for children and youth." This statement, which also excludes mention of mothers, aligns with UNICEF's focus on children as well. She noted, too, that UNICEF also began to "meet local costs where it is essential for their success . . . [and] assumes expenses of hiring qualified personnel."[18] Bernstein closed her remarks by noting that the "U.S. Government warmly supports UNICEF policies and programs" and "makes a substantial contribution to the objectives of the UN [in the amount of] twelve million dollars annually."[19]

This shift in tone and practice by the U.S. State Department seems to have occurred rather quickly given the continued Cold War tensions present in the United States. As recently as 1959, for example, the Daughters of the American Revolution had resolved to "carefully study and analyze the UNICEF contributions to a program to promote the World Welfare State and to remove Christ from Christmas," claiming that "the Christmas cards sold by UNICEF are devoid of the spirit of Christmas" and that "a very substantial part of the total funds [of UNICEF] goes to communist and communist-controlled countries." Pate wrote to Hoover for advice on how to handle this rebuke, noting that the only Communist countries receiving aid from UNICEF in 1959 were Poland and Yugoslavia—both of which also received direct aid from the U.S. government.[20] Hoover's reply two days later consisted of two sentences: "Don't get into a fight with these good people. It is profitless and not worth your while."[21] More likely, the U.S. State Department felt that UNICEF, guided by the foreign policies of the United States, would be a greater help in capturing the hearts and minds of children in Communist countries with its seemingly non-controversial relief aid assistance.

Focusing on children may have served a twofold purpose. First, it helped support U.S. foreign policy by reinforcing the good deeds performed by the United States to help others around the world; and second, it allowed UNICEF to provide aid to a group that was truly viewed as apolitical. In 1961, Pate had written an article for the *United Nations Review* titled "Helping Children: An Investment in the Future. A Statement Based on Fifteen Years of Work with UNICEF," which seems to reinforce the latter point. This article iterated UNICEF's continued relevance as a UN organization despite the concerns of its detractors by noting that "UNICEF has had two rather distinct careers since its founding in 1946." The first, which lasted four years, had been to provide relief aid "in countries whose children were the victims of the Second World War." The subsequent eleven years, he asserted, had been spent establishing "long-term programs to help the even needier children of the economically underdeveloped world." He proposed that "the next ten years should be as different again, not this time in terms of new goals, but in terms of the approach we take to our work and the methods we use to realize our objectives." Pate promised that UNICEF would "focus on how the emphasis on the welfare of children can be an important part of economic and social development," and closed by making it clear that UNICEF's policies in no way supported a world welfare state; "helping children," he proclaimed, "is not a form of charity—it is an investment in the future."[22]

Amy Staples notes that, at the end of World War II, "the United Nations system and its specialized agencies played a key role in promoting [the] process" of development. "World War II," she writes, had "witnessed a revolution in expectations that compelled the imperial and indigenous governments of most countries to contribute to the development of peoples throughout the Third World," and UNICEF's work paralleled that of the UN as a whole. "Newly independent Third World countries . . . pushed the specialized agencies to fund more and more services and projects that might improve the lives of their people."[23] Akira Iriye also found that, by pooling their resources, UNICEF and WHO could focus on disease elimination as a part of their program for "infrastructure development and primary health care programs."[24] UNICEF itself reported: "Emphasis [was] being put on extension of services of MCH [maternal and child health] services to new areas in countries which have not yet developed national coverage, rather than on aid for the elaboration of services already covered." The goal would be to ensure that, in developing regions, elementary health care services could be provided by UNICEF as widely as possible while at the same time training and supervision could be offered to local inhabitants to raise medical standards. This latter provision would also be important in ensuring prevention of diseases by attempting to guarantee that "more permanent schemes become an actuality."[25] Unfortunately, according to Staples, these programs did little to stop "malnutrition [and] infant mortality," which led many nations to "abandon the social programs urged on them" by the 1980s.[26] Iriye, too, writes that in the 1980s, "civil strife, debt crisis, and other afflictions in the poorer countries" led to the deterioration of health conditions—especially the health conditions of children.[27] But what of women, who had traditionally been made responsible for the care and well-being of children either as mothers or trained caretakers? Amy Staples writes that when the "top down, expert-driven" models of development failed to achieve their desired goals, it was women who led the way to a new, "post-development ideology" that brought about "amazing things."[28]

UNICEF historian Maggie Black argues that as early as the 1970s, the coming of second-wave feminism led to the first real changes in the ways UNICEF considered women, a conclusion Berkovitch's work affirms. Black asserted that "the movement for women's rights . . . concerned itself with . . . women from a very different perspective." Women, refusing to be narrowly defined in terms of their relationship to childbearing and their domestic roles, demanded equality with men instead. These women turned to UNICEF for help, but UNICEF changed its course slowly due to directions already charted for organization and programs.[29] The "Declaration of the Rights of the Child" and international concerns over ensuring child relief, for example, caused UNICEF to focus on child health, nutrition, and education, as well as community development and social welfare, and UNICEF continued to identify women primarily in their role as mothers or in other woman-identified occupations.[30] UNICEF did acknowledge in 1978 that "the integration of women in the process of development" had become essential, but determined that, once integrated, a woman could return to traditional roles and "improve nutrition, which because of its impact on health can reduce the load on health services."[31] It would not be until the 1979 Convention on the Elimination of All Forms of Discrimination against Women (CEDAW), which incorporated "most of the provisions in previous women's rights conventions and added new issues," that UNICEF would truly begin to incorporate women more fully into a greater variety of roles, acknowledging their status as or need to be full citizens of their respective nations.[32]

Yet another shift occurred during the 1970s when UNICEF's presence in rural areas of developing countries increased. Since these areas lacked a traditional infrastructure, UNICEF came to rely on women in new ways in order to successfully execute its programs. In countries where the traditional school feeding programs found in the West did not exist, UNICEF depended on women's clubs, mother's clubs, and community centers to distribute relief assistance and training.[33] Women also took on primary roles in training other women to become local health care providers, becoming the "barefoot mid-wives" and "barefoot teachers" mentioned in UNICEF publicity pamphlets that provided for a community's basic needs.[34] By acknowledging women's involvement beyond their "socially delegated" roles, many of UNICEF's programs that appeared traditional on the surface accomplished much more.[35] Virginia Hazzard writes that mothercraft and homecraft programs in Africa provided "an acceptable activity that women could do together and in which they would frequently be supported, and even encouraged by their husbands." She notes that these programs significantly decreased the illiteracy rate for women in Africa, and increased their participation in community affairs.[36] And, because by the end of the 1970s no permanent UN organization for women existed, they looked to UNICEF, the one organization that had recognized them in any capacity, for help.

Changes in UNICEF's programs, then, seem to have been influenced by both the women's movement, as Maggie Black contends, as well as by changes in the UN's direction. Another factor to consider is that programs in developing countries were not succeeding as UNICEF had hoped due to their conflict with local and national laws and customs. For example, Margaret Gann remembered that educating women in midwifery required trainees in Afghanistan to be transported on "a bus with blackened windows so the girls couldn't look out and nobody would look in on them" due to threats made against their lives. Family planning programs in Asia, too, faced hurdles according to Julia Henderson. She noted that UNICEF took an "over-timid approach" due to its focus on women only. UNICEF's program relied on the use of the inter-uterine device, or IUD, which she described as "difficult devices that had to be inserted." She expressed her frustration with the UN as a whole, asserting that it "never even tried to find out" how to deal with the male population. Income-generation programs for women, too, "were very bad." Run on a "charity basis," Henderson claimed they were "all done by rich women of the town who went out like Lady Bountifuls and taught poor women to crochet or embroider or knit, always the same things, and there was tremendous problems of marketing the stuff" because there was little demand for the goods produced.[37] Real change occurred when UNICEF could no longer ignore that the varied roles required of women, especially in developing countries, made their programs less appealing and successful than they had been in the Western world.

UNICEF's board found guidance in its efforts to redirect its focus after the first UN conference for women, held in 1975. This conference signaled a new awareness in UN policy and, by the end of the Decade for Women, provided UNICEF with the impetus for making truly meaningful adjustments in its commitments to women that exceeded their singular employment as mothers. The three programs of action produced by the conferences in Mexico City, Copenhagen, and Nairobi illustrated the need for a change in perception of women's roles all over the world. This helped to dispel the notion that women played little if any role in the family economy, bringing down the rubric based on the traditional middle-class Western family model.

By the 1980s, UNICEF acknowledged that women the world over undertook almost every task related to the survival of the family. The growing and processing of food in particular became identified with women despite the fact that it had traditionally been identified with men in the West. Women often spent eleven hours of sixteen on tasks heretofore defined as "domestic."[38] Amy Staples argues that much of the shift in UN policy resulted from the direct actions of women in developing regions. She cites the Deccan Development Society (DDS) that worked with women in India, noting that it allowed untouchable women to "meet, work, talk and sing together." The women, part of the lowest caste in India and living in a strictly patriarchal society, found they could develop "collective priorities" in order to "develop and maintain autonomy." These women, she writes, began by discussing "the most vital issue in their lives—food security." Once they had reclaimed the growth of a traditional food crop and ten thousand acres of land, the women turned their focus to "food sovereignty," resulting in the creation of a community seed bank as well as schools for their children, a Community Green Fund, and a willingness to challenge authority.[39]

This success story helped reinforce the fact that understanding the lives and work of women in most parts of the developing world helped to dispel the notion that "women in . . . communities in Africa, Asia and Latin America had not been perceived as making any significant contribution to the family economy."[40] Women also performed household maintenance, manufactured clothing, baskets, and mats, and engaged in commerce, often selling surplus food goods at informal markets. Based on differences in culture, customs, work, and citizenship status, UNICEF eventually conceded that compartmentalizing the work of women into the narrowly defined category of mother created an artificial identity for most women throughout the world. Any attempts to help mothers without taking into account the full range of their responsibilities would result in failing to help both mother and child in the end, a fact made obvious by the successes of a group like the one founded to help women in India.

With so much information to support the expansion of the roles of women, and the growing admission that gender operated as a fundamental organizing and constricting principle in society could not be avoided within UNICEF. By 1990, UNICEF acknowledged that women, girls, and boys lacked basic rights because of "inequities and impediments that prevent many national citizens from being able to participate fully in both the public and economic spheres."[41] Having already committed itself to consider the special needs of the girl child in 1995, UNICEF renewed its commitment to elevate the status of women in general. Under the direction of its first female executive director, Carol Bellamy, who assumed this position in 1995, child development replaced child survival as the organization's primary cause. This has allowed UNICEF to participate in the intellectual, psychological, and emotional development of children of both sexes equally while acknowledging the value of parents, demanding their recognition as full citizens of their nation and their community to a child's overall wellbeing.[42]

From the start, UNICEF faced criticism for its programs regardless of the fact that, without them, countless children and mothers would have died. While it did not always keep pace with the cultures and societies it attempted to help, it is clear that UNICEF did not undertake its mission in an attempt to constrict individual family roles. Instead, it used the roles accepted by benefactor nations in the West in order to ensure its survival as an organization, then found it difficult to change these roles once programs had been built around them. Jan Jindy Pettman writes that states "frequently reinforced masculine power," directly impeding women's "access to and experience of citizenship."[43] It is clear that both UNICEF and the UN as a body have left behind the prescriptions for families and their members that resulted from Cold War politics, and have made an unwavering commitment to full participation for both women and men in their families. Whether in economic or domestic activities or as caregivers for their children, UNICEF's recent programs have begun to challenge and break down the categories that "violat[e] the official criteria of universal entitlement."[44] Like the UN as a whole, UNICEF cannot escape the prevailing attitudes and trends present at any given time, and can do no more than UN members and its supporters will allow; however, its late twentieth- and early twenty-first-century policies and programs no longer rely on "pre-established cultural domains of female power and rightful ownership and responsibility."[45] UNICEF has expanded the definition of *woman* to afford more opportunity for women, boys, and girls to fully participate in their societies around the world.

NOTES

1. Charles Egger, Director, AMERO, to Dick (Mr. E. R. J. Heyward), Report-Visit to Spain, 11 December 1953, 1; Maurice Pate to Dick (Mr. E. R. J. Heyward), November 28, 1953; Maurice Pate to Charles Egger, December 14, 1953; Maurice Pate to Charles Egger, December 20, 1953; Maurice Pate, Notes for the Record (Middle East Trip), 1–4; Rachid A. Koleilat, Notes on Mr. Pate's Visit to Beirut, 24 December 1953-9 January 1954; "Mr. Pate Returns," UNICEF Staff News, No. 138, Item 1474, 22 January 1954. Maurice Pate Papers, Princeton University Library.

2. "Mr. Pate Returns," UNICEF Staff News, No. 138 Item 1474, 22 January 1954. Maurice Pate Papers, Princeton University Library.

3. Maurice Pate, "Helping Children: An Investment in the Future. A Statement Based on Fifteen Years of Work by UNICEF." In *United Nations Review* (July 1961), Volume 8, Number 7 (New York: United Nations Office of Public Information, 1961), 1. Maurice Pate Papers, Princeton University Library.

4. E/ICEF/111, *Report of the Meeting of the Sub-Committee on Medical Projects Held on 5 March 1949, Paris*, 1.

5. E/ICEF/111, 19.

6. Amy L. S. Staples, *The Birth of Development: How the World Bank, Food and Agriculture Organization, and World Health Organization Changed the World, 1945-1965* (Kent, OH: Kent State University Press, 2006), 9.

7. Staples, *The Birth of Development*, 10.

8. E/ICEF/168, *Summary of UNICEF Policies and Practices*, 32, 34.

9. E/ICEF/240, *Aid to the African Areas, Statement to the Executive Board on September 9, 1953, by Charles Egger, Director, UNICEF Office for Africa, Eastern Mediterranean and Europe Regional Office, 13th September 1953* (New York: UNICEF Archives, 1953), 13.

10. Katharine F. Lenroot, *United Nations Aid to the Developing Countries for Extending and Improving Their Services for Children and Youth* (20 April 1961).

11. Lenroot, *United Nations Aid to the Developing Countries*, 7–8.

12. Nitza Berkovitch, *From Motherhood to Citizenship: Women's Rights and International Organizations* (Baltimore: Johns Hopkins University Press, 1999), 1.

13. CF/HST/MON/1989-002, 58.

14. "Notes on Maurice Pate's Last Illness," 27 January 1965. Maurice Pate Papers, Princeton University Library.

15. "Acceptance Speech by Mr. Labouisse: Nobel Lecture by Mrs. Harman; Observations by Mrs. (Adelaide) Sinclair, Mrs. (Helekna) Pantaleoni, and Mr. Ling," *UNICEF Staff News*, No. 290-13. January 1966.

16. Blanche Bernstein, *UNICEF—the United Nations Children's Fund* (Washington, DC: Department of State Bulletin, 1966), 1–2.

17. Bernstein, *UNICEF—the United Nations Children's Fund*, 2–6.

18. Bernstein, *UNICEF—the United Nations Children's Fund*, 7.

19. Bernstein, *UNICEF—the United Nations Children's Fund*, 9.

20. Maurice Pate to Herbert Hoover, 24 April 1959. Maurice Pate Papers, Princeton University Library.

21. Herbert Hoover to Maurice Pate, 26 April 1959. Maurice Pate Papers, Princeton University Library.

22. Pate, "Helping Children," in *United Nations Review*, July 1961, Volume 8, Number 7 (New York: United Nations Office of Public Information, 1961), 1.

23. Amy L.S. Staples, *The Birth of Development*, 181.

24. Akria Iriye, *Global Community*, 173.

25. CF/HST/MON/1989-002, 45–46.

26. Staples, *The Birth of Development*, 181.

27. Akria Iriye, *Global Community*, 173.

28. Amy L.S. Staples, *The Birth of Development*, 187.

29. Maggie Black, *The Children and the Nations: The Story of UNICEF* (New York: UNICEF, 1986), 184–85.

30. HIST/50, 2–4.

31. HIST 46, 1.

32. Berkovitch, *From Motherhood to Citizenship*, 107.

33. E/ICEF/608/Add.9, *General Progress Report of the Executive Director: The First Twenty-Five Years of UNICEF: A Summary of Policy Evolution*, 6, 8.

34. Black, *The Children and the Nations*, 12.

35. Black, *The Children and the Nations*, 183.

36. Virginia Hazzard, *UNICEF and Women, the Long Voyage: A Historical Perspective* (Geneva: United Nations Children's Fund, 1987), 17.

37. Gann interview, 7, 11–12, 13; Henderson interview.

38. UNICEF News, "Development Begins with Women" (New York: Issue 104/1980/2, 1980), 2.

39. Staples, *The Birth of Development*, 187–88.

40. Black, *The Children and the Nations*, 186–87.

41. Alison Brysk and Gershon Shafir, eds., *People Out of Place: Globalization, Human Rights, and the Citizenship Gap* (New York: Routledge, 2004), 44.

42. Black, *The Children and the Nations*, 214.

43. Jan Jindy Pettman, "Globalisation and the Gendered Politics of Citizenship," in *Women, Citizenship and Difference*, Nira Yuval-Davis and Pnina Werbner, eds. (New York: Zed Books, 1999), 207.

44. Berkovitch, *From Motherhood to Citizenship*, 172.

45. Pnina Werbner, "Political Motherhood and the Feminisation of Citizenship: Women's Activisms and the Transformation of the Public Sphere," in *Women, Citizenship and Difference*, Nira Yuval-Davis and Pnina Werbner, eds. (New York: Zed Books, 1999), 221.

Bibliography

UNICEF ARCHIVES, UNICEF HOUSE, 3 UNITED NATIONS PLAZA, NEW YORK, NY EXECUTIVE BOARD

Committee on Administrative Budget, Committee Report. 19 April 1948. E/ICEF 58.

Compilation of Major UNICEF Policies. 8 March 1949. E/ICEF/107.

Consultation Concerning the Proposal of the French Government to Establish an International Children's Centre in Paris. Summary Record of the Consultation, Lake Success, New York, 26 September 1947. 15 October 1947. E/ICEF/33.

Director's Report to the Seventh Meeting of the Executive Board. 19 June 1947. E/ICEF/17.

Final Report of the First Executive Board of the United Nations International Children's Emergency Fund 11 December 1946-31 December 1950. 22 January 1951. E/ICEF/160.

General Progress Report of Executive Director. 26 October 1950. E/ICEF/155.

General Progress Report of the Executive Director. 15 October 1951. E/ICEF/182.

General Progress Report of the Executive Director. 15 March 1953. E/ICEF/221.

General Progress Report of the Executive Director: The First Twenty-Five Years of UNICEF: A Summary of Policy Evolution. 24 March 1971. E/ICEF/68 add. 9.

International Children's Emergency Fund Report of the Executive Board. 22–24 May 1951. E/ICEF/178.

Plans and Progress of Operations in UNICEF-Assisted Medical Projects in Europe. 19 April 1951. E/ICEF/174.

Proposed Section in Draft Board Report to 9th Session of ECOSOC on Cooperation with Other United Nations Organizations [WHO]. 11 June 1949. E/ICEF/W.62.

Recommendation of the Executive Director for an Additional Apportionment to the Philippines. 26 January 1951. E/ICEF/R.130.

Report of the Executive Board of ICEF Submitted to the Fifth Session of the Economic and Social Council. 10 July 1947. E/459.

Report of the Executive Board on its 43rd and 44th Meetings Held at the Palais de Chaillot 19 November 1948. 27 November 1948. E/ICEF/86.

Report of the Executive Board on its 63rd and 65th Meetings Held at Lake Success 6-7 March 1950. 20 March 1950. E/ICEF/145.

Report of the Executive Board on its 70-73rd Meetings Held 27-28 November 1950. 8 December 1950. E/ICEF/159.

Report of the Executive Board on the 40th through 42nd Meetings Held at the Palais de Chaillot, Paris 18th and 19th October 1948. 20 November 1948. E/ICEF/82.

Report of the Executive Board on the 58th through 62nd meeting held at Lake Success, 2, 4 and 5 November 1949. 9 November 1949. E/ICEF/136.

Report of the Executive Board to Economic and Social Council 6, 7 and 10 October 1952. 27 October 1952. E/ICEF/212.

Report of the Executive Director to the 10th Meeting of the Executive Board Held at Lake Success, New York 29 September-1 October 1947. 2 October 1947. E/ICEF/25.

Report of the Executive Director to the Nineteenth Meeting of the Executive Board. 9 March 1948. E/ICEF/46.

Report of FAO-WHO Committee on Child Nutrition (to Advise ICEF), 23-26 July, 1947. E/ICEF/23. annex 3.

Report of the UNICEF WHO Joint Committee on Health Policy: Statement by the UNICEF Rapporteur (Dr. Katherine Bain) to the 288th Meeting of the UNICEF Executive Board. 11 June 1962. E/ICEF/453.

Review of Maternal and Child Health Activities and Related Training of Professional and Auxiliary Health Workers Presented by the WHO Secretariat to the Tenth Session of the UNICEF-WHO Joint Committee on Health Policy, 2-3 May 1957. 22 July 1957. E/ICEF/347.

Rules of Procedure (As Adopted on 24 February 1947 and Revised 9 January 1948). 23 January 1948. E/ICEF/8/Rev. 2.

Statement Agreed to at the Sixteenth Meeting of the Executive Board. 8 October 1947. E/ICEF/29.

Statement Made Before the Fourth Meeting of the Executive Board of the International Children's Emergency Fund by Dr. A. P. Meiklejohn, Senior Consultant in Nutrition, European Office, UNRRA, Lake Success, New York, 24 February 1947. 27 February 1947. E/ICEF/12.

Statement Made to the 9th Meeting of the Executive Board of the ICEF by Mr. E.D. Marris, Assistant Secretary, Ministry of Education, U.K., on 19 June 1947. 19 June 1947. E/ICEF/22.

Statement of the Secretary-General of the United Nations Delivered on His Behalf at the Seventh Meeting of the Executive Board of the ICEF 17 June 1947. 17 June 1947. E/ICEF/18.

Summarized Plans of Feeding Operations in Europe. 16 February 1949. E/ICEF/10A.

Summary Record of the First Meeting Held at Lake Success New York 19 December 1946. 27 December 1946. E/ICEF/1.

Summary Record of the First Meeting of the Latin American Countries of the Executive Board New York, New York 24 January 1947. 6 February 1947. E/ICEF/6.

Summary Record of the First Meeting of the Work Committee Held at Lake Success, New York 27 December 1946. 7 January 1947. E/ICEF/2

Summary Record of the Fourth Meeting, Lake Success, New York 24 February 1947. 26 February 1947. E/ICEF/13.

Summary Record of the Third Meeting Held in Washington, DC (Children's Bureau) 13 January 1947. 31 January 1947. E/ICEF/5.

Summary Record of the Third Meeting Lake Success New York 7 February 1947. 10 February 1947. E/ICEF/7.

Summary Report of the Fourth Meeting. 3 March 1947. E/ICEF/16.

Summary Report of the Fifth Meeting, 28 February 1947. 28 February 1947. E/ICEF/14.

Summary of UNICEF Policies and Practices. 12 April 1951. E/ICEF/168.

UNICEF Aid to the African Area: Statement to the Executive Board on 9th September 1953, by Charles A. Egger, Director, UNICEF Office for Africa, Eastern Mediterranean and Europe Regional Office. 13 September 1953. E/ICEF/240.

PROGRAMME COMMITTEE

Communications between the Executive Director and the Secretary-General, 12 January 1949 and 17 January, 1949. 17 January 1949. E/ICEF 95.

Justification for Increased Allocation for Albania. 26 October 1948. E/ICEF/W.32.

Note by the Administration on the Anti-Syphilis Campaign. 15 July 1948. E/ICEF/W.19.
Note by the Executive Director on Voluntary Fund Raising in 1949 on Behalf of UNICEF. 11 January 1949. E/ICEF/W.42.
Programme Committee's Report to the Executive Board on Meetings Held in Hotel Majestic, Avenue Kleber, Paris, between 18th and 23rd August Inclusive, 1947. 17 September 1947. E.ICEF/23.
Proposed Plan of Operations for the Philippines. 20 January 1949. E/ICEF/W44.
Recommendation by Executive Director for an Apportionment to Syria for an Anti-Bejel Syphilis Campaign. 8 October 1951. E/ICEF/R.241.
Recommendation for an Allocation to Iraq for a Bejel/Syphilis Project. 31 May 1950. E/ICEF/R.63.
Recommendation of the Executive Director for the Allocation and Programme for Korea. 24 June 1949. E/ICEF/W.67.
Recommendation of the Executive Director for an Allocation for Finland. 18 October 1949. E/ICEF/W79.
Recommendation of Executive Director for an Allocation to Yugoslavia to Extend the Campaign Against Endemic Syphilis. 11 October 1951. E/ICEF/R.246.
Recommendation of Executive Director on Unutilized Portion of Hungarian UNICEF Allocation Following Closure of Hungarian Mission. 11 October 1949. E/ICEF/W.72.
Recommendation of the Executive Director for an Apportionment to China (Taiwan) for Control of Pre-Natal Syphilis. 12 September 1952. E/ICEF/R.371.
Recommendation of the Executive Director for an Apportionment to Morocco for the Control of Syphilis. 12 August 1953. E/ICEF/R.471.
Recommendations by the Executive Director for an Apportionment to Afghanistan for Continuation of a Maternal and Child Welfare and Anti-Syphilis Training and Service Programme. 2 October 1951. E/ICEF/R.230.
Recommendations by Executive Director on Yugoslavia. 29 June 1949. E/ICEF/W.70.
Recommendations of Executive Director for Additional Apportionment to India. 30 October 1949. E/ICEF/R.94.
Recommendations of the Executive Director Regarding Medical Programmes. 2 November 1948. E/ICEF/W.36.
Recommendations of the Executive Director Regarding Use of Anti-Syphilis Allocations. 14 October 1949. E/ICEF/W.76.
Report and Recommendations of the UNICEF-FAO Panel of Dairy Experts. 31 December 1949. E/ICEF/88.
Report by the Executive Director Regarding Supplemental Equipment for Penicillin Production Plants, Originally Provided by UNRRA. 17 June 1949. E/ICEF/W.66.
Report of the 58th Meeting of the Programme Committee. 17 August 1948. E/ICEF/76.
Report of the Executive Director to the 71st Meeting of the Programme Committee to be Held at Lake Success, 20 January 1949. 12 January 1949. E/ICEF/89.
Report of the Executive Director to the 93rd Meeting of the Programme Committee to be Held on 20 October 1949, New York City. 10 October 1949. E/ICEF/129.
Report of the Executive Director to the Twenty-Sixth Meeting of the Programme Committee on Current and Prospective Resources. 4 November 1947. E/ICEF/36.
Report of the Meeting of the Sub-Committee on Medical Projects Held on 5 March 1949, Paris. 6 April 1949. E/ICEF/111.
Report of the Programme Committee on the Forty-Seventh through Fifty-Second Meetings Held at the Paris Headquarters UNICEF, 3-5 July 1948. 11 July 1948. E/ICEF/73.
Report of the Programme Committee to the Tenth Meeting of the Executive Board Held at Lake Success, 29 September-1 October 1947. 1 October 1947. E/ICEF/26.
Report of the Session of the Medical Sub-Committee Held at Paris UNICEF Headquarters 9-10 August 1948. 5 October 1948. E/ICEF/77.
Report of the Sub-Committee on Medical Projects. 18 February 1948. E/ICEF/43.
Report of the Survey Mission to the Far East (Other Than China). 1 July 1948. E/ICEF/72.
Report on Special Missions to Korea by Dr. Marcel Junod Chief of UNICEF Mission, China 19-24 August 1948. 21 October 1948. E/ICEF/W26.

Report on U.N.I.C.E.F. Operations in the Middle East. 22 October 1948. E/ICEF/80.
Statement by Executive Director Regarding Allocations. 16 July 1948. E/ICEF/W.20.
Statement of Needs of Refugee Children and Mothers in the Middle East. 14 August 1948. E/ICEF/74.
Statement on Anti-Syphilis Campaign. 30 October 1948. E/ICEF/W.31.
Statement on Resources and Allocations as of June 30, 1948. 30 June 1948. E/ICEF/W8.
Yaws Eradication and Rural Syphilis Control Programme. 19 January 1950. E/ICEF/141.

INTERVIEWS (ACCESSED AT UNICEF ARCHIVES, UNICEF HOUSE, NEW YORK, NY)

Eliot, Martha May. Interviewed by Jeanette Cheek for the Schlesinger-Rockefeller Oral History Project. November 1973–May 1974.
Gann, Margaret. Interviewed by John Charnow. November 21, 1983.
Henderson, Julia. Interviewed by John Charnow. July 30–31, 1983.
Hyde, Henry Van Zile. Interviewed by Richard D. McKinzie for the Harry S. Truman Library. July 16, 1975 .
Sinclair, Adelaide. Interviewed by John Charnow. November 17–18, 1982.
Pantaleoni, Helenka. Interviewed by Richard Polsky for the Oral History Research Office, Columbia University. April 12, 1977.

OTHER UNICEF DOCUMENTS AND PUBLICATIONS

"50 Years of Goodwill Ambassadors for Children." 3 December 2003. UNICEF Press Release.
Alice C. Shaffer: Champion of the World's Children. July 1983. CF/NYH/OSEB/HST/1997-005.
Budget of Current Resources. 1947. E/ICEF/56.
Charnow, John. *The First Four Years of UNICEF.* 28 October 1985. HST/48.
———. *History of UNICEF* (Unpublished). 1964–1965. CF/HST 080.
Committee on Relations: Co-operation with United Nations, Relations with UNICEF. 29 January 1948. WHO.IC/R/44/Rev. 3. annexes 2 and 3.
The Contribution of UNICEF to the Peace Process. January, 1986. UNICEF History Project. HIST/50.
"Evolution of UNICEF's Programme Strategy." Excerpts of a paper prepared for the Rene Sand Award to UNICEF by International Council on Social Welfare. August, 1978. HIST/46.
Extension during 1949 of the United Nations Appeal for Children, December 8, 1949. General Assembly Resolution 215 (III).
"Fifty Years for Children." 21 September 1998.www.unicef.org/sow96/50years.htm.
General Remarks and Conditions of the VD Campaign in Slovakia. 6 July 1948. E/ICEF 68 add. 2, annex IV.
Grant, James P. "Our Departing Giants" (remarks made at the Farewell Party for Messrs. Heyward, Egger Charnow and Stein, 21 December 1981, New York). HST/51.
Lenroot, Katherine F. *United Nation Aid to the Developing Countries for Extending and Improving Their Services for Children and Youth.* 20 April 1961.
Letter from B. Kozusznik, M.D., to Earl H. Bell, Chief of Mission, United Nations International Children's Emergency Fund, Warsaw 18 June 1948. 6 July 1948. E/ICEF/68 add. 2, annex IV. *Letter from Dr. P. Gregoric, President of the Public Health Protection Committee, to Dr. D. Adler, Chief of UNICEF Mission in Belgrade, 9 June 1948.* 6 July 1948. E/ICEF/68 add. 2, annex IV.
Letter from F. Kopanaris, Director General of Hygiene, to Canon W.J. Edwards, Chief of the UNICEF Mission in Greece 17 May 1949. 6 July 1948. E/ICEF/68 add. 2, annex IV.

Letter from Olt Karoly, Minister of Public Welfare, to Dr. P. Descoeudres, Delegate of the UNICEF Mission in Hungary. 6 July 1948. E/ICEF/68 add. 2, annex IV.

Letter from Osk. Reinikainen, Chief Medical Officer and Taumo Putokonen, V.D. Control Officer, State Medical Board, Helsinki, Finland, to Dr. Henry Hemholz, United Nations Children's Emergency Fund, Paris. 6 July 1948. E/ICEF/68 add. 2, annex IV.

Main Trends in UNICEF's Policy: 1947-1980, by Charles A. Egger. January, 1986. HIST/45/ Rev. 1.

Maurice Pate: UNICEF Executive Director, 1947-1965. CF/HST/MON/1989-002.

Memorandum from Dr. Tibor Bielek, Chief Public Health Inspector, to Dr. Pierre Descoeudres, Chief of UNICEF Mission to Hungary 5 February 1948. 6 July 1948. E/ICEF/68 add. 2, annex IV.

Note Concerning the V.D. Campaign in Austria 26 May 1948. 6 July 1948. E/ICEF/68 add. 2, annex IV.

Note of WHO Secretariat on UNRRA Penicillin Plants. 9 March 1949. JC3/UNICEF-WHO/10.

Number of Syphilis Cases to be Treated by Penicillin. 6 July 1948. E/ICEF/68 add. 2, annex IV.

Nutrition and Health of Children in Five Countries of South America: Excerpts from a Report to the UNICEF Administration by Dr. R. Passmore, M.D. 15 November 1948. E/ICEF 83.

Plans for a General V.D. Control Campaign in the Federative People's Republic of Yugoslavia. 6 July 1948. E/ICEF/68 add. 2, annex IV.

Poland: Summary of Needs. 3 May 1948. E/ICEF/W.3 annex K.

Programme of the Campaign Against Endemic Syphilis in Yugoslavia. E/ICEF/68 add. 2, annex IV. 6 July 1948.

Progress Report of the Secretary-General on Implementation of Resolution 58 of the General Assembly on the Advisory Social Welfare Functions of UNRRA Transferred to the United Nations. 10 July 1947. E/458.

Provisional Report of Programme and Estimate of Expenses 1947 to be Submitted to the Fourth Session of the Economic and Social Council. 24 February 1947. E/ICEF/10.

Remarks by Miss Katherine Lenroot, March 8, 1971, at a Luncheon with UNICEF Friends on the Occasion of Her 80th Birthday. CF/HST/INT/LEN-001/M.

Report of FAO-WHO Committee on Child Nutrition (to Advise ICEF). E/ICEF/23 annex 3.

Report of the Fifth Meeting of the Committee on Administrative Budget Held at Lake Success, 15 March 1949. 31 March 1949. E/ICEF/110.

Report of the Special Technical Committee on Relief Needs after Termination of UNRRA, Rapporteur: Mr. J. H. Penson (United Kingdom). 23 January 1947.

Report of the Technical Agent of the Council on His Mission in China from the Date of His Appointment until April 1st, 1934. Series of League of Nations Publications, General, 1934, 1.

Report of the Third Session of the UNICEF/WHO Committee on Health Policy. 11 May 1949. E/ICEF/112.

Report on Nutrition and Health Aspects in Six UNICEF Countries in Europe by Dr. H.F. Helmholz and Dr. J. M. Latsky. 15 October 1948. E/ICEF/78.

Resolution on Relief Needs after the Termination of UNRRA Adopted by the General Assembly, Paragraph 8 (a) and (b) Report by the Secretary-General. 2 March 1947. E/300.

Romania. 6 July 1948. E/ICEF/68 add. 2, annex IV.

Roumania: Summary of Needs. 3 May 1948. E/ICEF/W.3 annex L.

Schmidt, William M. *Eulogy for Martha May Elliot, M.D.* Harvard University Memorial Church, Cambridge, Massachusetts, March 21, 1978.

Selskar Gunn to Dr. Vincent, April 7, 1928. League of Nations Health Section, January–May, 1929, Box 10, File 172. Geneva: Archives of the League of Nations.

Supplement to the National Plan to Combat Syphilis Among Pregnant Women and Children Under 18 Years of Age in Bulgaria. 6 July 1948. E/ICEF/68 add. 2, annex IV.

Supplementary Request for Supplies Additional to Those Included in the Original Plan. 6 July 1948. E/ICEF/68 add. 2, annex IV.

Trained Personnel Needed for the Field Survey of Endemic Syphilis. 6 July 1948. E/ICEF/68 add. 2, annex IV.

Trained Personnel Needed for the Medical Treatment of Endemic Syphilis. 6 July 1948. E/ICEF/68 add. 2, annex IV.

Treatment of Endemic Syphilis by Penicillin. 6 July 1948. E/ICEF/68 add. 2, annex IV.

UNICEF, A Pictorial Record: For All the World's Children. New York: United Nations International Children's Emergency Fund, August, 1952.

United Nations International Children's Emergency Fund, December 2, 1949. General Assembly Resolution 318 (V).

Yugoslavia: Summary of Needs. 3 May 1948. E/ICEF/W.3 annex M.

WHO/UNICEF Participation in Antisyphilis Campaigns: Progress Note by WHO Secretariat. 21 March 1949. JC3/UNICEF/WHO/9.

Who's Who in the UN, November, 1959.

MAURICE PATE PAPERS, SEELY G. MUDD MANUSCRIPT LIBRARY, PRINCETON UNIVERSITY LIBRARY, PRINCETON, NEW JERSEY

Box 4

Folder 1

Pate, Maurice. Letter to Edgar Rickard, April 6, 1921.

Folder 2

Hoover, Herbert. Address to the Gridiron Dinner, Washington, DC, May 10, 1947.

———. "Can Europe's Children be Saved?" Address delivered October 19, 1941.

Hull, Cordell, U.S. Secretary of State. Letter to Herbert Hoover, June 29, 1941.

Pate, Maurice. Letter to Herbert Hoover, August 9, 1944.

———. Letter to Herbert Hoover, March 4, 1947.

Folder 3

Hoover, Herbert. Letter to Maurice Pate, April 26, 1959.

Pate, Maurice. Letter to Herbert Hoover, April 24, 1959.

———. Letter to Mr. Harold Fleming, Editor, A.R.A. Association. March 16, 1961.

Folder 11

Maurice Pate. Letter to Mrs. John F. Kennedy, September 24, 1964.

Box 9

Folder 1

Buck, Pearl S. Letter to Martha Lucas Pate, March 15, 1965.

Campbell, W. Glenn. Letter to Mrs. Maurice Pate, March 11, 1965.

Fosdick, Raymond. Letter to Martha Lucas Pate, January 21, 1965.

Heyward, E. J. R. Letter to Mrs. Maurice (Martha Lucas) Pate, March 11, 1965.

Lindsay, Hon. John V. "Remarks on the Passing of Maurice Pate." Congressional Record, appendix, page A258. Washington, DC, January 25, 1965.

Pate, Martha Lucas. Letter to Mrs. D. S. (Adelaide) Sinclair and Mr. E. J. R. (Dick) Heyward, March 2, 1965.

"Rites Set for Prominent Ex-Denverite." *Rocky Mountain News*, January 20, 1965.
Thant, U, U.N. Secretary General. Information Circular ST/ADM/SER.A/984 20 January 1965 in re: death of Maurice Pate.
UNICEF Staff News. The Oslo Ceremonies, No. 290-13 January 1966.
United Nations. "Maurice Pate, UNICEF Executive Director for 18 Years, Dead at 70." New York, January 19, 1965.

Folder 4

UNICEF/Misc. 99. Statements made at the special meeting of the UNICEF Executive Board in memory of Maurice Pate. February 17, 1965.
UNICEF Staff News. *Maurice Pate, 1894-1965*. No. 287, 25 January 1965.

Box 13

Folder 1

Belgian League of Honor in the United States. Minutes of organizational meeting held December 1, 1936, New York.
————. Pamphlet including constitution, by-laws, members of Executive Committee, officers, and membership list. New York, 1936.
————. Receipt for lifetime membership fee of $5.00. New York, 1936.

Folder 2

"Banquet in Honor of Lieutenant Pate." *Morning Courier*, Warsaw, 29 August 1919.
Fitch, Don. "Denver Man Helps to Feed 50,000 Belgians."

Folder 3

Pate, Maurice. Letter to Ann, September 14, 1916.
————. Letter to his father, July 15, 1916.
————. Letter to his mother, June 27, 1916.
————. Letter to his mother and father, July 3, 1916.
————. Letter to his mother and father, July 11, 1916.
————. Letter to his mother and father, August 26, 1916.
————. Letter to his mother and father, September 22, 1916.
————. Letter to his mother and father, December 30, 1916.
————. Letter to his mother and father, February 28, 1917.
————. Letter to his mother and father, May 23, 1917.
————. Letter to his mother and father, June 14, 1917.
————. Letter to Richard, July 25, 1916.

Folder 4

Pate, Maurice. Diary, 1916–1917.

Folder 7

Directory of C.R.B. Members, May 1, 1939.

Folder 8

Pate, Maurice. "The Withdrawal of the American Commission from Belgium." 1917.

Folder 9

Pate, Maurice. CRB Identity Card, 1916.

Folder 11

American Relief Administration. "The Relief of the Children of Eastern Europe." Bulletin No.
2. New York, 1919.
The Commission for Relief in Belgium. *C.R.B. Bulletin.* Bulletins 5 and 6, No. 3. New York,
1919
————. Manual of Information for Representatives. 1917.
Smith, Robinson. Food Values and the Rationing of a Country, 3rd edition. New York: Commission for Relief in Belgium,1919.

Folder 14

Pate, Maurice. Letter to Dr. May Albuquerque, Women's and Children's Hospital, Bangalore,
India. May 24, 1946.

Box 14

Folder 1

Pate, Maurice. "Some Notes on Trip with Hoover Mission." President's Famine Emergency
Committee. *World Food Survey,* 1946.

Folder 12

Escudero, Professor Pedro. Letter to Maurice Pate, June 12, 1946.
Hoover, Herbert. Letter to President Harry Truman, May 13, 1946.
United Nations Relief and Rehabilitation Association. "Estimate for Providing a 2000 Calorie
Supplement for Children aged 7-9." Washington, DC: U.S. Government Printing Office,
1946.

Box 17

Folder 2

Commission for Polish Relief. Meeting minutes, June 8, 1942.
Paderwieski, I. J. Letter to Maurice Pate, January 21, 1941.

Folder 10

Galpin, Perrin C. Letter to Maurice Pate, February 13, 1947.
Hill, Martin. Letter to Ludwik Rajchman, January 10, 1947.
Hutson, J. B. Letter to Maurice Pate, January 27, 1947.
Pate, Maurice. Draft Letter of Resignation as UNICEF Executive Director to U Thant, Decem-
ber, 1964.
————. Letter to Annie, August 5, 1960.
————. Letter to Hallam Tuck, December 17, 1946.
————. Letter to Ludwik Rajchman, December 18, 1947.
————. Letter to Mr. Weir Stewart, August 5, 1953.
————. Letter to Trygve Lie, 27 January, 1947.
————. Memo to UNICEF Executive Board, August 24, 1953.

————. Notes on Conversation with Miss Lenroot and Mr. Schwartz of the Children's Bureau. January 30, 1947.
Ringland, Arthur. Letter to Maurice Pate, May 17, 1946.

Folder 11

Davidson, Al. Cable to Ludwik Rajchman, June 23, 1947.
————. Cable to Maurice Pate, 12:33 PM, July 15, 1947.
————. Cable to Maurice Pate, 2:45 PM, July 15, 1947.
————. Cable to Maurice Pate, July 17, 1947.
Pate, Maurice. Cable to Al Davidson, June 20, 1947.
————. Letter to Al Davidson, October 26, 1947.

Folder 14

Wechsberg, Joseph. "At the Heart of UNICEF." *The New Yorker*, December 2, 1961.

Box 18

Folder 2

Bernstein, Blanche. *UNICEF—the United Nations Children's Fund*. Washington, DC: U.S. Department of State, 1966.
United Nations Children's Fund. "UNICEF's Children." New York, 1952.

Folder 3

Davidson, A. E. Memorandum to T. L. Peers de Nieuwburgh, December 16, 1947.
Rajchman, Ludwik. Letter to Dr. Brock Chisholm, December 18, 1947.
————. Letter to Dr. Brock Chisholm, copies to Dr. MacDougall and Dr. Johannes Holm, 18 December, 1947.
————. Letter to Dr. Johannes Holm, December 16, 1947.
————. Letter to Dr. Madsen, December 17, 1947.
————. Letter to Dr. Madsen, Ref: C/14, December 17, 1947.
————. Letter to Wictorija Winnicka, December, 1947.
Rasmussen, Gustav. Cable to Ludwik Rajchman, 17 December, 1947.
Winnicka, Wictorija. Letter to Ludwik Rajchman, November, 1947.

Folder 4

Pate, Maurice. "Helping Children: An Investment in the Future." New York: UNICEF, 1961.
UNICEF Staff News. *Acceptance Speech by Mr. Labouisse; Nobel Lecture by Mrs. Harman; Observations by Mrs. (Adelaide) Sinclair, Mrs. (Helenka) Pantaleoni, and Mr. Ling*. No. 290, 13 January, 1966.
United Nations International Children's Emergency Fund. Lists of Field Personnel in Europe and Eastern Mediterranean Regional Office, International Children's Center, Asia Regional Office, Area Office for Central America and the Caribbean. June 1, 1951.

Folder 5

Egger, Charles. Report to Dick (Mr. E. R. J. Heyward) Regarding Visit to Portugal and Spain. December 8, 1953.
Koleilat, Rachid A. Notes on Mr. Pate's Visit to Damascus. 28-30 December 1953.
————. Notes on trip to Beirut, December 24, 1953-January 9, 1954.

Pate, Maurice. Letter to Charles [Egger], December 14, 1953.
———. Letter to Charles Egger, December 20, 1953.
———. Letter to Dick (Mr. E. R. J. Heyward), November 28, 1953.
———. Notes on trip to the Middle East, January 5, 1954.
UNICEF Staff News. "Mr. Pate Returns." No. 138, Item 1474, 22 January 1954.
United Nations Children's Fund. *The Compendium*, Vol IV, 1953–1954.
———. Notes on Maurice Pate's Last Illness, January 27, 1965.
Ward, Dudley. Letter to Maurice Pate, January 27, 1954.

OVERSIZED MATERIALS

Box 22

International Children's Emergency Fund. "Today's Children—Tomorrow's Leaders." Lake Success, NY, April, 1947.
Owen, A. D. K., Acting Secretary-General. Letter Template for Soliciting Contributions to UNICEF. January 23, 1947.
Pate, Maurice. Letter to the Honorable George C. Marshall, U.S. Secretary of State. January 23, 1947.
United Nations International Children's Emergency Fund. "Facts about U.N.I.C.E.F." April, 1947.
U.S. Department of Agriculture Famine Emergency Committee. "The Children Are Hungry." Washington, DC: U.S. Government Printing Office, 1946.

Box 23

"$9,814,000 U.S. Aid to Children's Fund Hailed at U.N. as Benefitting 20,000,000." *New York Times*, August 5, 1953.
"U.N. Child Fund Made Permanent in Face of Threatened U.S. Aid Cut." *New York Times*, Special, Geneva, July 20, 1953.
"UN Fires Woman Press Aide, Self-Admitted Red." *Evening American*, January 22, 1953, 6.
"Unicef Meets, Rejects Red Bid to Unseat Nationalist Chinese." *U.N. Yesterday*, September 8, 1953.

NATIONAL ARCHIVES OF THE UNITED STATES, MARYLAND FACILITY, OFFICE OF FOREIGN RELIEF AND REHABILITATION OPERATIONS, GENERAL SUBJECT FILE 1942–1943, RECORD GROUP 169, FILE LOCATION 169.5

Burland, E. G., Associate Chief, Division of Field Operations. Letter to Mr. Fryer, September 11, 1943.
Hildring, J. H., Major General, Chief, Civil Affairs Division, War Department. Letter to the Honorable Herbert H. Lehman, Director, Office of Foreign Relief and Rehabilitation Operations, 27 August 1943.
Jackson, Mr. H. R. Letter to Mr. Gulick, January 23, 1943.
Lehman, Herbert H., Director of UNRRA. Letter to Frances Perkins, Secretary of Labor, December 15, 1942.
———. Letter to Frances Perkins, Secretary of Labor, March 12, 1943.
Lenroot, Katharine F., Chief, U.S. Children's Bureau. Letter to Dr. Luther Gulick, Chief, Program and Requirements Division, Office of Foreign Relief and Rehabilitation Operations, March 15, 1943.

Schmidt, William M., M. D. Memorandum Regarding Rations for Infants, Children and Pregnant and Nursing Mothers in the Relief Program. September 10, 1943.

Sexauer, Fred H., President, Dairymen's League Co-Operative Association, Inc. Letter to Mr. Herbert H. Lehman, Office of Foreign Relief and Rehabilitation Operation, May 21, 1943.

Weintraub, David. Memorandum and Report to Mr. Lithgow Osborne, Department of State, Office of Foreign Relief and Rehabilitation Operations, May 21, 1943.

LIBRARY OF CONGRESS, WASHINGTON, DC, BUSINESS AND SCIENCE READING ROOM

"A Children's Charter in Wartime." Children in Wartime No. 2, Bureau Publication 283, United States Children's Bureau. Washington: U.S. Government Printing Office, 1942.

"America's Contribution through Food Administration: A Letter to the President by Herbert Hoover, United States Food Administrator." Washington: Government Printing Office, 1918.

"America's New Opportunities in World Trade." Planning Pamphlet Nos. 37–38. Washington, DC: National Planning Association, 1944.

Bradley, Frances Sage, MD, and Florence Brown Sherbon, MD. "How to Conduct a Children's Health Conference." Miscellaneous Series No. 9, Bureau Publication No. 23, U.S. Department of Labor; Children's Bureau, Julia C. Lathrop, Chief. Washington: Government Printing Office, 1917.

"Care of Children Coming to the United States for Safety Under the Attorney General Order of July 13, 1940, Standards Prescribed by the Children's Bureau." Bureau Publication No. 268, U.S. Department of Labor, Frances Perkins, Secretary; Children's Bureau, Katharine Lenroot, Chief. Washington: U.S. Government Printing Office, 1941.

Charnow, John. "Topics for Research Concerning Public Assistance Programs." Pamphlet Series No. 6. Washington, DC: Committee on Social Security of the Social Science Research Council, 1941.

Children in Bondage: A Survey of Child Life in the Occupied Countries of Europe and Finland Conducted by the Save the Children Fund. London: Longmans, Green and Co., 1942.

"Children's Health Centers." Children's Leaflet No. 5, Bureau Publication No. 45, U.S. Department of Labor; Children's Bureau, Julia C. Lathrop, Chief. Washington, DC: Government Printing Office, 1918.

"Community Action for Children in Wartime." Publication No. 295, U.S. Department of Labor, Frances Perkins, Secretary; Children's Bureau, Katharine Lenroot, Chief. Washington: U.S. Government Printing Office, 1943.

Dobbs, Josephine. *The Children's Charter (The Declaration of Genva).* Geneva: Save the Children Fund International Union, 1924.

"Economic Recovery in the Countries Assisted by UNRRA: Report Presented by the Director General of UNRRA to the Secretary-General of the United Nations." Washington, DC: United Nations Relief and Rehabilitation Administration, 1946.

"Fifty Facts about UNRRA." London: His Majesty's Stationary Office, 1946.

First Quarterly Report on UNRRA Expenditures and Operations. Seventy-Eighth Congress, 2nd Session, House Document No. 803. Washington: U.S. Government Printing Office, 1944.

"Food for Europe After Victory." Planning Pamphlet No. 29. Washington, DC: National Planning Association, 1944.

"Grants to States for Maternal and Child Welfare Under the Social Security Act, Approved August 14, 1935. Title V, Parts 1, 2, 3. Maternal and Child Health Services, Services for Crippled Children, Child-Welfare Services." Maternal and Child Welfare Bulletin No. 1, U.S. Department of Labor, Frances Perkins, Secretary; Children's Bureau, Katharine F. Lenroot, Chief. Washington: United Sates Government Printing Office, 1935.

"If Your Baby Must Travel in Wartime." Children in Wartime No. 6, Bureau Publication 307, U.S. Department of Labor, Frances Perkins, Secretary; Children's Bureau, Katharine Lenroot, Chief. Washington, DC: U.S. Government Printing Office, 1944.

"Laws Relating to 'Mothers' Pensions' in the United States, Denmark and New Zealand."
Dependent Children Series No. 1, Bureau Publication No. 7. U.S. Department of Labor;
Children's Bureau, Julia C. Lathrop, Chief. Washington: Government Printing Office, 1914.

Lowenberg, Miriam E. "Food for Young Children in Group Care." Children in Wartime No. 4,
Bureau Publication No. 285, U.S. Department of Labor, Frances Perkins, Secretary; Chil-
dren's Bureau, Katharine Lenroot, Chief. Washington: United States Government Printing
Office, 1942.

Lundberg, Emma O. "Public Aid to Mothers with Dependent Children: Extent and Fundamental Principles." Bureau Publication No. 162. U.S. Department of Labor, James J. Davis,
Secretary; Children's Bureau, Grace Abbott, Chief. Washington: Government Printing Office, 1926.

Mander, Sir Frederick, and J. G. Browne. "Billeting in Brief: The Care of Children in Time of
War." Bedford: Castle Press, Rogers G. Porter, Ltd., Printers, 1939.

McGill, Nettie. "Infant Welfare Work in Europe: An Account of Recent Experiences in Great
Britain, Austria, Belgium, France, Germany and Italy." Community Child Welfare Services
Series No. 1, Bureau Publication No. 76. U.S. Department of Labor, W. B. Wilson, Secretary; Children's Bureau, Julia C. Lathrop, Chief. Washington: Government Printing Office,
1921.

Meigs, Grace L., M.D. "Maternal Mortality From All Conditions Connected with Childbirth in
the United States and Certain Other Countries." Miscellaneous Series No. 6, Bureau Publication No. 10. U.S. Department of Labor; Children's Bureau, Julia C. Lathrop, Chief.
Washington: Government Printing Office, 1917.

Nesbitt, Florence. "Standards of Public Aid to Children in Their Own Homes." Bureau Publication No. 118, U.S. Department of Labor, James J. Davis, Secretary; Children's Bureau,
Grace Abbot, Chief. Washington, DC: Government Printing Office, 1923.

"Our Greatest National Asset: Is It Well with the Child?" London: Save the Children Fund,
1938.

"Recommendation of the White House Conference on Children in a Democracy, January 18-
20, 1940." Washington, DC: U.S. Government Printing Office, 1940.

"Relief for Children: Selected Statements, United Nations Resolutions, September 21-Decem-
ber 12, 1948." The Department of State Office of Public Affairs. Washington: U.S. Government Printing Office, 1949.

"Relief for Starving Peoples of War-Stricken Areas: Report on A Resolution on UNRRA
Adopted at the 21st Plenary Meeting of the United Nations General Assembly Held in
London on February 1, 1946." Committee on Foreign Affairs, House of Representatives,
Seventy-Ninth Congress, 2nd Session. Washington: United States Government Printing Of-
fice, 1946.

Report of the Director General to the Council for the Period 1 January 1946 to 31 March 1946.
Washington, DC: UNRRA, 1946.

Report of the Director General to the Council for Period 1 July 1946 to 30 September 1946.
Washington, DC: UNRRA, 1946.

Report of the Director General to the Council for Period 1 October 1946 to 31 December 1946.
Washington, DC: UNRRA, 1946.

Report of the Director General to the Council for Period 1 January 1947 to 31 March 1947.
Washington, DC: UNRRA, 1947.

"Report on a Joint Mission to Evaluate the Lesotho Expanded Programme on Immunization."
The Kingdom of Lesotho Ministry of Health, Save the Children Fund, United Nations
Children's Fund, World Health Organization. Lesotho: Mazenod Institute, 1982.

Report to Congress, U.S. Financial Participation in the United Nations Children's Fund.
Department of State B-166780. Washington, DC: The Comptroller General of the United
States, 1969.

"Services for Children of Working Mothers in War Time: A Manual for Child Care Committees of Local Defense Councils." OCD Publication 3625. The Office of Civil Defense with
the Cooperation of the Office of Defense Health and Welfare Services, the U.S. Office of
Education of the Federal Security Agency and the Children's Bureau of the U.S. Department
of Labor. Washington: U.S. Government Printing Office, 1943.

"Standards for Day Care of Children of Working Mothers: Report on the Subcommittee on Standards and Services for Day Care Authorized by the Children's Bureau Conference on Day Care of Children of Working Mothers." Children in Wartime No. 3, Bureau Publication 284, United States Department of Labor, Children's Bureau. Washington: United States Government Printing Office, 1942.

"To Parents in Wartime." Children in Wartime No. 1, Bureau Publication 282, Children's Bureau, United States Department of Labor (Washington: Library of Congress, May 23, 1942, Government Pub'ns. R.R., 1942).

"The Children's Bureau: Yesterday, Today and Tomorrow." United States Department of Labor, Frances Perkins, Secretary; Children's Bureau, Katharine Lenroot, Chief. Washington: United States Government Printing Office, 1937.

"The Nation's Concern for the Health of Mothers and Babies: Seven Years of Federal Aid for the Promotion of the Hygiene of Maternity and Infancy and the Effort to Secure Its Renewal." Washington, DC: Committee on Child Welfare, League of Women Voters, 1931.

"The Production, Distribution and Food Value of Milk: A Report to Herbert C. Hoover, United States Food Administrator." The Milk Committee. Washington: Government Printing Office, 1918.

"UNRRA: Gateway to Recovery." Planning Pamphlet Nos. 30–31. Washington, DC: National Planning Association, 1944.

"UNRRA: Organization, Aims, Progress." Washington, DC: United Nations Relief and Rehabilitation Administration Press of Graphic Arts Press, Inc., 1945.

West, Mrs. Max. "Child Care: Part 1. The Preschool Age." Care of Children Series No. 3, Bureau Publication No. 30. U.S. Department of Labor; Children's Bureau, Julia C. Lathrop, Chief. Washington: Government Printing Office, 1918.

———. "Prenatal Care." Care of Children Series No. 1, Bureau Publication No. 4, 2nd edition. U.S. Department of Labor; Children's Bureau, Julia C. Lathrop, Chief. Washington: Government Printing Office, 1913.

OTHER PRIMARY SOURCES

A Brief History of the United Nations. New York: United Nations Office of Publications, 2004.

Charter of the United Nations. New York: United Nations Official Documents, 1945.

"Development Begins with Women." In *UNICEF News*, Issue 104, Volume 2, 1980.

Food and Agriculture Organization of the United Nations. *World Food Survey.* Washington, DC, July 5, 1946.

Foreign Relations of the United States, Vol. I, 1941. Washington, DC: US Government Printing Office, 1958.

Foreign Relations of the United States, Vol. IV, 1934. American Consul in Geneva. "The Consul in Geneva to the Secretary of State, Geneva, July 13, 1934." Washington, DC: U.S. Government Printing Office, 1934.

Hoover, Herbert C. *An American Epic, Volume I: Introduction: The Relief of Belgium and Northern France, 1914-1930.* Chicago: Henry Regnery Co., 1959.

———. *Further Addresses upon the American Road, 1938-1940.* New York: Charles Scribner's Sons, 1940.

———. *The Memoirs of Herbert Hoover, Volume I: Years of Adventure, 1874-1920.* New York: The MacMillan Company, 1957.

"Hoover Says Poles Must Rise Again." *New York Times*, April 29, 1940.

League of Nations, Provisional Health Committee. *Minutes of the First Session, Geneva, August 25-29, 1921.* Geneva: United Nations Office at Geneva, 1921.

Lenroot, Katharine. *United Nations Aid to the Developing Countries for Extending and Improving Their Services for Children and Youth.* Presented April 20, 1961. New York.

Lenroot, Katharine F., and Emma O. Lundberg. *Juvenile Courts at Work: A Study of the Organization and Methods of Ten Courts.* Washington, DC: Government Printing Office, 1925.

Pilsudski, Joseph. *The Memoirs of a Polish Revolutionary and Soldier.* London: Faber and Faber, 1935.

Rajchman, Ludwik. "Why Not? A United Nations Public Health Service." *Free World,* 6, no. 3 (September 1943): 216–21.

Sixth Pan-American Child Congress, Lima, July 4-11, 1930. Report of the Delegates of the United States of America. Washington, DC: United States Government Printing Office, 1931.

The Story of UNRRA. Pamphlet issued by the Office of Public Information, United Nations Relief and Rehabilitation Administration. Washington, DC, February 15, 1949.

The Structure of the United Nations [1947]. United Nations Publication Sales No.: 1947.112.

The Structure of the United Nations, 1949. New York: United Nations Department of Public Information. Research Section, 1949.

Tacon, Sheila. Interviewed by Jennifer Morris. October 16, 1998. Interview in possession of the author.

Tenth Report to Congress on Operations of UNRRA Under the Act of March 28, 1944 as of December 31, 1946. Washington, DC: U.S. Government Printing Office, Department of State Publication 2800, 1947.

United Nations Interim Commission on Food and Agriculture. *The Work of FAO.* Washington, DC, August 20, 1945.

U.S. Congressional Record. Resolution by the U.S. Congress, November 9, 1943, Approving U.S. Participation in UNRRA. Washington, DC, 1943.

U.S. Department of State. "Declaration Regarding the Defeat of Germany and the Assumption of Supreme Authority with Respect to Germany by the Governments of the United States of America, the Union of Soviet Socialist Republics, the United Kingdom and the Provisional Government of the French Republic." June 5, 1945. *Treaties and Other International Agreements of the United States of America.* Volume 3.

U.S. Department of State. The United States and the United Nations: Report by the President to the Congress for the Year 1946. Washington, DC: U.S. Government Printing Office, 1947.

U.S. House of Representatives Subcommittee of the Committee on Appropriations. A House Joint Resolution Making Appropriations for the United Nations Relief and Rehabilitation Administration for the Fiscal Year 1946: Hearings before the Subcommittee of the Committee on Appropriations. Seventy-Ninth Congress, First Session, 1945.

U.S. Senate Subcommittee of the Committee on Appropriations. H.J. Res. 266, A Joint Resolution Making an Additional Appropriation for the United Nations Relief and Rehabilitation Administration for 1946: Hearings before the Subcommittee of the Committee on Appropriations. Seventy-ninth Congress, First Session, 1945.

Woodward, Patricia, Natalie F. Joffee, Marjorie Janis, and Eva Shippee. *The Role of Milk in American Culture.* Washington, DC: Committee on Food Habits, National Research Council, 1943.

SECONDARY SOURCES AND SCHOLARLY ARTICLES

Alvah, Donna. "'I Am Too Young to Die': Children and the Cold War." *OAH Magazine of History* 24, no. 4 (October 2010): 25-28.

Bacot, John. *A Treatise on Syphilis: In which the History, Symptoms, and Method of Treating Every Form of That Disease, Are Fully Considered.* London: Longman, Rees, Orme, Brown and Green, 1829.

Barker, L., Randol, John R. Burton, Phillip D. Zieve, eds., and Thomas E. Finucane, assoc. ed. *Principles of Ambulatory Medicine.* Baltimore: Williams & Wilkins Co., 1998.

Belfrage, Cedric. *The American Inquisition, 1945-1960.* Indianapolis: The Bobbs-Merrill Company, Inc., 1973.

Bennett, A. Leroy. *International Organizations: Principles and Issues.* Englewood Cliffs, NJ: Prentice Hall, 1988.

Berkovitch, Nitza. *From Motherhood to Citizenship: Women's Rights and International Organizations.* Baltimore: Johns Hopkins University Press, 1999.

Best, Gary Dean. *Herbert Hoover: The Postpresidential Years, 1933-1964.* Stanford: Hoover Institution Press, 1983.

Black, Maggie. *The Children and the Nations: The Story of UNICEF.* New York: UNICEF, 1986.

————. *Children First: The Story of UNICEF, Past and Present.* New York: Oxford University Press, 1996.

Blazanco, Andre. *VD: Facts You Should Know.* New York: Lothrop, Lee & Shepard Co., 1970.

Bock, Gisela, and Pat Thane, eds. *Maternity and Gender Policies: Women and the Rise of the European Welfare States, 1880s-1950s.* London: Routledge, 1991.

Bray, R. S. *Armies of Pestilence: The Impact of Disease on History.* New York: Barnes and Noble Books, 1996.

Breines, Wini. "Domineering Mothers in the 1950's: Image and Reality. In *Women's Studies International Forum,* Volume 8, Number 6, 1985.

Brysk, Alison, and Gershon Shafir, eds. *People Out of Place: Globalization, Human Rights, and the Citizenship Gap.* New York: Routledge, 2004.

Calder, Ritchie. "Growing Up with UNICEF." *Public Affairs Pamphlet No. 330.* New York: Public Affairs Committee, 1962.

Connelly, Matthew. *Fatal Misconception: The Struggle to Control World Population.* Cambridge, MA: The Belknap Press of Harvard University, 2008.

Digby, Anne, and John Stewart, eds. *Gender, Health and Welfare.* New York: Routledge, 1996.

Dobbs, Josephine. *The Children's Charter (The Declaration of Geneva).* Geneva: Save the Children Fund International Union, 1924.

Donovan, Robert J. *Tumultuous Years: The Presidency of Harry S Truman, 1949-1953.* New York: W. W. Norton & Company, 1982.

Dutcher, Addison Porter. *Pulmonary Tuberculosis: its Pathology, Nature, Symptoms, Diagnosis, Prognosis, Causes, Hygiene, and Medical Treatment.* Philadelphia: J. B. Lippincott & Co., 1875.

Dwork, Deborah. *War Is Good for Babies and Other Young Children. A History of the Infant and Child Welfare Movement in England, 1898-1918.* London: Tavistock Publications, 1987.

Eagleton, Clyde, ed. *Annual Review of United Nations Affairs.* New York: New York University Press, 1949.

Eder, Franz X., Lesley A. Hall, and Gert Hekma, eds. *Sexual Cultures in Europe: Themes in Sexuality.* Manchester: Manchester University Press, 1999.

Encyclopedia of Social Work, 18th edition, vol. 2. Silver Spring, MD: National Association of Social Workers, Inc., 1987.

Enloe, Cynthia. *The Morning After: Sexual Politics at the End of the Cold War.* Berkeley: University of California Press, 1993.

Everingham, Christine. *Motherhood and Modernity: An Investigation into the Rational Dimension of Mothering.* Buckingham, PA: Open University Press, 1994.

Faderman, Lillian. *To Believe in Women: What Lesbians Have Done For America—A History.* Boston: Houghton Mifflin Company, 1999.

Fildes, Valerie, Lara Marks, and Hilary Marland, eds. *Women and Children First: International Maternal and Infant Welfare, 1870-1945.* New York: Routledge, 1992.

Fisher, H. H. *The Famine in Soviet Russia, 1919-1923: The Operations of the American Relief Administration.* New York: The MacMillan Company, 1927.

Footitt, Hilary. "American Forces in France: Communist Representations of US Deployment." *Cold War History* 11, no. 1 (February 2011): 85–98.

Freeman, Kathleen. *If Any Man Build: The History of the Save the Children Fund.* London: Hodder and Stoughton, 1965.

Fuller, Edward. *The Right of the Child: A Chapter in Social History.* London: Victor Gollancz, Ltd., 1951.

Gardiner, Frances, ed. *Sex Equality Policy in Western Europe.* New York: Routledge, 1997.

Gordon, Linda. *Pitied but Not Entitled: Single Mothers and the History of Welfare.* New York: The Free Press, 1994.

Hambidge, Gove. *The Story of FAO.* New York: D. Van Nostrand Company, Inc., 1955.

Hazzard, Virginia. *UNICEF and Women, the Long Voyage: A Historical Perspective.* Geneva: United Nations Children's Fund, 1987.

Heilbroner, Robert L. "Mankind's Children: The Story of UNICEF." *Public Affairs Pamphlet No. 279.* Public Affairs Committee, 1959.

Henig, Ruth B. *The League of Nations.* Edinburgh: Oliver and Boyd, 1973.

Herman, Arthur. *Joseph McCarthy: Reexamining the Life and Legacy of America's Most Hated Senator.* New York: The Free Press, 2000.

Higonnet, Margaret Randolph, Jane Jenson, Sonya Michel, and Margaret Collins Weitz, eds. *Behind the Lines: Gender and the Two World Wars.* New Haven: Yale University Press, 1987.

Hirshberg, Lauren. "Nuclear Families: (Re)producing 1950s Suburban America in the Marshall Islands." *OAH Magazine of History* 26, no. 4 (October 2012): 39-54.

Hitchcock, William I. *France Restored: Cold War Diplomacy and the Quest for Leadership in Europe, 1944-1954.* Chapel Hill: The University of North Carolina Press, 1998.

Hogan, Michael J. *The Marshall Plan: America, Britain, and the Reconstruction of Western Europe, 1947-1952.* Cambridge: Cambridge University Press, 1987.

International Children's Center.http://childhouse.uio.no/childwatch/key/cie/index.html.

Iriye, Akira. *Global Community: The Role of International Organizations in the Making of the Contemporary World.* Berkeley: University of California Press, 2002.

Judt, Tony. *Postwar: A History of Europe Since 1945.* New York: The Penguin Press, 2005.

Kandal, Terry R. *The Woman Question in Classical Sociological Theory.* Miami: Florida International University Press, 1988.

Keeney, S. M. *Half the World's Children: A Diary of UNICEF at Work in Asia.* New York: Association Press, 1957.

Kellogg, Charlotte. *Women of Belgium: Turning Tragedy into Triumph.* New York: Funk and Wagnalls Company, 1917.

Kellogg, Vernon. *Herbert Hoover: The Man and His Work.* New York: D. Appleton and Company, 1920.

Kennedy, Paul. *The Parliament of Man: The Past, Present and Future of the United Nations.* New York: Random House, 2006.

Kessler-Harris, Alice. *In Pursuit of Equity: Women, Men and the Quest for Economic Citizenship in Twentieth-Century America.* Oxford: Oxford University Press, 2001.

Killick, John. *The United States and European Reconstruction, 1945-1960.* Edinburgh: Keele University Press, 1997.

Koonz, Claudia. *Mothers in the Fatherland: Women, the Family and Nazi Politics.* New York: St. Martin's Press, 1987.

Koven, Seth, and Sonya Michel, eds. *Mothers of a New World: Maternalist Politics and the Origins of Welfare States.* New York: Routledge, 1993.

Kraus, Allen Kramer. *Environment and Resistance in Tuberculosis: A Presentation of the Environment and Resistance and Their Relation to the Pathology, Diagnosis, Symptoms and Treatment of Tuberculosis.* Baltimore: Williams & Wilkins Co., 1923.

Kundanis, M. "'Baby Riots' and 'Eight Hour Orphans': A Comparison of the Images of Child Care in British and U.S. Popular Magazines during World War II." In *Women's Studies International Forum*, Volume 19, Number 23, 1993.

Latour, Bruno. *The Pasteurization of France.* Translated by Alan Sheridan and John Law. Cambridge: Harvard University Press, 1988.

Leitch, Alexander. *A Princeton Companion.* Princeton: Princeton University Press, 1978.

Lerski, George J., ed. *Herbert Hoover and Poland: A Documentary History of a Friendship.* Stanford: Hoover Institution Press, 1977.

Letherby, Gayle. "Mother or Not, Mother or What? Problems of Definition and Identity." In *Women's Studies International Forum*, Volume 17, Number 5, 1994.

Lindenmeyer, Kriste. *"A Right to Childhood": The U.S. Children's Bureau and Child Welfare, 1912-1946.* Urbana: University of Illinois Press, 1997.

Little, Marjorie. *Sexually Transmitted Diseases.* New York: Chelsea House Publishers, 1991.

Mahood, Linda. *Feminism and Voluntary Action: Eglantyne Jebb and Save the Children, 1876-1928.* New York: Palgrave Macmillan, 2009.

Maier, Charles S., ed. *The Cold War In Europe: Era of a Divided Continent*. Princeton: Marcus Wiener Publishers, 1996.

Margulies, Herbert F. *Senator Lenroot of Wisconsin: A Political Biography, 1900-1929*. Columbia: University of Missouri Press, 1977.

Marr, Lisa. *Sexually Transmitted Diseases: A Physician Tells You What You Need To Know*. Baltimore: The Johns Hopkins University Press, 1998.

Marrus, Michael R. *The Unwanted: European Refugees in the Twentieth Century*. New York: Oxford University Press, 1985.

Martin, R. B. *Save the Children: The Story of Eglantyne Jebb*. London: Lutterworth Press, 1969.

May, Elaine Tyler. *Homeward Bound: American Families in the Cold War Era*. New York: Basic Books, Inc., Publishers, 1988.

Mazower, Mark. *Dark Continent: Europe's Twentieth Century*. New York: Vintage Books, 1998.

———. *Governing the World: The History of an Idea, 1815 to the Present*. New York: Penguin Books, 2013.

———. *No Enchanted Palace: The End of Empire and the Ideological Origins of the United Nations*. Princeton and Oxford: Princeton University Press, 2009.

Melman, Billie, ed. *Borderlines: Genders and Identities in War and Peace, 1870-1930*. New York: Routledge, 1998.

Meyer, Oscar Daniel. *That Degenerate Spirochete*. New York: Vantage Press, 1952.

Michel, Sonya. *Children's Interests/Mother's Rights: The Shaping of America's Child Care Policy*. New Haven: Yale University Press, 1999.

Middlemas, Keith. *Power, Competition and the State: Britain in Search of Balance, 1940-61*. Stanford: Hoover Institution Press, 1986.

Milward, Alan S. *The Reconstruction of Western Europe, 1945-1951*. Berkeley: University of California Press, 1984.

Moeller, Robert G. *Protecting Motherhood: Women and the Family in the Politics of Postwar West Germany*. Berkeley: University of California Press, 1993.

Morant-Sanchez, Regina Markell. *Sympathy and Science: Women Physicians in American Medicine*. New York: Oxford University Press, 1985.

Murpy, John. "Shaping the Cold War Family: Politics, Domesticity and Policy Interventions in the 1950s." *Australian Historical Studies* 26, no. 105 (October 1995): 544–68.

Murray, Robert K. *The Harding Era: Warren G. Harding and His Administration*. Minneapolis: University of Minnesota Press, 1969.

Mutari, Ellen, Heather Boushey, and William Fraher IV, eds. *Gender and Political Economy: Incorporating Diversity into Theory and Policy*. Armonk, NY: M.E. Sharpe, Inc., 1997.

Nash, George H. *The Life of Herbert Hoover: The Humanitarian, 1914-1917*. New York: W.W. Norton & Company, 1988.

Nash, Lee, ed. *Understanding Herbert Hoover: Ten Perspectives*. Stanford: Hoover Institution Press, 1987.

Northedge, F. S. *The League of Nations: Its Life and Times, 1920-1946*. New York: Holmes and Meier, 1986.

O'Brien, James J. *The Great Humanitarian? How Hoover Brought America into the World War, Prolonged War Two Years by Feeding German Army in Belgium and People in Germany, Hoover and Franquie Sold Food at Three Profits to Belgians and Germans*. New York: Multiple Duplicating Check Co., Publishers, 1932.

Offner, Arnold A., and Theodore A. Wilson. *Victory in Europe, 1945: From World War to Cold War*. Lawrence: University Press of Kansas, 2000.

Oriel, J. D. *The Scars of Venus: A History of Venereology*. London: Springer-Verlag, 1994.

Ortner, Sherry B. *Making Gender: The Politics and Erotics of Culture*. Boston: Beacon Press, 1996.

Parish, Henry James. *A History of Immunization*. Edinburgh: E & S Livingstone, 1965.

Patenaude, Bertrand M. *The Big Show in Bololand: The American Relief Expedition to Soviet Russia in the Famine of 1921*. Stanford: Stanford University Press, 2002.

Patenaude, Bertrand M. "Herbert Hoover's Brush with Bolshevism." Washington, DC: The Kennan Institute for Advanced Russian Studies at the Woodrow Wilson International Center for Scholars, 1992.

Pedersen, Susan. *Family, Dependence, and the Origins of the Welfare State, Britain and France, 1914-1945.* New York: Cambridge University Press, 1993.

Pettman, Jan Jindy. "Globalisation and the Gendered Politics of Citizenship." In *Women, Citizenship and Difference,* Nira Yuval-Davis and Pnina Werbner, eds. New York: Zed Books, 1999.

Phillips, Kim M., and Barry Reay, eds. *Sexualities in History: A Reader.* New York: Routledge, 2002.

Pietila, Hilkka, and Jeanne Vickers. *Making Women Matter: The Role of the United Nations.* London: Zed Books, 1990.

Pinder, John. *The Building of the European Union.* Oxford: Oxford University Press, 1998.

Pirkey, Janet B. *A Gift from the Heart: Profile of Helenka Adamowska Pantaleoni, American Volunteer and Founding Spirit of UNICEF.* Franktown, CO: JP Enterprises, 1986.

Piven, Frances Fox, and Richard A. Cloward. *Poor People's Movements: Why They Succeed, How They Fail.* New York: Pantheon Books, 1977.

———. *Regulating the Poor: The Functions of Public Welfare.* New York: Pantheon Books, 1971.

Prior, Katherine. *UNICEF.* New York: Franklin Watts, 2001.

Quack, Sibylle, ed. *Between Sorrow and Strength: Women Refugees of the Nazi Period.* New York: Cambridge University Press, 1995.

Richardson, Diane. *Women, Motherhood and Childrearing.* New York: St. Martin's Press, 1993.

Roberts, Mary Louise. "The Price of Discretion: Prostitution, Venereal Disease, and the American Military in France, 1944-1946." *American Historical Review* (October 2010): 1002–30.

Ruttan, Vernon W., ed. *Why Food Aid?* Baltimore: The Johns Hopkins University Press, 1993.

Sainsbury, Diane, ed. *Gendering Welfare States.* London: Sage, 1994.

Saltman, Jules. *Immunization for All.* New York: Public Affairs Committee, 1967.

Schrecker, Ellen. *The Age of McCarthyism: A Brief History with Documents.* New York: Bedford Books, 1994.

Schulze, Max-Stephan, ed. *Western Europe: Economic and Social Change since 1945.* London: Longman, 1999.

Scott, James C. *Seeing Like a State: How Certain Schemes to Improve the Human Condition Have Failed.* New Have: Yale University Press, 1998.

Scott, Joan Wallach. *Gender and the Politics of History.* New York: Columbia University Press, 1988.

Sen, Gita, and Caren Grown. *Development, Crises and Alternative Visions: Third World Women's Perspectives.* New York: Monthly Review Press, 1987.

Sidel, Ruth. *Women and Children Last: The Plight of Poor Women in Affluent America.* New York: Penguin Books, 1992.

Siim, Birte. *Gender and Citizenship: Politics and Agency in France, Britain and Denmark.* Cambridge: Cambridge University Press, 2000.

Skran, Claudena M. *Refugees in Inter-War Europe: The Emergence of a Regime.* Oxford: Clarendon Press, 1995.

Spiegelman, Judith M., and UNICEF. *We Are the Children: A Celebration of UNICEF's First Forty Years.* New York: The Atlantic Monthly Press, 1986.

Spongberg, Mary. *Feminizing Venereal Disease: The Body of the Prostitute in Nineteenth-Century Medical Discourse.* New York: New York University Press, 1997.

Staples, Amy L. S. *The Birth of Development: How the World Bank, Food and Agriculture Organization, and World Health Organization Changed the World, 1945-1965.* Kent, Ohio: The Kent State University Press, 2006.

Stokes, Donald E. *Pasteur's Quadrant: Basic Science and Technological Innovation.* Washington, DC: Brookings Institution Press, 1997.

Surface, Frank M., and Raymond L. Bland. *American Food in the World War and Reconstruction Period: Operations of the Organizations under the Direction of Herbert Hoover, 1914-1924.* Stanford: Stanford University Press, 1931.

Thane, Pat. *The Foundations of the Welfare State.* New York: Longman, 1982.

Thomas, Evan W. *Syphilis: Its Course and Management.* New York: The MacMillan Company, 1949.

Thompson, Jana. "Women and War." In *Women's Studies International Forum*, Volume 14, Nos. 1 and 2, 1991.

UNICEF. *Fifty Years For Children.* Available online at http://www.unicef.org/sow96/50years.htm. 21 September 1998.

Van Bueren, Geraldine, ed. *International Documents on Children.* Boston: Kluwer Academic Publishers, 1993.

Varga-Harris, Christine. "Homemaking and the Aesthetic and Moral Perimeters of the Soviet Home During the Khruschev Era." *Journal of Social History* (Spring 2008): 561–89.

Vedder, Edward B. *Syphilis and Public Health.* Philadelphia: Lea and Febiger, 1918.

Walters, F. P. *A History of the League of Nations.* Oxford: Oxford University Press, 1952.

Weindling, Paul, ed. *International Health Organizations and Movements, 1918-1939.* New York: Cambridge University Press, 1995.

Werbner, Pnina. "Political Motherhood and the Feminisation of Citizenship: Women's Activisms and the Transformation of the Public Sphere." In *Women, Citizenship and Difference*, Nira Yuval-Davis and Pnina Werbner, eds. New York: Zed Books, 1999.

Wilmer, Harry A. *Corky the Killer: A Story of Syphilis.* New York: American Social Hygiene Association, 1945.

Wilson, Francesca M. *Rebel Daughter of a Country House: The Life of Eglantyne Jebb, Founder of the Save the Children Fund.* London: George Allen and Unwin Ltd., 1967.

Wolfe, Harold. *Herbert Hoover: Public Servant and Leader of the Loyal Opposition, A Study of His Life and Career.* New York: Exposition Press, 1956.

"Women and Gender in Countries in Transition: a UNICEF Perspective." New York: Regional Office for Central and Eastern Europe, Commonwealth of Independent States and Baltic States, 1994.

Young, John W. *France, the Cold War and the Western Alliance, 1944-1949: French Foreign Policy and Post-War Europe.* New York: St. Martin's Press, 1990.

Yuval-Davis, Nira, and Pnina Werbner, eds. *Women, Citizenship and Difference.* New York: Zed Books, 1999.

Zahra, Tara. "The Psychological Marshall Plan: Displacement, Gender, and Human Rights after World War II." *Central European History* 44 (2011): 37–62.

Index

About the Author

Jennifer M. Morris began her examination of UNICEF during a graduate seminar on women and the United Nations at Miami University at a time when the history of the United Nations went largely unnoticed. Since then, she has published on UNICEF as well as having presented papers at both national and international history conferences. She is pleased that this work on UNICEF will become part of the rich history of the United Nations. Dr. Morris currently teaches European, world, and women's history at Mount St. Joseph University in Cincinnati, Ohio.

Lightning Source UK Ltd.
Milton Keynes UK
UKOW01n0735280616

277224UK00011B/317/P